HUMAN LOVE

HUMAN LOVE

by
JEAN GUITTON
de l'Academie Francaise
Introduction by
ROBERT W. GLEASON S.J.

FRANCISCAN HERALD PRESS
Chicago, Illinois 60609

HUMAN LOVE, by Jean Guitton, translated from the second French edition of *L'Amour Humain*, with permission of the publisher, Aubier, Editions Montaigne, Paris VIe, France. Library of Congress Catalog Card Number: 66-17110. Copyright 1966 by Franciscan Herald Press, 1434 West 51st Street, Chicago, Illinois 60609. Made in the United States of America.

NIHIL OBSTAT:
  Lucan Freppert O.F.M.
  Censor Deputatus

IMPRIMATUR:
  Most Rev. Cletus F. O'Donnell, D.D.
  Vicar General, Archdiocese of Chicago

February 3, 1966

PREFACE
by the author

CERTAIN subjects are like mirrors in which the whole universe is reflected. And I confess that I have always liked to take as a theme for my reflection a problem which enables me to find all other problems, as a man can find the whole world, heaven and earth, in the gaze of his spouse. That is precisely the subject you will find in these pages: their theme is married love. For, when speaking of human love, I have paradoxically sought to ponder, not on the raptures or the deviations of love, as do most poets, philosophers and mystics, but on its most common and constant, humblest and most vital, most Christian, most natural and also most supernatural form, namely the long and slow love between man and woman in marriage.

That is the originality or the paradox of this book. The sum of my purpose has been to substantiate what men and women in the world secretly feel and dare not say, because the most common experiences are the ones which remain forever unknown; the things of everyday life are the most mysterious and the most unspeakable of all. In this book I have tried to convey the sound of everyday life, grasped in its continuity and in its depth, like the rolling of the ocean or the beating of the heart.

* * *

I must now tell you the circumstances under which these pages were composed. It was during the winter of 1945 in a prisoners' camp in Silesia, then in the Ango-American reprisals camp of Colditz in the heart of Saxony. When I chance to reread any page from this book of mine, I am unable to detach it from the circumstances of its origin: behind the lines I can see the bleak horizon of a prison, the discomforts of the last wait, I can hear the sound of human voices. Five years of captivity are a true ordeal for young men. Five years at the time when homes are founded, when a man and a girl bind their love firmly for an everlasting adventure, when the hearthstone is laid, when the children appear, each an unpredictable universe and destiny, and give meaning both to your existence and to your partner's, and still more to the mysterious bond that knits them together. Now, being thus far away from their homeland, far from any person of the opposite sex (which thought alone could conjure up), my comrades, whether they were French, Poles, English or American, would often speak of the wife desired, the woman they hoped to marry, to whom some of them were already engaged. One by one I collected these sundry experiences. My book is the fragrant essence of all those confidences. If it is worth something, it is because in this abstract form, detached in appearance and extremely chastened — the form used by philosophers and suitable to the proprieties of French prose — I have not spoken of myself, but of a universal human experience, gathered in hard times by young men in the course of a most cruel conflict.

* * *

I am pleased to see this book published once more in America, and to see it reappear especially at this time when the work of Vatican II must be implemented, especially in tackling the problems of life in the world, the action of the layman, the greatness and the hardships of Christian marriage, love and its blessedness.

In an introduction to the first English edition, I asked my great friend, the third Lord Halifax, who was British ambassador to the United States for a long time and during crucial days, to kindly grace the English edition with a preface. I think that what he then said cannot be improved upon, and I beg permission to quote him here.

"The author is one of that generation of his countrymen who, having still been at school or college during the first war, was caught up in the cataclysm of 1939, and experienced all the strains, material and moral, of prolonged captivity. It was this association with thousands of others, condemned like himself to separation from all the human companionship which had hitherto been one of the principal foundations of life, that led M. Guitton to this analysis.

And this little book, therefore, is the outcome of what concentrated searching of thought, which to those who are able to take advantage of it may offer relief from the worst restrictions of physical confinement.

"In that sense this contribution of a French thinker and Christian philosopher is one of the finest fruits of the war, and against such background the author brings his readers to the deepest appreciation of the part that Love, in all its manifold expression, plays in the human heart and mind. By such study, precious light can be thrown upon the eternal problem of man's existence. For there is no area of man's relations to his fellows, or, so far as we may apprehend them, of his relations to his Maker, that is untouched for better or for worse by the operation of this deepest of all elements in human nature.

"Many years ago when my father had come to know well the Abbe Portal, with whom he worked on the basis of close and enduring friendship in the Cause of Catholic Reunion, M. Portal introduced him to M. Guitton.

"The latter shared all the aspirations and longings of the older friends to do something for the healing of our unhappy divisions; and from that introduction and from common devotion to their ideal of Unity, there grew naturally the affectionate friendship that to the end of his life my father enjoyed with the author of this book. That friendship, to which I have been happily heir, has given me the opportunity of knowing something of the quality of M. Guitton's thought, and enables me with the greater confidence to commend this study to the interest of all."

J. G.

Vatican Council II
Rome, November 1965

CONTENTS

INTRODUCTION
by Robert W. Gleason S.J.

DURING the last few decades books on marriage and human love have proliferated. Many of them have made important contributions to a Christian understanding of the sacrament of marriage and the divine invitations implicit in interpersonal relationships. The twentieth century has been called the age of the person and the deepest strata of personal life, touched in human love, have been given new light by the analyses of contemporary theologians.

While admiring the distinct contributions of all who have worked in this field, we believe that Jean Guitton has achieved something quite unique in *Human Love*. No single book on marriage contains such a wealth of insights, so clearly structured. Guitton brings to his task an extraordinary equipment. A sure grasp of the Christian ideals of love, an historical perspective that sets problems accurately and a rare psychological finesse contribute to make this a uniquely valuable book.

Many analyses of love which have been made in the past have concentrated on love in its genesis as its first splendor. But love is a developing thing with its own history and its own inner dynamisms. Guitton traces love from its first beginnings to its culmination in old age, with the hint of an eternal dyad after death. Each period of love's history has its own dangers and difficulties and these are portrayed by the author with luminous clarity. The invitations to growth implicit in each stage of love are marked and the temptations concretized in a static view of love are shown for what they are.

1

It is rare that the whole course of love is taken seriously by authors who speak of it. Such an approach however can be seriously misleading if it conveys to the reader the unspoken assumption that love is something given once and for all with no inner laws of development.

With extraordinary perception Guitton describes in concrete phenomenological terms the dangers to love that will appear at each stage of the life between a changing man and a changing woman, both immersed in a changing situation. It has often been said that books which deal with sociology or reflect the social conditions of one country do not translate well. It is the merit of Guitton that his analyses are orientated to point up rather what is permanent and unchanging from country to country and culture to culture, because founded on the nature of man himself.

The reader will notice constantly how the attitudes — so diverse — of both the man and the woman towards the love situations are described. Two fundamentally different images of God, man and woman, are here taken seriously in the whole plenitude of their personal existence as enfleshed spirits. The different ways in which a man and a woman, think, feel, choose, relate to persons are noted with extraordinary accuracy.

It is to the *whole* person that Guitton addresses himself and it is the *whole* person who will find unchanging guidelines here. The nature of sexuality is exposed, not from a moralistic point of view, but from the viewpoint of a profoundly Christian metaphysic of the person. The domain of human affectivity, its counterfeits and cul-de-sacs are observed. The intellectual and spiritual components of love are located in their proper sphere so that a fully integral understanding of love in the Christian sense is made possible. The opening to divine, supernatural charity inherent in every love is pointed out not in any aprioristic fashion but rather emerging from the analysis of the love-relationship itself.

In conclusion, I can honestly think of no single volume on love that will contribute more to the understanding of this great gift — the greatest *human* gift the Lord of the universe can grant to a man or woman. Although the principles sounded here are profound and exquisitely difficult of analysis, the author's sureness of treatment and unerring sense of the concrete make for effortless and delightful reading. I could only hope that *Human Love* would be read, re-read and wholly absorbed by all those to whom God has given this gift, task and vocation.

1 *The difficulties and the languages*

N A T U R E is a prodigal sower.   She scatters seeds everywhere;
one might almost be tempted to say that she is over-lavish.
Very few of these seeds spring up or even reach maturity.
Many seem called but few chosen.   On this apparently royal
road of love to which every man seems summoned (for every
man believes that this desire of mankind has sounded secretly for
him alone), how many are there who find no fulfilment, who
squander themselves, who engulf themselves, who attain to love
in its deformities alone?   It seems as if nature had both desired
to summon man to love and, at the same time, allowed him to
be prevented from loving.

This is true of all loves, of human as of divine love: counterfeit love abounds.   The very word is delusive in every tongue,
as is shown by the simple fact that it is applicable both to God and
to the relation between man and woman.   Everyone, according
to his soul and slant, conceives it differently.   Sin, error,
ambiguity are in their own element here, and this, it seems, has
always been so.   In the first of all Books, from the first page of
it, it is with the problem of man's sin that history begins and
this sin, it seems, is bound up with the abuse of sex.   Duns
Scotus attributes the fault of Adam to an immoderate love for

the affections of his spouse, *immoderatus amor amicitiae uxoris*. The expositions of this problem by both the theologian and the psychiatrist only confirm the impression that sexual love is not to-day what, by nature, it should be, that it has gone astray and, there seems no doubt, done so at a very early date.

Whatever its origins, which are so difficult to determine, the tender and noble sentiment which, in the West, we call *love* seems a somewhat belated achievement. For the emotion that we call by this term implies a certain equality between woman and man; and it seems that originally woman was never anything but a privileged servant dominated by the male. Woman is a kind of domestic organism, here more submissive and more humiliated, there at long last held in honour. The most burdensome tasks are often allotted to her because she is the more feeble creature and cannot refuse to perform them. Woman is, moreover, the food of the life-force and it is notable that those two functions which, for modern man, are combined in a single being, formerly appeared as two distinct categories: the woman of the home was not the mistress of the market-place and, to satisfy the citizen of the ancient world, both were needed. If desire received the name of *Eros* and friendship that of *Philia*, the love of man for woman was for long to be nameless and, since there is no name which befits it, to some extent it still remains so.

Even in Israel, woman long remained the property of man, his most precious chattel over which he ruled like a Baal. The adulterer seems there to fall into the category of the thief. Polygamy is authorised and, with the kings, practised on a large scale. Woman is a slave and, even if monogamy were the law of the first couple, a special revelation was required to establish that law in the realm of love. The success of the prophetic movement in Israel and the preaching of Jesus, slowly transform this attitude and reveal the pre-existent germinal idea of love. Christ restores the Mosaic régime. He revindicates the equality of man and woman in the name of their original creation.

Thenceforward monogamy appears as a right. Woman is no longer merely *mater*, she is also *uxor*, *sponsa*, *soror*. She is no longer *meretrix* but *peccatrix*. This new law is indeed too hard for human kind. The gulf between the purity of the law and the impurity of man is called sin. It is more and more conceived as inward.

Christianity revealed, perhaps even aroused, the notion of a conflict, radical, bitter, bloody, between the flesh and the spirit of which the ancients had hardly a notion. For centuries this conflict caused torments of conscience, and until the threshold of our own era, no essentially new element seems to have been introduced into this development of love. Then, however, we seem to enter a new phase; and these changes, being contemporary, are not easy to define or assess. To speak a primitive language, let us say that man began to taste the tree of knowledge. Until then *sex* and *love* were on the plane of instinct. Consciousness of sex was scarcely aroused, or was at least hardly to be distinguished from life itself. There was a kind of radiance lighting up such instinctive acts as the motions of love which could elevate, enrich and expand them, but did not become detached as knowledge, which barely distinguished self from its object.

From that time consciousness has moved away from instinct. The intellect comprehends what life enjoys; much more than that, it apprehends the mystery of the mechanism. It is mistress of creation and of love. Formerly, even when the means for the control of life were known, they were screened by ignorance and secrecy. The nineteenth century dared to approach these forbidden shores; it defined the elements of a kind of *positive sexology* capable of totally transforming the economy of love, the status of the family, custom and even morality itself.

We have not yet recovered from this revolution. It confronts us with certain consequences which seem disastrous. Almost unspeakable prospects threaten to transform the situation of man. The Churches are disturbed. Man feels that love itself is threatened and is either pleased or troubled by the fact. The whole situation suggests that we have already entered upon a new era. Will it destroy the past? Or will it return to its origins by a détour? Such are some of the questions which it is possible to pose.

I have tried to study them, combining traditional conceptions with insights which I believe to be modern, remembering always with Vauvenargues that it is easier to utter new ideas than to reconcile them with those which have been uttered. And in this respect these reflections will not be to the taste of our desperadoes. I am indeed sometimes inclined to think that this new epoch upon which we are entering will transform the specifically Christian phase of love and, after many tribulations, fulfil it in some new way. Thus love, the oldest of all topics, can also be the most up-to-date. In any case it is one which may be revived by the rising generation. For the application of the knowledge of this tenebrous theme of love may also be a source of illumination.

Such is the problem which, in my scanty leisure, I have put to myself. For five years I have lived with two or three thousand comrades of between the ages of twenty-five and forty years who, at the age for love, have been starved of love. Starved for years and thus, so to speak, enjoying an experience rare in the annals of mankind. Starved of love in actuality but not in spirit. Very abnormal situations were to be seen in those purgatorial circles: men who had known their wives for a few days or hours only, on leave granted on 10 May 1940, husbands of a marriage in the past, now sadly separated; men cheek by jowl and alone, with the opportunity of considering the abnormal experiences which, in such matters, can happen to men. Those experiences became common property. For captives, though normally silent upon such subjects or only referring to them crudely, also long to confide in order to confute their incongruity.

Solitude and deprivation, those mothers of reflection, sometimes beget curiously accurate analyses. No doubt it is almost impossible to obtain the conditions necessary for exact experience in these matters, for some have known too much or too soon while others have no experience or, happily, that only of peace. Rare are the spirits who, according to Foerster, possess "a penetrating knowledge of the forces of life and an incorruptible freedom in relation to them". Who could boast such a poise, a poise perhaps impossible to man? However, it should at least serve, ideally and within due bounds, as a pattern.

The reading of certain books which chance had placed in our barracks supported me in my purpose; Rilke and his *Letters to a Young Poet*, Morgan and his essay *On Singleness of Mind*, the *Cadences* of J. Chevalier, Dr. Biot, de Rougemont, G. Thibon. I regret not having known at that time of Camille Mayran's *Dame en Noir* in which love is for the first time studied from the feminine point of view, or still more Henri Rambaud's *Voie Sacrée*, in which the dialogue with M. Mauriac is most illuminating. As for Dr. Allendy's book, it has given me the salutory stimulus of discussion with a sceptic.[1]

I then conceived the idea of a work of this kind which should do for human love what the Georgics had done for the labours of the soil, showing how, in different phases of history, the idea takes shape, how human thought approaches it; in what way it emerges and matures; the corruption which dogs it; the place of love in the architecture of the universe and the design of creation, its future in the human odyssey, its rôle in the ascent of spirit; what, in the end, is the relation between all loves; if it is true that there is only one love, and, if so, how the share of the spirit and that of the senses in this unity is to be conceived. How many are the questions which I would have liked to consider separately or rather to perceive in relation to one another!

This work does not then seek to sound any original note but, on the contrary, to make an inventory of what has been apprehended by the best minds. It is a book written for pleasure and

[1] Stendhal, Michelet, Proust, Gide and Claudel have also been always in my mind.

not as a duty, no doubt because it was begun in a state so little free that it needed compensation. I could write with ease a work conceived as an introduction to another, a work defined indeed but destined never to see the light. In fact, the majority of human affairs are like that. We set ourselves grandiose projects; but life passes and anti-climax comes. Then one adopts the attitude of the testator and gathers together what is left for legacies: thus, with its omissions and its gaps, with a kind of patina associated with souvenirs upon it, there emerges what is called a book.

What attracted me in this eternal riddle was the hope of being able to approach it on a more lofty level of generalisation than most men have attained. It did not so much concern me in itself as in relation to the primordial questions which have always arrested the attention of philosophers. Plato, whose *Symposium* is ever in my mind (like an unattainable ideal where the different points of view, the different possible languages about love have been expounded for the first time and then set each in its proper place and assessed by a sage), Plato, I say, thought love was essentially a mediating spirit. And I suspect him of having glimpsed the mysterious truth that sexual love is the means for transcending itself: at all events he taught that to reflect upon love was the means of raising thought towards the ineffable in the scale of being.

It will be seen that the problem of love has provided me with a taking-off ground for considerations of another order, relating to philosophy, religion, the understanding of existence in time, the study of humanity in its history and development. I have pursued this analysis of love together with a consideration of the nature of being; and have treated it also as a study with a metaphysical significance. When a thoughtful reader compares these two types of work, he will see that they complement each other, that the one illuminates the other, that what, in the one, is too abstract and remote from the common life is redeemed by the humanity of the other.

It seemed to me that this problem of human love provided a fit point of view for the study of the mystery of our being to which it is necessarily and intimately related, and perhaps that of being itself. It is a meeting-point for so many questions; on the one hand those of near-sublimity, touching the divine element in our being: on the other those which concern the conjunction of body and spirit. For of love one might say what Scripture says of the Word: that it is "quick, and powerful, and sharper than any two-edged sword, piercing even to the dividing asunder of soul and spirit, and of the joints and marrow". Love confronted me with a unique case of ambiguity or rather of a compound of essences, of intricacy and of conjunction, since there I constantly noted the coinherence of two natures in the unity of the person.

★

During these researches I also pursued a lengthy enquiry into the Christian understanding of life and its relation to modern thought and to the kind of adaptation which it should undergo in order to ensure its development. These latter studies have been of interest in connection with this work.

A friend, very conscious of the difficulties of Christianity at the present time, told me that Catholics would have to solve three riddles of the Sphinx. Otherwise, he added, they are in danger of losing the ear of our world. The first of these questions, he said, is that posed by Spinoza: it concerns the historic character of the written documents which are the foundations of the faith. The second is that which Nietzsche posed: the question whether the values taught by Christianity, such as gentleness, submission, humility, pity, have not enfeebled and enervated human nature. The third question is posed by Marx; it concerns the organisation of labour and the distribution of goods. Has Christianity conduced to a total justice; is it not tantamount to an economic revolution?

The problem of love is not, apparently, concerned with any of these riddles. Nevertheless, Christianity and human love are so closely linked in history that their fate is almost conjoined. It cannot be denied that Jesus introduced a revolution in our conception of the relation of flesh and spirit. The problem of knowing what good (or, maybe, evil) gift Christianity has revealed to man is thus posed—and a dialogue with Nietzsche is involved. It may be asked, moreover, if the organisation of the city and the family, bound up, in the West, with Christian civilisation, can be maintained—and a dialogue with Marx ensues. We must know whether, during the coming century, love will manifest itself in the same form or whether, in a new scientific and economic environment, it will undergo such profound changes that humanity will not recognise it.

Another idea which has influenced me equally in this work has been that of *sublimation*. The reader will, I believe, find this conception present throughout: I have represented human love as an essence doomed to imperfection which can only preserve its own identity by changing in form, in aspect and in nature. This change, moreover, takes place at the summit; it integrates the past and the flesh in a higher reality; it moves from level to level, conserving that which it seems to destroy by causing it to participate in an existence of another order. A symbolic saying of the Church of the Fathers concerning the Incarnation, declares that the Christ took flesh *non conversione divinitatis in carnem sed assumptione humanitatis in deum*.[1] And Plotinus had similar ideas concerning the relation between soul and body, suggesting that the soul is not cast into a body but that the body is raised up to the soul, which enlightens it. This is, in fact, the mystery of all love which allows the images of the lower life to rise to its own level and subsumes them in its own light.

The word 'sublimation' would perhaps be the best with which to describe this process, had its meaning not been distorted by Dr. Freud's use of it. It occurred to me to choose the word *assumption* which implies fundamentally the same thing. It is,

---

[1] Not by the conversion of divinity into flesh, but by assumption of humanity into God.

perhaps, love's ennobling and transforming influence upon the flesh that will reconcile the conflict between the flesh and the spirit. The Christian tradition seems to carry with it the idea of a radical and irreconcilable opposition between the spirit and the senses: the formulas of St. Paul and St. Augustine will be remembered. Perhaps it has not been sufficiently noted that there is in Christianity another current of thought which has not had the good fortune to find interpreters as popular as St. Paul. In the problems relating to love, one sees practical and pastoral considerations constantly interfering with the real and, if one might venture to say so, the ontic point of view.

When one deals with love from the point of view of the moralist one can hardly avoid the idea of safeguarding morality. From this angle it is well to insist on the conflicts; but that has the effect of infecting words with a contrary adverse significance. Thus the word *flesh* will not readily recover from the sombre sense given to it by St. Paul. St. John, however, did not follow St. Paul in this respect: for him, since the Word made His abode in it, the flesh was a neutral, not a damnable element. It is within the Johannine perspectives that my thought took shape: every man is entitled to his own preferences.

It may be asked whether the rôle of spirit is not that of assuming and sublimating what should be spiritualised in matter and life, of thus preparing a final metamorphosis of the energies of the universe. It may even be asked whether, in the history of humanity, there is not a rhythm of growth directed towards a more perfect spiritualisation of all things. It may be hoped that the integration of the sensual in the spiritual (which is surely the goal of the present creation) will find more favourable conditions in the age to come. The idea of a third age of the world, of a third state of humanity and love was not absent from my horizon.

I would have wished that thus all the aspects of my work would be inter-related and interdependent in spite of appearances to the contrary. Are the books which we dare to publish anything more, after all, than interrupted thoughts compelled to *appear* before they are ripe, only really comprehended when completed? In the meantime we must resign ourselves to ignorance of their final and true meaning and to patience, even with oneself.

★

Now, since first thoughts on every subject should be directed towards the tools at our disposal for its investigation, it is fitting that, at this point, we should go back a little and offer certain remarks on the languages of love. Apart from observing its rhythm in ourselves, the chief means at our disposal for the knowledge of love is the sign or symbol. For even in experiences which he believes to be original to him, man is under the influence of customary language.

Mind only knows itself in its projection in a language-pattern which at once translates and betrays it. Thought and expression are not separate, but expression is only possible with the aid of formulas received from others with the imprint of custom and usage upon them. And those languages which existed before thought and now transmit it, have a kind of secondary significance which is liable to abuse. Let us try then to define the associations contained in the terms in which love is expressed and the gap which sunders them from the reality which they seek to depict.

★

I will first consider the *poetic* language. Its advantage consists in the fact that the knowledge of love blossoms in the climate of beauty. Love and beauty are linked together and seem mutually to beget each other. And, just as poetry requires metre and numbers, even when it seems to abandon them, so love also has its own discipline and discovers its own law and liturgy; and thus it is that a mystique of profane love, almost as well defined as that of poetry, is seen to emerge. A kind of code, almost a poetic religion of love, exists which varies hardly at all with the passage of time and the centres of civilisations. In spite of all other differences it has its own devotees; it supplies them with words, symbols and a ritual which make for a certain constant element of conventionality in the language of love as its divine comedy unfolds before us, since each lover, whether he likes it or not, is far less original than he likes to think.

Poetry lifts love out of the ordinary and familiar and the biological and social order; it translates it into an unreal world. In poetry woman is not this particular woman but a nameless, abstract, glorious creature. To continue along these lines would be to approach an ecstasy hardly to be distinguished from that of the mystics. The rhythm of poetry paves the way for it; it imitates it; it is a substitute for a wholly ineffable experience. It should be added that the poetry of love sustains itself upon the sufferings which are inseparable from it: absence, separation, jealousy, the impossibility of arresting the instant, the irrevocability of the past, the presence of death though only as an hypothesis. These sufferings make their way into the liturgy of which we speak, and from Diotima, Amaryllis, and the Shulamite to the most recent times, the poetic tradition represents love as disinherited.

The poetic expression of love suggests that the norm of love is excess and that it should beget hyperbole and dithyrambics. Perfect love is so rare that man is driven to pretend to so sublime a grace. Insincerity creeps into the telling of all loves and most of all that of God. The acts of adoration which children are made to repeat in the catechism are far beyond their experience; one hears adolescents declare in hymns that they are dying or transfixed, although their placid expression, their air of indifference and abstraction, give the lie to these fireworks. Man finds solace in hyperbole, he finds there what at heart he lacks. If men did not express themselves in this superlative language they would, no doubt, have no means of giving significance to emotional states which would remain merely physical phenomena, biological or psychological events. Moreover, those who can compute their grief and be sufficiently lucid to sing their rapture either do not experience it so intensely or at least free themselves from it.

★

I call the language of those who study love as professional moralists and with a view to the sins which it brings in its train, the *ascetic* or pastoral language. The casuist in particular has to enter into very meticulous considerations which have the effect of casting a crude light upon the act of love and of allowing one to suppose that it can be reduced to its most gross corruptions. Language such as this is indeed a necessity, just as are the clauses of a penal code in a society of delinquents. How else can due weight be given to the gravity of the sins or, from the start, the line dividing that which is licit from that which is illicit be drawn? Yet who does not perceive that, for an assessment of the human reality of love, the use of this method is a stumbling-block?

In the treatises of which I speak love is reduced to 'the act of the flesh' or the culpable pleasure which this act procures when it exceeds the limits of normality. It is studied as if it were merely instinctive, like, for example, an act of violence or gluttony, or even as though the object of love were a thing and not a person at all. In reality, however poignant the stir of the senses may be, we do not love a human creature as we desire some material thing, this fruit, this piece of bread. From the very fact that love appeals to a body inhabited by spirit, or rather to a spirit touched to sensitivity, it is difficult to distinguish the throng of joys and sorrows which it brings in its train from the struggle to break out of solitude and unite oneself with another being, a lively desire, a need for fulfilment, an estranging passion, an acquiescent freedom, flesh, spirit, soul. In any case, to try to express this bundle of emotions merely in the terms of a debased pleasure, is to risk seeing the essence of the matter evaporate.

In what morality calls fornication there is often something wholly other than bestiality, and, too, something wholly other in the adultery which revolts against convention—and that because man is not an automaton subject to temptations but a person engaged in his bodily existence in a very special history and because the flesh contains that which is more than the flesh. On this point the romancers supplement the moralists happily enough except, however, when, with an inverted extravagance, they suggest belief in the fatality of the race. Moreover, anyone wishing to apply a kind of tariff in these subtle matters would invite a return to a state of primitive justice and to inability to distinguish between physical and moral purity, as is the case with certain ordinances of Leviticus or the Koran.

More than that, by dint of considering love from the angle of sin and gross satisfactions, it will be difficult for him to say why the same human action, though remaining fundamentally identical, becomes lawful in marriage and remains culpable outside it. Must he bring himself to say that the grace of sacrament covers with a veil that which, without it, would remain vile? That would be tantamount in fact to throwing back upon the Creator the responsibility for evil: many religious thinkers since Marcion have fallen into that pit. We thus arrive at a failure to comprehend man: either in the evil which he commits or the good which he achieves, since there is no difference between good and evil other than the legal and the illegal.

What I am seeking to define here is a subtle danger which, because of this very innocence, menaces those who sit in judgment upon love. For those who have renounced the life of the flesh risk the reaction of not understanding love in its relation to the flesh. It may be added that the ascetic tendency inclines to consider love in its generative function as though it existed and redeemed itself through that alone. But it is also a restriction of the range of love to see in it no more than a means to the end of progeny. It is not limited by that alone, but, without doubt, contains its own justification.

★

I shall not dwell long on the *erotic* language such as one finds in Ovid, in La Fontaine and in Voltaire, in Pierre Louÿs and in so many other self-deceiving writers. It presents all the degrees from crudity to subtlety and even to beauty. It is to be seen in our day coming to terms with the analysis of essences. And it is, moreover, very difficult to find any merit in it except that it makes the spirit loath to penetrate a mystery—a mystery which from its very nature should remain secret and even without utterance, in spite of the curious temptation of the mind to depict it clearly. It finds, no doubt, a malignant and iconoclastic delight in such a false revelation. It would be particularly pertinent to enquire why the male sex, when gathered together, can scarcely speak of love without debasing it. This would lead to the enquiry, as is the tendency of a certain philosophy of our age, as to what relation there may be between perversity, the sense of nothingness, and the consciousness of existence.

★

The *biological*, medical, psychiatrist's language is more important. Freud and Allendy employ it with scholarly care, studying a phenomenon objectively and without confusing it with any valuation revealing that they are men and, above all, moralists. Love is reduced to no more than the conduct of a rational and social animal. He, therefore, who knew the play of instinct and the influences emanating from society would be able to define it fully, seeing that it is found at the intersection of these two worlds. That is, biology subordinated to sociology should be able to comprehend and reconstitute it—a profound error which tends, moreover, to empty love of all that is precious and essential in it, particularly as it appears to be the application of a method which is not easy to contest!

The origin of these methods and views might be sought in the earlier philosophy of A. Comte. But he specifically renounced such views when, under the influence of Clotilde, he discovered the dimension of love. These so-called positive methods have the merit of reviving an eternal topic which had become antiquated. The novelty consists primarily in the practice of an objectivity, a clinical detachment in a region where, till then, subjective experience had alone mattered. Psycho-analytic methods have also the cure of certain mental ailments to their credit. But to study love as a biological and social function is to extract from it its essential human character; under the pretext of gaining a more accurate and unrivalled, merely 'scientific' knowledge, with harsh determination we discard for ever all that constitutes the psychic and moral reality of love.

The results of these studies would seem intolerable to us were we not habituated to them: in the past century, this preliminary reduction of a sublime phenomenon to its lowest terms was almost a law of exposition. The effect of such a method, and, if one might venture to say so, its chastisement, is the abolition of every norm in order to discern the normal and the abnormal. Then, in the next place, it leads us imperceptibly to a reversal of the terms of the problem, to forget the hierarchy of values, or rather, in the name of science, to deny it, and finally to perceive in the normal merely a specific case of abnormality. This is doubtless due to the fact that the abnormal, being a distortion of the order of things, falls more readily into the clutches of medical and psychological analysis, since it is the abnormal cases who unbosom themselves most freely, either from lack of self-control and modesty or to escape from anguish. Moreover, being more susceptible, they are wont to reflect back upon us the picture of themselves which we foresaw; they say to us the words we expected to hear, making observation more easy still since it shows us nothing to contradict our preconception.

Under these conditions, we are tempted to perceive in the description of states of insanity or aberration a privileged method offered to us for penetrating into the very heart of the phenomenon of health. It is still more tempting when it proceeds to deal with love and all those states of inspiration which might seem, to a crude common-sense view, to suggest an unwonted quickening of the humours. But who cannot perceive the peril of these methods? We study love by the methods used to analyse diseases, hallucinations and obsessions (which, in certain respects, it resembles); then we reach the point of superimposing the mechanism of our method on the structure of the experience, and of believing that we have discovered the essence when we are, in fact, limited to observation of the accident. Freudism, the invention of a doctor, often falls into this kind of excess: such confusions taint psycho-analytic studies of love and give them a very deceptive truth.

Moreover, even if this language were untainted it would have the defect of standing alone: and in such solitude language corrupts. The confusion which language breeds does not consist so much in the multiplicity of tongues as in this encompassing seclusion confining us to a single language and begetting the belief that this is the universe—and the only conceivable one. We would have to be able to speak all these tongues at once and check them against each other, or rather to set them one against the other in order to perceive, where they conflict, the form of the truth which they conceal. Yet he who thus tried to speak them all would, no doubt, like a polyglot, be pledged to a false facility, for he would believe himself to be altogether superior—even God Himself.

It is here that the philosophic spirit can help us, for philosophy is not just a special supplementary language, but it seeks to mount to a point of view above the symbolic patterns of language in order to gauge unceasingly the gap which separates the sign from the thing signified. Since nature, in niggardly fashion, has granted to Plato alone the privilege of being independent of all languages by the very fact that he was the master of them all, it remains for us, having catalogued them, to permit of no beguilement by any one of them.

Some will doubtless be surprised that we have maintained a cautious style in speaking of love, for the contemporary world is accustomed to a more garish light, and that divine modesty cherished in the pagan world, which could say all it wanted to say quite inoffensively, after the serene and chaste fashion of Virgil, is now unknown. It is in the same spirit that I have laboured long to prune this work, to suppress rather than flaunt my sources, to set the foundations out of sight so as to exhibit my thought alone. It seemed to me that, in an age when matter is so dense, and in dealing with so disturbing a subject, it would be well to return to the tradition of the ancients who held that a book should be brief. In my view, the task of the philosopher consists above all in the discernment of liaisons and analogies in order to allow the reader to perceive everything at a glance: since human concentration has its limits that means that one must be resigned to limitation.

★

The three sections of this book correspond to three points of view, three methods at the same time ancient and modern.

The first concerns the history of Ideas; it is an analysis of the expositions of love which man has made, and of the problems which he has set himself in the course of history under the influence of philosophy, poetry and religion. The reader who wishes to follow our course will already be prepared for the radiant obscurity which love displays. For sexuality is enfolded by spirit: it is that which constitutes its mystery.

The second section is an analysis of that which emerges in the human consciousness throughout its existence. We would wish to review the visions, the crises, the slow metamorphoses of love in its development, as though love were a non-temporal essence moving in time. There we follow a development in the precise and full sense of that word.

Then, in the study of love and sex we shall need finally to rise higher; to enquire into the significance of animal and human sexuality; to confront it with the claims of reason; to justify it, if need be; to try to divine to what future our species moves and whether the conditions of love will be modified. After having described the modes of being, we will need to seek the reason of being. Even if one fails in the task, it is a great adventure.

2   Themes of exaltation

IN all matters, and especially in relation to love, the mood of excess should be carefully considered. For here excess is no accident; it is love's desirable and normal course, it is at least what love wants to experience and what it forces itself to strive after, even though impotent to attain it.

As I have said, hyperbole is the customary language of this feeling whether directed towards God or the creature. The feeling begets the language which expresses it. And one can even affirm that when one meets hyperbolical language then hate or love is at hand. Love exists in this world, but as an extremely ethereal essence; it is the property of perfumes to diffuse themselves over an area immense for so insignificant a morsel of matter. It is true that one breathes love everywhere and chiefly in oneself; but that does not mean that one experiences it.

Three great themes in history have expounded love: the Platonic theme, the theme of Solomon and the theme of Tristan. Each of these corresponds to a civilisation: the Greek, the Jewish and that of the modern world. Henceforward they will supply us with the three 'harmonics' of love among men.

It would be inaccurate to say that the Greeks did not know

nuptial love, for the episode of Andromache and Hector in the most ancient of literary works shows us this sentiment in an enduring form. But the theme of conjugal love does not seem to have inspired the philosophers or poets. In any case, in Plato's dialogue on love there is not the least hint of marriage. It is the State of love which interests him and still more, perhaps, the life of the spirit and the means of access to the loftiest moments that the mind can know.

We have there a very singular point of view which is perhaps unique in the history of this conception of love. It is no longer found with that very precise meaning which the author of the *Symposium* and the *Phaedrus* gave to it; but ideas culled from Plato were for a long time to nourish reflections upon love and for a long time to colour the experience.

Plato is not interested so much in love itself as in the vibrations which love causes in the soul, and in the incentive which this passion gives to the aspirations of the spirit. Love is the medium of ecstasy, a kind of intermediary or 'demon', as he calls it, which inspires flight towards the intelligible world. Within these perspectives, the loved being is only an accident and a stimulus to the attainment of a content in which there is no need for this being to remain, where he is even out of place, for his palpable presence might disturb the ecstasy. It is a spark kindling a fire which then feeds itself. One realises that Plato did not pay great attention to the quality of the individual who causes the kindling of love; his sex is for him a matter of indifference. The loved being only exists in order to be constantly surpassed; and if one is to label as dialectic every process which attains only in order to surpass, one can say that Platonic love is dialectic itself: one must pass from the love of beautiful bodies to that of beautiful souls and from the love of beautiful souls to that of the supreme and formless Good.

With Plato there is a hidden relation between the theory of knowledge and the doctrine of love. One knows that for him the acquisition of knowledge is not concerned with the mere concrete facts which are presented to us, but with isolating a pure and abstract essence, abandoning the sensible, the individual and the historic. To take the rose as an example, one would say that it is divisible into two aspects: the 'roseness' which abides eternally in the realm of Ideas, and the particularities of the rose which pass and vanish in the course of its existence: *this* rose does not exist. Knowledge consists in just such a division; so too does love. This particular being, worthy of my love, is divided into two parts: the evanescent image which is his distinct personality, and the idea of Beauty which he incarnates and leads me to perceive. Never is he loved in himself or for himself and eternity will transfigure him into an impersonal essence. We consider that a dissection of this sort is implicit in idealism also and is to be found too with Kant's successors. No doubt there is an unsuspected relation between the asceticism of the abstract and the ardour of Eros, for these two contraries are compensatory: they feed each other and think to come to terms without actually vindicating the unity of being or the simplicity of true love.

Plato cannot indeed neglect the elementary data of experience in its biological and social aspects: he wants love to engender and serve the city. But, disintegrating genius that he is, here too he divides without being able to reassemble. For the author of the *Symposium*, love moves in two directions: one is temporal and, so to speak, horizontal, the desire to engender bodies for the sake of society; the other, which I would fain call vertical, soars towards ecstasy and eternity. And, without doubt, with his sense of the coincidence of contradictories, Plato perceived that these loves are indebted to each other. The desire to perpetuate one's species in time is not a pure vital instinct, since it functions in beauty and the thirst to engender conceals and symbolises the desire to be immortal in one's progeny. And, inversely, the labour of the philosopher who begets souls by education begins with lovely bodies.

These two directions are, at least in principle, opposed. The popular Aphrodite who begets is one thing and the celestial Aphrodite who comes to the aid of the philosopher is another; the State should give to each of these her task. When the need is for artisans and warriors it will for the time being couple the best parents. It will apply rigorous methods with a view to the conservation of the human stock; and, above all, it will avoid propagation until provision for progeny has been made.

Why is it that, in this matter, mankind differs from other species? When, on the other hand, it is a matter of moulding minds for art, for mysticism, for thought, nay even for the government of men, it is Eros that is needed to lead man from abstraction to abstraction and from ardour to ardour. There is no question of family here: the first act of the legislator is to expel parents. Human stud-farms and monasteries suffice for this; the biological and the mystical, the *infra* and the *supra*, but nothing between those extremes.

This division is admirable logic for it combines the most racial eugenics with the most lofty aspirations. By this system these opposites do not wholly negate each other provided that either *City* or *Culture* profits from this state of affairs.

Deliberately neglecting the family and the person, adopting one isolated point of view of either *State* or *Spirit*, Plato tends to see in Eros merely a means of generation or of ascent of spirit. It can be said of him that he has wholly comprehended and justified everything, except love. In the *Symposium*, that inimitable dialogue, Plato has assembled all that was worth saying about love. Although only on the threshold of the history of this idea among men, he has distinguished every conceivable type of thought, and all possible attitudes whether sublime, grotesque or mediocre. Then, bearing out these opinions by the sayings and example of Socrates, and vindicating them in their truth, he has exalted the subject to the highest possible level: he has envisaged love in its spiritual sense, in its relation to well-being and, better still, in its function as mediator at the heart of being. But, in spite of these astonishing flights, there is never, in his dialogue, any question of what is commonly called by the name of love (whether directed towards God or man), that which is neither aspiration nor a means to an end, but possession, rest, fidelity. And that, without doubt, is why the spouse is never mentioned.

★

Let us now consider the Biblical theme. At this point I ask the reader to accept that the intention of the *Song of Songs*, as I believe that I have demonstrated,[1] is to contrast two loves of which the one, for all its splendour, is only the image and semblance of the other. The idea is that of exalting the love which gold cannot buy. Solomon represents the will to possess all to oneself, the desire, aggressive though tamed by courtesy, which complacently believes that it can *ravish* that which it prizes, allure it by display, by luxury, by the promise of a crown. As though this were a matter of bargain, contract, *quid pro quo!* This love suffers from the fact that it is not love at all; though it may not be able to confess the fact, it is passion.

In contrast to Solomon the shepherd represents the love of mutual consent. The origin of such a love is to be sought in God Himself.

> His brands are brands of fire
> A flame of Jahveh.

In this case there is nothing one fears to lose; one desires and possesses. Love burgeons then without mishap; it is sure of its goal, because it knows the freedom of its origin.

But this ambivalence of the two types of love should be pondered. The Jewish author has carried it to the highest possible degree in depicting, according to the conventions of Syrian poetry, a young woman caught between the solicitations of her king and the vows of a shepherd who is her spouse. It is a theme popular among all peoples because it makes salient a difference of rank and grandeur upon which the simple soul

[1] The *Song of Songs* (Gabalda).

instinctively seizes in societies in which the human person has attained to self-consciousness. In fact, if it is admitted that the difference between man and woman does not imply any fundamental inferiority in woman and that their identity is the result of their likeness to their Creator, polygamy and all those customs which degrade woman are condemned in principle, however long, owing to habit and necessity, they have persisted. In creating two united beings Jahveh-Elohim twice sealed them with the sign of His freedom: woman has in consequence the right of choice and, if this feminine choice is rather a compliance with convention and is perhaps in accordance with feminine nature, it remains none the less fundamentally free.

The *Song* easily surmounted the stages which separate human from divine love; and it has been the text-book of those who refuse to separate them. Its profound idea is, without doubt (that which St. Paul brings to light in a mysterious passage of his *Ephesians*), that the love of man and woman is not so very different from the love of God and man. It is true that the love of God for man is not reciprocal, since, by a prevenient grace, it is the Creator who first loves. But if one enters into the spirit of the *Song*, one perceives clearly that to reciprocate does not imply that the two loves are simultaneous: only freedom in the response is demanded. The shepherd too, 'under the apple-tree', has been the first to love. Yet he imposes no burdensome yoke. In the same way the love between God and His creature who calls himself man attains perfection only if human acquiescence corresponds to the divine gift.

Already, between the *Symposium* and the *Song*, an unfathomable difference is to be seen. For the Greek *Eros* the object is only the opportunity, as in every branch of idealism. But the Jewish *Agape* supposes the creation of the other as a real being. It would certainly be an imperfect definition of the relations between the Greek *Eros* and the Judaic Aaba (the first conception of *Agape*) to pretend that *Eros* was known only among the Greeks and that *Agape* should be considered as the peculiar property of Christians.

The Jews were, indeed, better equipped to vindicate human love owing to their conception of the creation of the first couple, which contained in embryo the consciousness of the equality of persons and of the full reciprocity of gifts. But the *Symposium* and the Orphic tradition were not wholly strangers to the love whose exalting and divine nature they had comprehended. . . . The difference seems one which should be sought as follows: in the thought of Plato, the creature, if creature there be, can be no more than the spark which causes the exaltation, while, for the author of the *Song,* the exaltation cannot be separated from the tender and nuptial union of the two creatures who have chosen each other. In both cases, love is lifted to the level of divinity, but Platonic love is an ecstasy which detaches man from the social order, while the love sung by Solomon does not take the person away from his life-work but on the contrary makes love incarnate there.

For the rest, this song is an antiphonal chorus; it is thus the song of two beings who respond to each other, and who, though exchanging their mutual ardour, always redeem it from self-centredness.

There is certainly a difference between the theme of Solomon's *Song* and that of the *Epistle to the Ephesians* which elevates nuptial fervour to the height of a sacrament charged with mystery, typifying the union of Christ and the Church. But Solomon is on the track which leads to Paul since the love which he celebrates is essentially a dyad and this dyad originates in the flame of Jahveh; that is to say, it is itself divine in essence.

Platonic love longs only to attain to an Idea which cannot be loved and cannot love. At first sight, indeed, the *Song* seems more erotic and carnal and the *Symposium* more ethereal, more spiritual, more mystical. But the appearance is deceptive, for the love-values contained in Plato approximate more to the unreal than to the human; they dissociate instead of combining and, since they do not correspond to the true nature of man and woman in that they sunder instead of uniting, they risk a false sublimation instead of a real incarnation of love. Therefore the Platonist runs the risk of passing from ecstasy to despair, and even from peaceful innocence to the vice of the Greeks; it is but a step from summit to abyss. It is a love garnered in a fleeting moment which yearns to be everlasting; it is not a love adapted to time and society.

On the other hand the Judaic man stands on the rock of his convictions, love does not ravish him, it sheds its light over him from on high to illuminate the activities of his senses and to lift to the level of the divine and the eternal what would otherwise be nothing but lust.

There should, however, be a constant commerce between these two traditions of love. They resemble each other, they complement each other too much not to intermingle and sustain each other, above all since Christianity, in encouraging the asceticism of virginity, was disposed to detach love from its nuptial foundations. The monks, the orthodox moralists, the celibate of both sexes found, in the tradition and terminology of the *Symposium*, the mould into which their experience could best run; for in retirement from the world of the senses, they preserved in themselves the flame of a pure attachment directed towards beauty alone, which at times induced in them states of entrancement not unlike those which Plato has described.

As for the *Song*, it could also be preserved, but on condition of being submitted to a transformation in its interpretation and of being seen as an allegory of the relation of the soul to God: a greater modification in the text is involved than in the case of the *Symposium*. From this combination of these two traditions a Christian conception of love could emerge. Platonism, its scheme retained, was transplanted into an absolutely new climate where love could at last be born because in it persons were respected and the human order maintained.

There is reason for affirming that Jesus revealed love. Before his coming the elements were given but they were as though strangers to each other. There was *Philia*, that social affection of which Aristotle had written, and the platonic *Eros*, of such a nature that it could be employed in the mystery-cults. That which, imperceptible yet essential, was lacking was a bond of union, of close accord, without which these two sentiments of duty and of ardour were in danger, each in its own way, of degeneration. Even the prophets of Israel, if one excepts the unknown author of the *Song*, had approached but not attained that consummation, for the exaltation or zeal which consumed them was bound up with social conditions or solitary movements of soul in the presence of Jahveh. And neither fervour nor ardour is love, that joy, serene and effective, which devotes itself to service, that interflow between persons. The love which emanates from Jesus is not relished for its own sake alone; here there is no ecstasy, love has come to fruition. It leads us to the individual. It does not divorce itself from a sacrificial affection for a person present in the flesh who can be called by a proper name. It is condescending rather than ascending, because a person exists more by virtue of the gift which we bestow upon him than by the delight which he causes in us.

The *Agape* of the first Christians, wholly occupied with their mission, with the tasks of the common life and of charity, was above all a gesture of patience, of loving-kindness and self-forgetfulness, as is to be seen in the passage where St. Paul describes it. Perhaps, at least in the expression of it, it lacked warmth a little? It was the Platonist mystique which, owing to the intervention of the school of Alexandria, was to supply Christianity with the language of fervency and the science of transcending the senses, of the night of the powers and of the fruition already tasted on earth. It might have been a most perilous gift seducing love from its true way if the Christian ferment had not assimilated these riches. And the mystique which emerged had so much the more to adopt the Platonist language, its degrees, its methodical initiations, its philosophic and intellectual harmonics. For it contains an ever-present corrective in the Jewish conception according to which the love of God and the love of man for man were fundamentally one and the same thing, a conception which brings ardour down to earth and comes to terms with duty.

★

Taking the epithet from the literary style which this theme of love has so continuously inspired in the West, I call romantic or romanesque the passionate love of man and woman which develops outside the bonds of matrimony. A critic of extreme penetration has associated this love with the mediaeval myth of Tristan and Iseult and has seen there one of the most enduring of speculations concerning love and of the feeling of modern man in love. So true is it that a theme expressed in literature has power over morality, and that by a reciprocal causality it interprets and at the same time demoralises it.[1] What makes this myth of Tristan more easily intelligible to-day is the fact that without doubt it has almost exhausted its force. We shall soon see that we have come to an epoch of transition in which it tends to be dispelled. It is the right time to study a subject, when it is about to disappear.

The theme of which we speak is to be found in *Tristan*, in *Phèdre*, in *Hernani*, in the *Lys dans la vallée*, in *Dominique*, and in the *Soulier de Satin*. We find there from the very first, and welded together, the ingredients which we have just defined. The metaphors which signify love are taken from the nature of fire: it is a fire, it is a furnace which, however, burns rather than illuminates. Here again are the states which the *Symposium* outlined and Christian contemplatives have ended by enumerating and classifying in a hierarchy: ravishment, rapture, the wounding which brings ecstasy, the identification of excess of suffering with excess of joy, the absorption of the joy in an eternal felicity. All that, in the Christian climate, had been tempered, moderated, associated with the relation of the soul with the Christ. But one could always dissociate these states from the humanity of Jesus and study them for themselves. The equality of man and

---

[1] M. Denis de Rougement.

woman is no longer contested, above all in the lands of the extreme West whence the Celtic genius extends its empire and where it would not be far from admitting the superiority of woman over man even as regards political and religious authority.

What is new is that, for the first time, woman appears as the instrument of fatality. The Greeks had conceived the idea of a necessity to which man must yield, in that it turned against them even the deeds by which man thought to preserve himself from its decrees: we see it in the first Oedipus legend. But fatality was not allied to love. It may be said that Dido fails to seduce Aeneas from his duty as a founder by a passion which has all the characteristics of a fatal folly: but, in fact, Aeneas escapes from these infatuations. And Eve no doubt offers Adam the fruit of sin: "It is by woman that sin enters into the world and that we perish," said St. Paul, so that it might be inferred that, for the Jews themselves, woman maintains the mechanism of evil and precipitates us into it. But her rôle is episodic and remains external. It is not love which is the seat and substance of fatality. Woman leads man into a temptation which is distinct from love; woman is not the temptation itself.

Let us now turn to the myth of Tristan: here there is no longer any question of sin. The new Adam and Eve find fulfilment in the exaltation of their love and enjoy the food of Eden, a food of which no repentance can deprive them. Paradise is regained, even in 'hell' itself: when Dante meets Paolo and Francesca, that Tristanesque couple, he puts no repentance into their mouths. What fatality can be more absolute than this! We are beyond all that can separate and in the presence of a double and eternal suicide.

Claudel, in his two plays, *Partage* and *Soulier*, would have us perceive that grace can come to terms with the myth of Tristan and make use even of this evil. Perhaps? In any case, with Tristan we are at the antipodes of Christianity. The Middle Ages with their courts of love where love was judged by a peculiar code contrary to the law of morality had perceived this: for example, the question was posed whether a woman should prefer the knight devoted to her service to her husband.

The conflict between this justice of the heart and the justice of the law appears again in the *Lys* of Balzac as well as in the *Affinities* of Goethe. Henriette tries to fulfil both her wifely and her courtly obligations: she dies of this double fidelity which, in *Dominique*, is to wear out Madeleine, and, to which, earlier, Odile has sacrificed herself. In fact, this modern myth has no solution—unless it be deceit, duplicity, a consuming fire and at last, by way of a sort of slow suicide, death.

Tristan steels himself to meet these ills. The torment of it is a necessity for him. He knows it so well that he dreads the attainment of his desire, being assured that, on the day when it is consummated, love will be consumed. His is the strategy of the strait and narrow way and of suffering. He accumulates obstacles in his path; he defers his journey's end. Although so recent, Kierkegaard and Gide also conform to the tradition of this cult of suffering. It is no mere verbal accident that, in many languages, the word *passion* implies excess of love and suffering.

Passionism has been perhaps one of the most characteristic traits of love during the past eight centuries. There is reason for seeing in it one of the most rarely specified but most persistent of Christian heresies. It is true that it had little influence upon the masses, for it required an idle existence, leisure and boredom. I would be ready enough to believe that, like most of the mythical notions dear to the imagination in Christian times, passionism was the result of an insufficiently digested Christian influence. Heresy in matters of doctrine is not so much rebellion, nor even, properly speaking, the choice of one doctrine from among several, as the realisation of a true idea out of its vital and natural context.

If that is so, heresy may well be a very general and persistent phenomenon in the history of Christianity and one as modern as it is ancient.

Of such a kind is the concept of liberty which takes its title, its origins and its climate from Christianity but, when detached and existing for its own sake, becomes a cult of its own. But why should only ideas be detached like this? Why not also feelings? And what is to prevent our consideration of, or rather consent to, love and sorrow apart from their object which, for religion, was of man, God or Man-God? What is to hinder us from experiencing love and sorrow, with woman as interpreter, apart from their origin and their end? The fruit of such dissociation is bound to be bitter.

To detach love from family and religious society is to run the risk of bringing into being, on the one hand, a loveless conjugal society or still more a loveless religion, and, on the other, a love beyond the pale of natural society and established religion.

We are not far from describing what came to pass in the eighteenth century while adding, nevertheless, that epochs of dissociation, like the prism, are more favourable to analysis than those of establishment and construction, since the errant elements, following factitious ways, can then be fully apprehended by the mind. But, whenever love is dissociated, the risk is run of destroying its very exaltation, just as reason is corrupted when desired in too pure a form. The eighteenth century is, indeed, in Europe, the century of these profound corruptions, so conducive to Idealism: then *purity* in feeling, *purity* in reason, *purity* in government were all alike exalted. And, in the domain of emotion, the most tender and ferocious of sentiments succeed each other (Sade and the Terror follow Rousseau), precisely because the spirit sought feeling, not being, and because feeling, fugitive when thus detached from its human and abiding subject, can only be sustained by shock tactics.

The myth of Faust, the contemporaneous character of which the genius of Goethe perceived (for the Dr. Faustus of the Middle Ages was an anachronism) well expressed this decomposition of love. Faust, like Don Juan, does not belong to the category of those who love. To love, one must go forth from oneself, discover and create the other at the same time that one allows oneself to be discovered and created; this supposes equality and reciprocity within sex-differentiation.

Now Faust is too fond of himself to love; he seeks not so much to excite love as to experience his own power which is all the more flattering when innocence is its object. In that he is blood-brother to Don Juan, that desperado, who no longer believes in the power of intoxication to forge an eternal bond with a single being, who makes use, therefore, of all the love-potions and loves as many times as there are nights.

Marguerite is for Faust only a means to a sweetness, an exquisite naïveté, a seemingly absolute non-existence, which permits Faust to feel himself to be a demiurge in this domain of the heart in which it is so difficult to create. In all his states Faust remains lucid and in the experimental attitude, which here, for the eyes of faith, is 'devilish' since Faust plays with the mystery of being.

Faust is the type and prophet of the man who is to come, more *intelligence* than *heart*, Narcissus not Adam, lonely in the midst of multitudes whom he rules by propaganda, who dissipates the boons of nature, who dissociates the indissociable, who dissipates himself and would soon fall unless by a last thread he remained attached to the mystery or were redeemed by his victim.

Woman is here at once abased and exalted since, after having been only the tool of intelligence, in eternity she becomes a saviour. But here perhaps Goethe remembers Dante. . . .

Henceforward, love will allow itself to be dissociated, no longer with the old dissociation which, after the pattern of Plato, exalted the eternal and ardent element in it (like fire snatched from the fuel which fed it), but with a new dissociation which falls upon the fiery substance and resolves it into its elements in the hope of recomposing it. And I am not speaking here of the superficial analysis of the romantics, of Hugo or Lamartine, or even that of *Volupté*, of *Dominique* or the *Lys*; there the mediaeval myth is adopted. But, already in this nineteenth century, another method for the analysis of love has made its appearance: that which consists in apprehending how this passion is engendered, how it can be produced by the subject himself.

The authors of whom we think, Stendhal and Proust, Freud and, in our day, M. J.-P. Sartre, have this much in common in that they exorcise the existence of *the other*; love for them is an essentially solitary phenomenon. With Stendhal the exaltation remains: love, conquest, war are closely akin. But, in all these cases, it is not, as in the time of Corneille, the end which is important; will is cultivated only in order to relish the exercise of it. Heroism and eroticism have this in common; they allow those violent moments when male power finds its satisfaction in risk, in seduction, in the abasement of the partner to be enjoyed. We are at the meeting-point of two worlds: Stendhal retains the classic Spanish and Italian conceptions of the love-passion, but he heralds the new age by this pitiless character of an analysis which takes a delight in dissolving the object of love at the moment when it is experienced. Julian and Fabrice create lucid experiences in themselves as, later, does Robert Greslau in Bourget's *Disciple*.

From now on love becomes a receptacle for self-love. Woman tends to be no longer only a means for obtaining the satisfaction of conquest: this is truly a *conquest* and so much the more precious since the man who loves in this fashion is usually infirm or ugly and doubts himself. Profit is made of the idea that love renews itself in secret and appears to be suddenly and immediately precipitated, like the crystals admired by Stendhal in the salt-mines of Salzburg. That has certainly been observed many a time, but we are now in an age when substructures are explored, when that which is lofty is explained by the hidden operation of base causes; Marx writes in the middle of this century.

It is the century which brings to light the laws of becoming which, beginning with the most lowly grades of being, necessarily also regulate the most lofty. Man at last feels himself to be emancipated from belief in creation and in freedom, master at last of nature and of himself, not in that he is independent in the cosmos but because at last he recognises necessity.

Transpose this attitude into the domain of love and we understand how significant explanations by inferior causes are here. We find ourselves again confronted with fatality, but it is on a field of battle where this enemy can be overcome. If love has its roots in a primitive unconscious impulse, in an imperceptible event, if it is the emergence to consciousness of an instinctive pre-history, then it becomes possible to explain its mystery as due to ignorance of its real causes.

Since Spinoza had already *explained* the free act, it was left for Proust to carry to a morbid perfection what Stendhal had only sketched. In the eyes of Proust, it is very clear that the beloved is an illusion created by human art, reflecting back upon man his own image. It is no longer a matter for astonishment that this love emptied of reality is so easily menaced by those accidents which are *vices*. If one primarily loves oneself in the other, is it even necessary that the other should be truly other, is it even necessary that he should exist? Whereas Proust gave an aesthetic explanation to the illusion essential to love, aided by a kind of analysis and talent apt for retracing obscure lines of approach, see how Freud sought to explain the amorous fixation by an altogether different method, at once biological and medical! It was indeed still at the cost of negation of the essence of it, for love was not based upon deep choice and mutual self-giving, but upon the metamorphosis of a life-impulse, upon associations perversely knotted by infantile repressions. With M. Sartre, love cannot cause us to meet the other person any more than, on the other hand, knowledge can elevate us to self-knowledge. This line of thought was moving towards the annihilation of the object in love; with this bold author, it at last dares to confront its implications. One recalls the saying of a father of the early Church: "And not even the nothingness which they seek shall be granted to them."

Love once again becomes an evil thing. But while, for the Middle Ages, it was a delightful evil, here it is conceived rather as a hell or a neurosis and is frequently symbolised by the story of Sodom. By means of medical or psychological analysis of the unconscious, the exaltation of love is reduced to nothing. We smile at such exaltation as at a danger overcome, free to make use of it from time to time if it feeds mind or senses, if it gives access to the realm of art and mysticism or overcomes the idea of death. We have, it seems, returned almost to our point of departure. But with Proust as with Morgan, there is an element of Platonism which saves him by seeming to coincide with both the Christian tradition and the needs of more exquisite natures.

It may be that the history which we have just summarised is that of the human spirit and that it presents to us, re-enacted through the changing centuries, the scene which *Genesis* placed at the threshold of history: that of knowledge, of the attempt of the mind to rise to the eternal in time while tasting an ever-lasting fruit reserved for eternity.

Absolute *amorism* in the order of sense would then correspond to the same illusion which moderns have called *idealism* in that of the intellect. *Intellect* tends to dissociate life. Wherever it applies itself to it, it diminishes it; but the conjunction of intellect and life produces neither nothingness nor death but forms of false truth, of an empty fulfilment and a temporal eternity; in brief, this inverted image of being upon which intellect still fastens and which the senses also are willing to enjoy.

I have described this process in another work.[1] Love is a reality of fire to play with which is a formidable game; one knows that well enough upon the plane of the flesh; but this law applies on all levels. And it may be said that the history of the themes of love, with the exception of that of the *Song*, is the history of these recurring aberrations. They are more dangerous than those of the senses, for these are the aberrations of innocence and they are practised in pride, whence their power to seduce. But, without wishing to anticipate thoughts still to come, I would say that the resemblance between the ultimate conclusions

---

[1] *La justification du temps.*

of both the *Symposium* and the *Temps Perdu* suggests an ineluctable necessity. What would, without doubt, strike an observer ignorant of humanity—some Micromegas from a loveless planet— would be the disproportion in the relations between men and women and the effect of those relations upon human psychology. Plato was well aware of it and Proust still more so.

But when a phenomenon is quite disproportionate to its antecedent cause, when a powder-magazine is exploded by a spark or a beauty-spot upon a face brings an empire to ruin, it is proof that the antecedent event is not really the cause but rather the instrument setting in motion a latent power which reason is forced to infer in order to account for the magnitude of the effect. If that is the case, one cannot fail to be surprised at the fortuitous character of sexual causality. The ancient sages spoke of vanity, fascination, triviality; they almost imagined some trickery of God or devil. And in the modern world we find this idea also. Freud has named an unknown force analogous to the 'concupiscence' of the theologians. Proust would have us envisage a pure potency creating worlds within us to which we give free play in artistic creation, or in the desire for immortality by means of memory, which also is a creation and one most in conformity with our essence. For Morgan, whose novels have so much fame in Europe, love seems to be no more than the desire to transcend death and win unity and eternity of spirit. For Valéry it is the means to a total self-love.

Is it conceivable that a glandular phenomenon should secrete incentives such as these? One cannot help thinking of what the ancient world called a *sacramentum* or *mysterion*, that is, a reality endowed with two aspects: the one normal, common and symbolic, the other ideal and hidden in the senses; the one temporal, the other non-temporal. Or, rather, one is led to suppose that, in duration, some eternal seed insinuates itself into the human act of love. In other words, owing to the very inadequacy of the physical, love must have a metaphysical explanation. In order to explain love we must go far beyond love.

3   *The conflict of flesh and spirit*

IN the preceding chapter we tried to apprehend love in its mystery.   Through the mediation of the poets, through study of the language of exaltation, we have seen in love a sort of sacrament of eternity.   But, while developing this theme, we perceived clearly that, for at least twenty centuries, it has not been the sole concern of the human spirit.   A second theme, that of conflict and sin, always superimposed itself upon it.   Love has always contained a disturbing element.   Is it a matter of man's conflict with society or a wholly inner anguish?   The question is crucial.

In the first case, in order to resolve a conflict of spirit with flesh, a new order of society or a revolution in convention would suffice.   Reform the censorship and the tension will disappear; peace will be reborn and for ever.   But if love, owing to its own essence or the duality of our nature, arouses an inward strife, the problem changes its aspect: it can only be resolved by the annihilation of one part of ourselves for the benefit of the other, and this entails sacrifice.   And that would mean that, in order to escape from anguish, man would represent to himself as external a conflict that was purely inward.   Imagining it in the shape of an external event or a constraint derived from some other source, he would save himself from that anguish. The idea of the devil is curative; one thinks one can kill the devil and one cannot kill the anguish in oneself.

This explanation, which consists in attributing to social censure the crucifying divisions of the inner being, has been revived in our time. The Freudians and the Gidians, united in their conclusions, although they set out from quite opposite points, explain the conflict in the terms of prohibition. For the disciples of Freud in particular, the love-drama proceeds from tabus of indefinite origin, from prejudices, laws of religious purification, social conventions allied to the economy of goods and classes, disrupting the life-force and counteracting the simplicity of nature; whence come unreasonable accusations, unhealthy restrictions, scruples, neuroses, frigidity and also many excesses and aberrations.

This explanation, which derives at once from sociological analysis and psycho-analysis (less different, to tell the truth, than one at first believes), finds favour in our thoughtful circles; for our age, more than any other, owing to the decadence of morals, is aware of a cruel hiatus between conduct and outwardly professed morality; man who calls himself moral, often wears the mask of virtue without the habit of it, and without undergoing its renunciations. Indeed, every moral society, compelled to appear what it wishes to become but has not yet the power to be, is condemned to a provisory hypocrisy. But, when man is conscious of his weakness at the same time as of his obligations, hypocrisy becomes a necessity.

From that point to suppose that by suppressing convention, by throwing off the mask, one would rediscover the simplicity and integrity of nature, is only a step, often taken, and one which M. Gide has achieved many times. And, indeed, it is undeniable that the justification increases the magnitude of the fault when it does not anticipate it: for a consciousness free from prohibition, instinct could believe itself to be the voice of nature and almost spiritual; man would thus return to his vital unity. Now, if the *Non facies* (Thou shalt not) gives light but not power, the prohibition carries the latent conflict to a dramatic intensity. Duality appears and it is insurmountable.

But, in this domain as in many others, a creative influence is attributed to society when in fact, it has only a rôle of envelopment and protection. Since this notion influences all forms of social life, it has no doubt a powerful effect upon this conflict also. It does not materially affect it, however, as is proved by the fact that the method proposed by the immoralist of rejecting convention in order to regain innocence does not produce a return to the original simplicity. M. Gide, for example, admits in man, not indeed an essential duality, but a duplicity deriving from the ambiguous relations imposed by the social factor. Are we not on the point of recovering the paradise lost in the fabrication of the economy of sacrifice? Seductive doctrine! But does Gidian man attain simplicity? It seems that he is not even a *double* but rather a *doubled* man with, so to speak, two existences: the one supra-sensuous and mystic in type, but with a void mysticism, and the other as though infra-sensuous and sensual in type but with a sensuality full of unrest.

We do not believe that it is possible in any case to escape this law of innermost being. The duality is already engraved in our nature before any moral specification is made. Indeed, society defines the offence; her variation of codes and customs according to time and scene may lead one to suppose that her injunctions are relative. But, through the instrumentality of these laws, society travails towards unity of being. Thus, the so-ancient prohibition of incest has already the effect, in subduing instinct, of diminishing the area of conflict to the benefit of reason. And if, at this point, the objection is raised that society, in order to diminish duality for reasonable beings, exasperates it for the others, the reply must be that every penal law is in like case. The drama of love is an inner drama and it does not depend upon social pressure or upon an arbitary belief but upon the very pattern of our being as it is given to us.

Must an initial catastrophe now be supposed to explain this conflict? Such is the Jewish and Christian idea of an original sin the repercussions of which have extended to us.

It is remarkable that Allendy, in order to explain the neuropathic character of love in contemporary society, infers that, at the origin of the human species, there must have been an initial fault, a kind of dementia præcox which, as a matter of experience alone, very soon disturbed the equilibrium of the species.

What seems more probable is that a profound disequilibrium in man was almost inevitable since an exhaustion of will under the pressure of instinct must one day necessarily take place, and in an enduring and inter-dependent world faults which heredity transmits are likely to brand the stock. Without a compensatory influence and constant restoration, humanity is doomed to degenerate. The conflict of flesh and spirit does not arise from social existence. It might rather be said that social life makes it more salient.

But might it not point to some historic circumstance? Might it not be due to the Christian graft? Might it not be Christianity, inventing the hitherto unknown sin of the flesh, which has caused the conflict? Has not Christian doctrine the effect of alienating and denaturing man? One meets this conception again with Feuerbach and Marx; in his black moments Sainte-Beuve accepted it and it is not absent from the *Journal* of M. Gide. But it was Nietzsche who expressed it in the most ruthless fashion when he said: "Christianity has given Eros venom to drink; he is not dead but he has degenerated into vice"

★

In order to understand this conflict of flesh and spirit and to note the influence of the Christian contribution to it, it is necessary to study history. It is true that the notion of the conflict between the spirit and the senses is scarcely to be found in the ancient civilisations nor even in the Jewish. Doubtless no one can consider human nature as it is presented to us without remarking its tendency to resemble the beasts, and no society of men however primitive is imaginable without a constraint imposed upon instinct in that which concerns death and life. From the beginning we see instructions, rules and sanctions introduced into these matters; but it is a long way from these external condemnations and regulations to the idea of an inward conflict personal to each one of us.

The ancient civilisations had indeed the idea of guilt and even of unpardonable guilt; but, although they introduced the concept of fatality into this idea, they saw in the guilt much more a defilement, as it were external to the soul, which ritual purification could cleanse, than a deed which shakes the conscience to the depths. In so far as the flesh is concerned it is only wrong if the social order is affected; it may even be that the life of the flesh is dependent upon this cult, as was to be seen in Canaan with the temple priesthood. And, no doubt, moralists like Plato often suggest the idea of a slavery of the senses, a derangement produced by sensual passion. But, there too, to go to the heart of the matter would be to perceive that it is rather a case of immoderate lack of balance than of latent and irremediable conflict. If the notion of moral guilt appears with Plato, it is not with regard to the abuse of the flesh, but to the excesses of tyranny and injustice.

It is true that Plato admits zones of life dependent upon distinct principles: under the diaphragm reigns *epithumia* representative of instinct, and we should be very near to the concept of conflict if intermediaries did not succeed in attenuating it and preventing it from appearing: for Plato envisages a power in the central part of the body, a power which assures the subordination of *epithumia* to *nous*. With the healthy man the economy of the soul functions naturally, as in a well-ordered city. Conflicts appear only in times of decadence, like revolutions in the city. Moreover, Eros is in no way condemned: Plato thinks only of capturing its force in order to divert it towards the Whole.

To believe that, after the fashion of most of his greatest disciples, Jesus fastened the attention of men upon these problems of the relation of flesh and spirit would be to deceive ourselves. Most certainly Jesus is terrible towards the adulterer and pursues him to his root-motives; He restores the primitive law of absolute unity between husband and wife, He places fornication in the list of the fundamental sins which defile man, beside covetousness and wrath. But he does not attach any especial significance to this because He knows how easily the weakness of women can be abused and how their love-instinct can be led astray. It would not be alien to His thought to say that the sin of the flesh can arise from a debased and as it were inverted love, and that if this sin is overcome in time by repentance, the sinner in the flesh can become a tender lover of God and man.

Jesus places virginity in a separate category which it requires a special reinforcement of intuition, power and even violence to enter. In teaching that all sex-differences are abolished in the kingdom of heaven, He shows clearly that the carnal economy is a provisional dispensation which does not, in the depths, affect love. But, once again, He does not, as in several other cases, burden this matter with a legislation peculiar to it. When He gives a rule for conjugal love it is by relating it again to the primitive ordinance, to the very law of creation, that of the solitary couple. If He finds the solution of the problem of sex and love, if He introduces a new element into these matters as into so many others, it is as though by way of increase and grace, or rather by that process peculiar to genius which can transcend a problem and cause it to disappear in one more exalted. Had Jesus perhaps the feeling that, if the human spirit became fixated and deluded over this question, it would risk deceiving itself and dissipating an energy precious for prayer and charity? It would be better to return to an incontestable and wholly uncorrupted wisdom, to an extremely simple law, but one whence all else is to flow; it would be better to recall incessantly this *Diliges proximum sicut te ipsum*[1] and the identity of this principle

[1] Thou shalt love thy neighbour as thyself.

with the love of God, since this ordinance of the new law gives a rule for the love of the sexes also. The scene of the Last Judgment has no allusion to trespasses against carnal love: there it is a question of lack of charity alone.

Moreover, if conflict is stressed in the Gospel, it is not that of spirit and flesh, but that which sets pride and obedience in opposition or, as St. John says, the light and the darkness. The other conflict, which opposes to the three-fold lust the purity of the single eye, certainly remains: but, as is to be seen in the *Epistle* of this same St. John, it is subordinated to the great drama of faith. It is true that, if the Christ did not speak of this inner conflict, he aroused it indirectly and dealt Eros a blow from which it will never recover: monogamy humbles it.

Jesus substitutes *Agape* for *Eros* as the law of life. He demands from His own a total gift at the same time as He lays upon them a duty to love all men by means of the sacrament of love for our neighbour. He thus substitutes for this principle of sensuous ardour concentrated in oneself, for which the object is never anything but opportunity and means, a principle of non-sensuous activity, oriented towards service, for which the object is at once end and goal. We shall soon see how the *Supper* makes the *Symposium* pale, as the sun at dawn extinguishes the lights of the nocturnal feast.

But this substitution does not change human nature. Eros remains very much alive. And thenceforward it is to a warfare that man is bidden; the power of the new principle is not such as to dissolve instinct, unless, however, it arouses a sublime passion for the person of Christ: that which caused St. Ignatius of Antioch to say: "My *Eros* has been crucified". But that would always be an exceptional state.

The most characteristic example in this respect is that of St. Paul whose conversion was not so much a gradual advent as an event which in a flash transformed the spirit, leaving blood and flesh intact. The more that grace elevated Paul, the more salient it made the gap between the aspirations of the new man and the sinister resistances of the as yet unconquered nature which he called the 'old man' or the 'body of death.' It is a consequence of the challenge of grace that this sense of impotence to do what should be done, this cruel disproportion between what is possible and what is wished, this curse which we are surprised into pronouncing against a Law which denies the power to accomplish its demands, gives rise to a source of sin to which man is at once enslaved and responsible.

Grace itself will assuredly supply the answer to the crisis engendered by grace. In the eyes of the apostle it was good that it should make man aware of his misery and impotence before filling him with its flood. Nevertheless the conflict abides henceforth in the depths of ourselves and arouses a fatal sense of infelicity: *Infelix ego sum!*[1] And that which the immediate disciples of Jesus had experienced during the course of their Master's agony (the willingness of the spirit and the frailty of the flesh), Paul seems to suffer constantly as a condition inseparable from experience of existence. That experience will be found again with many spirits who were to exercise a powerful influence upon our civilisation: St. Augustine, Luther, Pascal; and others could be cited in our own time. They represent a poignant succession of living victims for whom the problem of love is indivisible from that of the flesh transcended and overcome.

During the first Christian centuries, however, attention was not directed to this conflict. It is a law of nature that two values, two evils, two loves cannot coexist in the spirit; a minor value is destroyed by one more strong. While to profess the mere name of Christian was a delight which made death alluring, the whole system of religion was different from what it was bound to become in conventional and peaceful times.

Then the great deed was witness, the capital sin, apostasy. But as soon as the danger of death disappeared or became exceptional, the struggle was no longer against an external enemy but

[1] Unhappy man that I am!

against oneself, or rather against the so-complex spirit of the world. Christian strategy was turned towards perils which, though less terrible than those of the amphitheatre, were more insidious. And the manifest oppositions which history records are a small matter compared with this new state of tension, this radical opposition of man to himself. Combat with beasts is perhaps more simple than pitting oneself against a vigorous instinct which is, moreover, not external.

It might be said that the simplicity of man is now assailed, that henceforward there are two men in us: *Homo duplex*. Every individual will in some way be conscious of this duality, in proportion to the acuteness of his sensibility. And, as Nietzsche said, it is true that Christianity, in the course of this war waged against the age and against its own spirit of lust, can manifest and arouse complex and vicious shapes, morosities, hypocrisies, reversions, neuroses, revolts. But the cause of them is not its own weakness; it resides rather in the impotence of those who receive it. Whenever a value is too strong for us and we feel ourselves forced to attempt what we are neither able nor willing to perform then we create a fictitious value, apparently more perfect than the former, but really no more than a travesty of our own incapacity. Those who repudiate authority find satisfaction in indiscipline; yet at the same time they exalt the value of pure liberty to the skies. Those who refuse to have children speak of the right to life. Those who make no change in their own moral life are the apostles of a pure and virtuous morality.

It is characteristic of our time that this lofty notion of law, this inability to submit to it, this duplicity in twisting its meaning, this facile compensation for insufficiency by devotion to ideals, disguise its real ills from itself. In other words, every elevation of the ideal in a still imperfect society develops recurrent zones of hypocrisy with consequent spiritual disorders, since our psychology is not adapted for so persistent an effort to deceive. This much must be conceded to Nietzsche.

The problem of rendering Christianity responsible poses that of progress in education. In a world in which there is compensation in full, need we wait till man is what he should be before helping him to live in it? And might it not be better, in the meantime, to let him *appear* to be what, in behaviour, he is not but what, in intention, he desires to be? The evils which this struggle for appearance brings with it are certainly less than those which stem from cynicism.

It is true that, into the development which we are considering, a fortuitous circumstance with far-reaching effects has entered, complicating everything: I refer to the influence of St. Augustine, or rather of the connection which has grown up between the history of St. Augustine and the experience of Western man.

For St. Augustine would not have been so much imitated and loved if the Latin soul and flesh had not recognised themselves in him. With Augustine the division of flesh and spirit had been carried to its greatest intensity by his sensual temperament, by those Manichean years in which he had canonised his own nature, by his reading of St. Paul, by the experience of an almost unexpected conversion, by the opposition of Pelagius, the Breton monk, impregnated with optimism, who certainly admitted the conflict of flesh and spirit but believed that will and asceticism were sufficient to suppress it.

By reason of so many concurrent circumstances, to which must be added the charm of a nature deepened by love, St. Augustine is thus found to diffuse a kind of luminous cloud in which the Middle Ages lived and which, in the sixteenth century, broke in a thunder-storm. For the Augustinian mentality, flesh and spirit appeared like two mutually opposed kingdoms. Man seemed to be torn between two constraints and two attractions. Freedom consisted in choosing between them, or rather in accepting the stronger force. The history of this conflict is that of the Augustinianism latent in the Western tradition. From this original flaw how many followed!

Presently man takes delight in opposing these two kingdoms

of nature and grace, of instinct and flesh. And that leads to a double confusion: on the one hand a little more beauty than it can carry and a quality calling for adoration are read into instinct; on the other a little more fatality and necessity than it needs are ascribed to the operation of grace, leading to the subordination of obedience to grace, almost to the point of disappearance.

But thus to distinguish these two planes, and to wish to realise that of nature alone, is to fall into the temptation of the licentiousness which, on Christian soil, will always be tainted with a protesting impiety, with a tone of revenge and resentment. Or, indeed, it is still possible to separate grace and seek to apprehend it in isolation, discarding all that is nature. To teach that all that comes from us is evil and only that which is given to us is good, is to cause morality to fluctuate between a state of despair in which man cannot live and a state of indifference where he lets his inclination take charge. He thus lives on two levels, the one that of instinct from which he extricates himself, the other that of pure soul in which he deems that he adores.

Jansenism and quietism could, historically, be opposed: but for thought, seeking the essence of things, they are near neighbours. For if nature be judged, it is as true to affirm that it is wholly bad as that it is wholly good. The choice between these doctrines will be one of temperament: the tough, the violent, the intractable and those who find peace only in denial will be with Saint-Cyran and Pascal; the sensitive, the tender, whose peace consists in obedience, will be with Fénélon. Then, when faith has ceased to concern an age which no longer has the power to believe, the same attitudes, transposed into literary sentiment, which is religion laicised, will reappear. Thus nature will not, indeed, be condemned but glorified as wholly good; and we behold the birth of a second quietism with those who would fain separate the domain of spirit from that of the senses, leaving to each its own felicity: in this respect Rousseau and M. Gide are at one.

★

Humanity is not always of the same age. It passes through periods. The idea of love knows its phases also; and the conflict which we are considering is transformed when refracted in the modern atmosphere. What characterises this new age is a predominance of intellect over spontaneous life, of calculation over instinct, and, in so far as sin is concerned, of aberration over guilt. The sins of yesterday were like wounds inflicted by the sword; their contours were clean and the blood which flowed from the wound was healthy. Those of our own day might be likened rather to internal injuries, to those maladies which attack the cellular system. Modern guilt envelops itself in a web of justification, compensation, sublimation which makes it almost invisible to its subject. The conflict of flesh and spirit is disguised and tends to become no longer apparent to the consciousness. The comparison of three works and the names of three sinners should suffice to make this characteristic clear.

In St. Augustine's *Confessions* a typical case of the first kind of conflict, such as Christianity can cause, is to be seen. The opposition of the two principles is deployed in a wholly African light. It is so acute, so little disguised, that Augustine's temptation is precisely that of deifying each of these two forces conflicting in his life and so, as it were as a bystander and outsider to it, of escaping from responsibility for the struggle between good and evil. And even when Augustine is converted, he again confronts this same secret conflict in himself; it is like an incessant refrain running through, not only individual life, but also through universal history.

In the Middle Ages the letters of Héloïse to Abélard give us, as it were, a second edition of this inner tragedy. Like Augustine, Héloïse is fully conscious of a conflict between flesh and spirit. More courageous than he, she does not try to escape from it with some theory ascribing evil to a second god. She accepts *her* evil; but, loving woman that she is, she loses herself in him whom she would save; and, to satisfy both Abélard's love which desires this liaison and Abélard's glory, which is that of remaining chaste like the sages, she agrees to become his wife in secret, as though accepting a certain evil for the sake of a good deemed to be greater. She knows that she is giving way to the flesh and in that she is an Augustinian. But she tries to justify herself: whether by the violence of her passion (as later with Racine) or by her love for the glory of her master (after the style of Corneille) while, in her tendency to seek her justification in *motive*, she gives an insight into the modern age.[1]

Jean-Jacques Rousseau was familiar with these two antecedent narratives, and he so much wished to include his own case in their company that he made this clear in the title of his works: like Augustine, he writes his *Confessions* and he believes that he has created a new *Héloïse*. Nevertheless, let not words deceive! The drama of Augustine and that of Héloïse consisted in the conflict of flesh and spirit. No doubt they tried to escape from it by blinding themselves. But reality was abjured, it was not denied. Héloïse did not deem herself to be virtuous: she was crucified by a conflict which seemed to her to be almost insuperable. Rousseau, on the contrary, 'confesses' his 'virtue'. Soon instinct is glorified under other and purer names; soon spirit is elevated above instinct, stripped of a reality with which it wishes to have no connection.

Marx and Nietzsche understood this transmutation and segregation of values at the very time when the process became established in Europe. Under their different conditions they had seen clearly that the base values of cupidity, cowardice or lust tended to assume the mask of lofty values, and that much of the social and psychological superstructure was founded upon shameful substructures. But the solution of the problem usually given by them and the world with them was as defective as their exposition of the problem had been lucid.

By no artifice can the inward conflict in everyman be denied: it has no other solution than the subordination of the flesh to the spirit and the act of renouncement of the self, the I which

[1] *Cf.* E. Gilson, *Héloïse et Abélard*.

cannot identify itself with two contrary movements. Denial of the conflict ends in multiplying abnormal, ambiguous and sub-human states in ourselves and in society. Better be willing to concede the paradox and recognise division in this inwardness where it exists and so be absolved from surmounting it by virtue!

And it is doubtless true that Christianity has revealed this duality and by so doing accentuated it. But it is an aspect of the state of drama in which the world and the individual have found themselves since this gently cruel religion appeared: the new doctrine brings, as it were, a new dimension to being, that of grace. And this, in the order of morality, adds depth to good as to evil. But in that moment of emotion when He increases understanding, the Christ cures the wounds of his faithful with a succour more sublime. The danger is lest the spirit of man should introduce division even into this indivisible gift; that even there he should create disunion after his wont, and preserve the growth of evil and the deepening of human nature without accepting the superabundant aid of grace, and the depth, if it could so be called, of the divine. It is this which has happened in history: thus the balance is disturbed by a succour insufficiently accepted which often leaves man more dispossessed than before. Such, until now, has been the arduous history of love in the West.

THE DEVELOPMENT OF LOVE

4 *The initial crisis*

THE time has come to deepen the concept of love, no longer by directing alien rays upon it, but by trying to penetrate into its mechanism and its essence.

In spite of appearances we shall have little assistance in that task: so hard it is to comprehend an everyday and commonplace reality. The too frequent repetition of experience has the effect of blunting it. And that which occurs in all orders of reality when a certain degree of awareness has been attained, happens here too: the technique which assists our knowledge distorts the object of it. At the moment when we think we have grasped love we substitute some scholarly formula for it.

But, in this attempt to define love in its more metaphysical aspect, we shall stress the illusion which we have called *eternism*: that which inclines us to deny the incarnation of the eternal in time and to substitute for it the idea of a timeless moment, having the value of eternity. What created essence could better symbolise the presence of the eternal in time? On the level of feeling, the ecstasy of love typifies the timeless moment. On the level of consciousness its exaltation proclaims it. And since love is linked to creation, the spirit tends naturally to think that, if it comprehended this act, it could grasp the secret of the insertion into time and nature of something which transcends them and is able to prolong the movement of life in the universe through the generations. Love, an instantaneous moment like that of death (which it redeems and prefigures), would thus enable us to be present at the very act of creation and, at the same time, in the experience which it offers, enable our immediate participation in our own creative eternity.

There is, no doubt, a kinship between this logical myth and that which, from age to age, inspires revivals of idealism. For, in the one case as in the other, here through the sense of exaltation, there through pure intelligence, it is a matter of identification with the process of generation of being. This is indeed the real reason why the mind delights to substitute the analysis of passion in its crisis (but is there not also something other than *crisis* there?) for the study of love in duration. And that too is why we find authors preferring to study conditions of the least normal kind. For these convey just those aspects of fervour, confusion, dissociation which analysis can grasp so well, which will reflect back upon the mind the very picture of love which it looks for and wants.

Since the exaltation of love beyond the norms of society and the very laws of being drives the inner opposition between flesh and spirit to its extremity, love comes to be conceived as an exhausting and consuming strife between two vital forces in ourselves. It is thus that the two myths studied in the preceding chapters are begotten and sustain each other. For this exaltation takes its excess of colour and fire from social prohibition and, over-stimulating the spirit while revitalising the flesh, carries the inner dichotomy to its farthest point.

But a candid consideration of these common fallacies and their inter-action helps to dissipate them or at least to distinguish their influence. If it be true that, in the final analysis, they are rooted in a confusion as to the relation of eternity to time, that they arise from the temptation to reduce divine *creation* to human *genesis*, it follows that these same fallacies would themselves be rebutted, were a principle more in accord with the very law of being to be substituted.

Eternity does not enter time in some privileged moment, but in the course of a slow and common duration. In the moment, moreover, which compels the individual to withdraw from society and its laws and customs, it is lost and dissipated. But in duration, which impels him to accept the bonds of promise and the yoke of institutions, it is preserved and redeemed. The moment, divorce, fornication, anarchy, revolt, passion have a secret affinity with each other, as, on the other hand, have duration, vows, community, consent and love. To elucidate these analogies, helping us to understand the variety and the unity of being, would be a fit task for a friend of being.

Like every reality in creation, love is composed of two elements which in fact are indivisible but by right supremely distinct, one of which, at least if love develops in an ordered fashion, is subordinate to the other. The one derives from the body and animality, the other from freedom and the spirit. And in each impulse of desire, though language and common carelessness may confuse them, analysis perceives these two elements.

To deal with the problem satisfactorily one would need to use new terms and to discern that which lies beneath the confusion of desire: for example, to call what is never more than the echo of instinct, *allurement*, keeping the name of *attraction* for that which derives from an idea, an image or from human consent. We should then find that the reality of love is to be sought in the transformation of allurement into attraction, or better still in the exclusive character of attraction which renders us insensible to all persons of the other sex other than the chosen one. Attraction, a property peculiar to man, binds instinct to a single person.

The fact that man seeks to dissociate these two aspects is, moreover, a proof that they are not fictitious: he wants to experience sexuality without love and love without sexuality.

The first of these dissociations, so common, so vulgar, as so many cases sufficiently attest, imperils inner integrity. It is not for nothing that man imitates the animal; in this he acts from the very rudiments of his being. Even though a coupling originating in instinct alone should ripen into love in the end, it would still suffer from its original blemish: it is not easy to breed freedom from urgent necessity or to transform constraint into choice.

In the contrary case, sexuality, incessantly denied and transcended, as in the tradition falsely called Platonic, is so far removed from love that it is no longer apparent. But, for the most part, it produces only unsatisfactory adjustments and, when the effort does succeed, it is, save for some rare and peculiar grace, owing to an artifice of absence, courtesy, poetry or mysticism. It is true that passionate friendship does exist and that there are illustrious examples of it. But it calls for exceptional qualities of soul; the ground gives under the tread; one has the sense that nature does not enter into this transaction at all.

It is clear that nature has ordained the union of sex and love, a union which it is at least not easy to sunder. It is a law which, in the institution of marriage, society has sanctioned. The problem of the difference between friendship and love is often posed. Those who hold that love is signalised by the exclusion of all save the chosen person will cite Montaigne and La Boëtie. But the question arises whether we are not here concerned with abnormal cases; it is difficult to avoid the impression that, were a confused feeling of sex-difference to be added to it, the sentiment described by Montaigne would at once become that of love. We find ourselves still confronted with the mystery of sex which, however singular its manifestation, remains one of *otherness*. It is a mystery which man can hardly be said to have elucidated and has vastly profaned.

When the human person becomes conscious of sexuality, he is astonished as though this were an accident, which, though inalienable from his existence, yet seems alien to him. *Genesis* sufficiently reveals this surprise in the tale of Adam's and Eve's realisation of their nakedness after eating the fruit; it was then that they plucked fig-leaves and made girdles for themselves. Modesty is this surprise perpetuated and become a habit of the soul. There are various explanations justifying this feeling of modesty, peculiar to man among living creatures, which present themselves to the mind.

It has always been observed that, in animality, modesty already exists; the beasts are sometimes to be seen concealing their amours. Human modesty might be the climax of this kind of behaviour which is useful for the selection of the fittest. For, to foment his desire, it is well that the female should excite and evade the male. Coquetry, the artifices of the toilet and all the innocent mechanism of make-believe which retard the moment of love would thus find their origin or at least their first form in the animal world.

But, in our species, modesty is not confined to the weaker sex; it goes very much further than feint and retreat. Should modesty be ascribed to the suggestions, the constraints of society? It is understandable that society should be interested in the regulation of this life-force which is so essential to it: from that need these prohibitions, the source of modest behaviour, would thus be derived. It is sometimes said that it even causes the notion of a diffused guilt or, at the least, of a blemish in so far as sexual behaviour is concerned, even when this behaviour occurs in conformity with its own laws; this was so with the ancient Jews. *Et in peccatis concepit me mater mea,*[1] says the Psalm.

The family adopts these attitudes on its own account. Parents often keep the young in ignorance, often enough from a mixture of awkwardness and fear, allowing a vague disapproval to cloud such subjects. It is chiefly in the relation between mothers and daughters that this is to be seen in bourgeois societies. There are mothers who evade the instruction of their daughters from a kind of jealousy and secret revenge, rather like school-children

[1] And in sin hath my mother conceived me.

who, having endured a painful initiation in their first year, take their revenge by humiliating new boys. Thus these misunderstandings which are so hard to disentangle are transmitted from generation to generation.

As for the father, he does not speak either, thinking that the young man ought to find out for himself as he himself has done. All this excites in the adolescent nature a feeling of attraction, curiosity, fear which, in its ambivalence, is very near to dread. One would and one would not, and so it comes to pass that this unhealthy modesty, through dizziness, plunges towards the forbidden thing. But the influence of society is not creative: it is limited to illuminating what is already there. Modesty can be modified by the blunderings of education or by the pressure of convention; but it is engraved in our nature from the first.

Has one ever reflected that, if the psycho-analysts and sociologists are right, the apprehension of sexuality by consciousness should be analogous to that of the other physical functions? The fact that we have to become conscious of our essential functions, as though they were foreign to us, as though by right we were pure spirit and only body by accident, is already in itself surprising. But how then does it happen that, when confronted with that function by means of which the species exists and is renewed, the spirit has an almost religious wonder, so that all our knowledge begins with an *initiation*, whether healthy or unhealthy?

This word 'initiation', which one seems bound to employ, suggests a kind of mystery to be penetrated only by degrees and under direction. Many features contribute towards making the functions of life, apprehended in this great social and family silence and by his own brittle inductions alone, an enigmatic affair for the young mind. His respect for his parents who represent all that is sacred for him conflicts with his experience of the quasi-animal instinct which he encounters. The identity of the vital organs with other, according to common notions, less noble functions makes him suspect some mystery inherent in the very nature of things. In this confused context he is aware of spirit incarnate in his sex which is, at times, recognised and desired by another person. In the experience of existence thus obtained how could it be possible that there should not be a very acute distress?

It is at this point that modesty intervenes. But there are two kinds of modesty: that derived from society and that already described which, being rather shame or resentment than modesty, should be called by another name. It is a parasitic condition of the nature of group-constraint. It is not the same thing as that profound modesty which is related to the incarnation of spirit. It is conceivable that acquiescence by spirit in animal and incarnate existence could not occur all at once or without stages of development. As Joubert once remarked, in the spiritual order modesty is like those integuments with which nature envelops plants so that they may survive till their flowering-time.

It is a diaphanous envelope with which nature surrounds the senses in order to prevent *spirit* from coming too soon into contact with *life*, so that it may accustom itself to it little by little. Modesty exists in its first timid form since our character is not yet set and is still incapable of exercising that function of sublimation to which we shall return later. But, even should reason and personality not be formed, modesty would still remain to safeguard the use of the body and the emotions, so violent sometimes, which spring from it, and which, to assist our growth, should remain as friends of the soul and become integrated without damage to the person. Modesty is thus not only a protective mechanism for a being sexual and yet spiritual; it is also and in many ways the organ of spiritual development, the auxiliary of duration, the medium for the union of soul and body.

It must be recognised that between the induced modesty of which we have just spoken and this deep modesty there are close ties and connections. Who knows if the constraint, the jealous silence of parents are not due to some necessity? Can he who has begotten unveil this mystery to those who are the fruit of it? Would he not fear to emphasise an incomprehensible difference between the materiality of his act and the beauty of existence? Could he make it comprehensible that he has not always desired what he now believes to be the best part of himself?

It is here that the manifest difference between *problem* and *mystery* should be fully emphasised. A problem is a difficulty caused by ignorance; it can therefore be resolved by knowledge. A mystery is a difficulty concerning nature or the thing in itself which knowledge increases. If society makes a problem of sex it is because of its impotence to dissipate the mystery; it transforms into a seeming secret something which should remain sacred, even for the mind.

In the spiritual being who is bound to it, sexed existence is fated to arouse a vague sense of solitude and incompleteness. In one of the discourses in the *Symposium* Plato evokes the myth of a being originally one but cut in two: the two halves want to recombine and this is the reason for sex-attraction. But the real problem is not that. The incompleteness resented by the human being is something very different from that which an animal endowed with consciousness might know. Unless he submits to sink in the scale it is not merely a mate that man seeks. If it be true that the words *always, for always, for ever* enter into the most ordinary vocabulary of love, it is for another being, like himself entangled in the flesh, but personal, unique, even eternal, that he seeks.

It is surprising that this characteristic of the function of generation, when permeated by spirit, is not more often stressed. Apart from the fact that it thus becomes far more free and that its disuse does not in any way disturb the vital equilibrium (whereas the function of nutrition could not be interrupted without causing suffering and, in the end, decay and death), it is, as we have said, remarkable that it localises and concentrates itself upon one particular person. In the animal world selection has no effect upon inwardness. When the wolf devours the sheep or couples with the she-wolf, it makes only a passing demand upon them. It is the 'sheepness' which concerns it, not a certain sheep, the she-wolf and not a certain she-wolf. It would be so with man also were he no more than a more refined animal.

The concept of racialism consisted in denying precisely this radical difference, which, if one remains on the level of intellectual experience, is imperceptible. I would freely affirm that this is an ontological difference perceptible only by the man and the metaphysician. When it is a matter of nourishment no distinction is made between this or that partridge, this or that trout. The most delicate taste discerns the wine, perhaps even the vineyard, but not the vine nor the grape. The individuality of the substance escapes us and we content ourselves with *some* bread and *some* wine as the wolf contents himself with sheep. If man were not freedom and spirit before being flesh, one cannot see why it should not be so with generation also.

Now the feeling of vague expectation which precedes love is already a selective feeling: it is the expectation of a being who will cross our path and consequently be encountered. But, in order that this expectation oriented towards choice may produce its full effect, it must gestate for a long time within the spirit. A too precocious fixation might mutilate love with a mere parody of it. It is better that the object of love should, for a long time, be foreseen, pre-imagined and, as it were, pre-loved, before even the features take form in a face; and this person should then remain no more than a pure and impalpable possibility. That is why, when society wishes to encourage love, it avoids premature association. The more the other dissimulates, the more the quests are furtive, the language elliptic, the reality charged with mystery, the more facile will be the idealisation. Camaraderie is directly opposed to love. Because of this retreat, this reserve, this incubation, every cognition will seem to be a recognition. The person loved will seem to be familiar even before being known.

Because of this bias, love is readily superstitious: it believes in pre-existence; it almost accepts the idea of an eternal book in which the names of the lovers are inscribed. It has the character of *already* being, of seeming to precede itself, of having existed before being perceived. Inescapable illusion! In every sphere realisation is projected upon its antecedents; it deems that it perceives its image there when in fact it is only one possibility among many. Thus, as with every fulfilled event, love transfigures that which precedes it; it creates its own preparations, it invents its own forms. It is at the breaking of bread that the pilgrims of Emmaus know themselves: then they could relive and refashion that immediate past of which, at the moment itself, they had been unconscious.

So it is in the progress of love. That is why he who loves always finds that he is late. *Sero te amavi*. "Too late I have loved thee," said St. Augustine to his Creator. And he tried to discern the antecedents, the first flights emanating from himself. The soul which recognises God is overwhelmed with regret at the thought that it has lost time; but this regret is compensated by the joy of knowing that, in another sense, it has always known Him: it is the groping search which has come to an end. Love manifests itself after the manner of every great Idea: it makes its début by an emergence.

Love thus begins with a crisis. In every existence it is an event situated in place and time, a surprise, a shock, a date. This event is unique; like all that is historic, it does not repeat itself. The crisis can indeed recommence with another subject, but then it is only an imitation which takes its mode and colour from the first event. If one loves truly several times, it is without doubt by a repetition.

Although profoundly logical, the explanation which the subject of loves gives of his love is nearly always erroneous. He who explains why he loves argues according to a syllogism which might be formulated thus:

MAJOR   It is quite impossible not to love that which possesses outstanding qualities.

MINOR   Now, X, quite evidently, possesses those qualities.

CONCLUSION   X is lovable.   X is loved.   I love.

In truth, he who reasons thus is not deceived as to his first premiss.   All logic of feeling supposes a similar postulate, but love inverts the historic and logical sequence of the two final factors of the syllogism.   In reality, one begins by loving; one affirms that the object is lovable and then goes back to the qualities and confers them; the syllogism of the heart follows this sequence:

MAJOR   It is quite impossible not to love one who has outstanding qualities.

MINOR   Now, I love X.

CONCLUSION. . .

It must be noted in passing that, if one at least wishes to respect the profound order of love, this syllogism is not so fallacious.   Let us refer to the model of all love which is the love of God.   What Christianity has revealed and reason might have foreseen is the fact that God does not love the creature because of his merits; but because He first loves him he has his merits.   It is true that we are considering a case unique in kind, since it belongs to God alone to create by love an object worthy of that love.   Moreover, quality seems always to precede admiration.   Man refuses to admit that the beauty of the loved object is no more than the effect of his desire to find it beautiful.   But it may be observed that human love, by projecting the quality, aids the discovery of it.   The syllogism of the heart is based upon the presentiment that love must have a cause, that this cause can only be the ideal incarnate in the flesh, and that love alone perceives that which remains hidden for others.

Since there are seeds of goodness and even of beauty everywhere (even in this insignificant face, in this apparently mediocre and sluggish person), love, by dint of its faith, makes them grow; potentialities are revealed only to him who believes.   If love and faith seem to create qualities by a kind of evocation, it is because the innermost being needs to be believed or to be loved in order to manifest itself. How many there are who remain sullen, hard, jealous, non-existent because they have never been loved!

★

This is how psycho-analysis might account for the birth of first love. It poses the most supreme of all problems, that of the unity of the person. The adolescent does not realise this unity. His inclinations are unfulfilled, often incoherent, contradictory. In the adolescent there is a depth of uncertainty, of uneasiness and of doubt, and, as it were, a latent anxiety which society scarcely cures, which it rather enhances. The mechanism of perception has already made us forget. All that we have not willed, all that we have suffered, all that we have not registered and have only perceived, all that we have felt and have not tested, all this remains within us in a state of latency. To this is added all that society forbids us to do: the controls, the censures, the repressions, the hindrances, the obstacles. We must also include the secrets which we are not told, the promises postponed till the time when we shall be 'grown-ups' which tend to make children so jealous of adults: all this nourishes a state of uneasiness, of fear, of curiosity in us.

Can one say that those who have experienced love very early do not feel this dread? Yet a mere adventure rarely satisfies, and is usually accompanied by a feeling of failure, of impurity or guilt which adds still more to the dread and brings the desire for purification so that real love can also be nourished by false and pure by impure.

In order to dispel the uncertainty and distress of his thoughts, to find the unity of his being, the youth imagines a kind of second ego, a super-ego, as the Freudians say. This super-ego is not yet an *alter ego*, that is to say the image of another being who will come for my fulfilment; this would rather be an *ego alter* and, as it were, the reverse of my own ego. Owing to the fact that we are limited and incomplete, we are continually forming (willy-nilly) the abstract image of the one who is to fulfil our destiny. This image is different from the image of the being loved, although the latter is nourished by the former.

What are the characteristics of this duplicate image thus produced by our own self-consciousness? It is both that which we desire to be in order to fulfil ourselves, and that which we fear that we shall never be able to become. It is the consciousness of a double lack: that which is lacking in order to perfect and develop ourselves, just as the flower is lacking to the bud or the fruit to the flower, and, on the other hand, it is that which we lack for our completion, as the lily lacks the rose to make the bouquet. The duplicate image is our obverse, and maybe the dim outline of its features will be shown in our expression, the sign both of that to which we aspire and of that which we lack.

Thus the most amorous nature will be that which has the most unfulfilled propensities and, at the same time, feels most incomplete in itself. Picture the soul of an artist with manifold desires but, at the same time, with an insatiable sense of emptiness and thirst: it would be love itself. St. Francis of Assisi is an example of it. If God is defined by love, it is without doubt because in love there is an infinite multiplicity of manifestations and possible participations and at the same time, as it were, need to humble oneself.

We can thus understand that the love of another is inseparable from self-love, and can divine the unfathomable riches of the formula 'to love another as oneself.' To lose ourselves in another is to live to perfection, since we then find the being who all at once consummates, fulfils, and consequently unifies us.

We understand also that inability to love comes from poverty of soul: he whose propensities are few and easily satisfied will never love. He who is happy, he who is blissfully satisfied does not love, nor he who knows no anguish.

When the psychological situation is thus ripe, anything will liberate the anguish, cause the image to be projected and become real. The circumstances in which love has the chance of establishing itself may even be defined. It can, perhaps, even be explained why, when I am capable of loving a very great number of persons, my choice becomes fixed upon this particular one.

The more the other is plastic, indeterminate in appearance and mysterious in her novelty, the more capable she will be of exciting masculine love. That is why the young girl, of whom Novalis said that she was the image of the possible, will always attract. It is remarkable to observe how many women who have become the objects of great spiritual loves have been incomplete and, as it were, potential creatures: such as Beatrice for Dante, Sophie for Novalis; and one wonders if this is also true of Marguerite in *Faust* or of Violaine in *l'Annonce*. This is probably due to the fact that potentiality attracts the creative spirit since there it can find scope for its powers. The summit of desire is to escape from the frustration of creative power and, in the reflection of oneself in water which no breath ruffles, where one can at once behold and cleanse oneself, this can come to pass.

To explain our preferences psycho-analysts often adopt the method of reviving some remote memory, some situation of our early infancy. That is why it has been observed that the wife often resembles the mother; it should be added that contrast is also resemblance.

The problem we are considering is very like that of dreams. It may be asked why we should dream of this and not of that. A psychologist gave the answer that the probability of dreaming of a fact increases with the vividness of the impression produced, and diminishes with the amount of attention paid to it: that is to say, our dreams are produced by the impressions which have not been apprehended by consciousness. They return all the more readily for being neglected or rejected at the time.

Dreams are filled with furtive dramas which have not crossed the frontiers of the watcher's consciousness. Everyone knows how dangers which we have escaped while scarcely conscious of them readily reappear in dreams. Now it is possible that, in our first infancy, we have known many very vivid impressions which have not, however, been gathered and sifted by reflection. This is, in fact, the first stage of life, an age when impressions are strong and reflection upon the impressions is very feeble; when the consciousness is open to receive new imprints of things and quite incapable of grasping them or even of realising what they are.

If that is so, impressions lying latent in a sort of sub-memory may return and set the dream of love in motion. The mechanism of love would thus be the reverse of that of the dream, in which it is the daytime emotion that gives rise to the phantasmagoria of the night. Here it would be the nocturnal emotion of the primitive history which would cause the lucid fixation of love to arise in the conscious phase. Thus the sudden shock of love suggesting a flash of lightning would be explained, and too, this mobilisation, this swift and total concentration of the soul upon a single being to the exclusion of all others.

It must be recognised that, if the problem is confined to the provisional sphere of the mechanism of love, the hypothesis has some truth. In particular it accounts for this paradox, that it is possible to love profoundly that which is ugly or mediocre. What strikes us in such cases is not the quality of the object but its resemblance to another figure met in the past which gave us a juvenile emotion. That would also explain the fact that melancholy women are often the object of a *grande passion* on the part of those whose infantile memories are sad.

This return of the dream on waking is no doubt connected with what Allendy calls the desire to recompose a *situation-type*. Here we touch upon the problem of destiny in relation to character. Everything happens as if the events which occur to us resembled each other. The events which we encounter resemble us and they resemble each other because they resemble us. If I slip twice on orange-peel, it is because the peel is in me; what makes me fall is not the peel but clumsiness.

Let us remind ourselves that our propensities are incomplete. We are in search of the keystone to complete the building and of the buttress to support it. We cannot create that which would assure our peace, but we can suggest an imaginary diagram for it. Each one of us projects the outline of a situation which could satisfy our propensities; or rather, we project an infinity of potential situations corresponding to our propensities, just as the point O projects an infinity of points equidistant from O to form a circle. It is remarkable that these potential situations may be favourable or unfavourable. If we have a tendency to believe ourselves persecuted or to feel guilty, we project a situation in which we shall be persecuted or condemned. If we love conflict, retort, irony, we project a situation in which we invite attack. If we love to be the one who re-establishes order and is alone able to do it, we project a situation where everything is desperate, we attract catastrophe in order the better to be able to remedy it.

Drama (tragic or comic) is often founded upon such repetitions of situations. Georges Dandin, for example, exhibits a vainglorious and sensitive temperament. Since vanity, for him, is a way of reassuring himself by the spectacle of his power, and since sensitivity is the dread of being deprived of what he has, a character of this kind should develop a situation in which he can act in accordance with both these traits at the same time. He therefore encounters the situation of an unhappy husband. He is led on to marry above him, to believe that he is deceived, to provoke what he dreads. We have the impression that he is the plaything of fate and human injustice. In reality, he himself creates three times over the situation corresponding to his own character, and, for his own satisfaction, three times over forges his own unhappiness.

Now, no event is more capable of causing the *situation* corresponding to our character to pass from possibility into reality than that of meeting with a woman. It is probable that of all the women whom we meet the one we choose is not so much the one to whom a vague memory of early infancy corresponds as she who happens to realise the situation in which we are involved. That is why we often choose the woman who will bring us happiness or unhappiness according as our bent is towards one or the other. And there again the profound law is fulfilled which ordains that a man gets what he deserves and that events precipitate us along the way we have already chosen. He who loves tormenting will fall in love with a person devoted to self-effacement; a pure soul will attach himself to a soul yet more pure. Everywhere we seek the being who will let us complete our own inner circuit. That is why the lost soul is rarely cured by love, for he fastens upon another lost soul. That is why the most perfect persons are called upon to suffer; for the difference between complementary and contrary, between those who fulfil and those who enrage us is not great.

Thus of all life's happenings, love is outstandingly unique. While ordinary events are passive phenomena introducing no disturbing element into the innermost being, the encounter with another being is like a germ which reacts upon us, which seizes us, which creates a new polarity in the circuit of our thought. But love has this admirable feature, that the service which, in loving, we render ourselves, we also render to another by means of our love. Still more, in allowing ourselves to be loved, we render that service to ourselves over again. It is not so much the unification of the self through the projection of one's own image which is the most characteristic feature of this phenomenon of love as the reception in oneself of an image of oneself which derives from the beloved. In other words, the most remarkable experience is not that of loving but that of being loved.

Let us try to analyse this second aspect of the mechanism of love. In love the lover substitutes the other's image of him for his own image of himself and, in that act, is cured of the self-hatred which self-love engenders. It is a new image, fresh and innocent, in which all our physical and moral characteristics are idealised, which replaces the always somewhat tormented consciousness of oneself. This image is incessantly projected by love upon our own self-consciousness and thus forms a veritable duplicate of it.

Thus what an ideal morality impels us to realise 'this second person superior to ourselves who is our "type" ' love lets us attain upon easy terms, too easy terms. . . . But this, maybe, reinforces the moral effort? For just as it is not easy, by oneself, to raise oneself to the level of a super-self, so, when this model of oneself is projected upon us by one who loves us, it becomes easy to become like it. In both cases a sort of illusion is present since an image is imposed which does not yet really exist. But when this image proceeds from the love of another, it has a creative power. That is why each of us acts, is real, even exists at all, according to our capacity as envisaged by those who love us.

The secret of education is to suppose everybody to be a little better than, in fact, he really is. What am I if not what those who love me believe me to be? When consciousness is self-enclosed it dessicates and torments itself. When it opens itself to love it frees itself from its inner bonds. But it is only when the consciousness welcomes love that it expands. Thus, in the ambit of love, the response means more than the demand and the gift received more than the gift bestowed. To love is good; to be loved, on condition always that the love received is that of admiration, is yet more fulfilling.

We conclude that the mechanism of love involves two 'hallucinations', each of which has an advantageous effect: by means of the first we project the image of that which we lack upon another person; by the second we ourselves receive the image of our possible perfection enabling us to surpass ourselves and fulfil ourselves at our best. The first mechanism frees, the second uplifts us.

Such, at least in its state of perfection, is love. And already it can be foreseen how difficult, how almost impossible to attain love is. For its mechanism, if simple, is delicate. In fact it may be inferred that, if the reciprocal emotion did not occur with equal force, that is to say, if one should love without being loved, or at least were not loved as much, love would become a cause of torment; and of a very cruel torment, since it attacks our very being in its most vital propensities, compelling us to belie ourselves without ceasing to be in love.

If the other, instead of loving us, loves another, the torment becomes an agony. If we cease to admire the person we have loved, then the life of love is a grievous condemnation, and most of all for those who find themselves compelled to dwell amidst the ruins of their love.

★

This is the place to examine the mechanism of *inversion*, a process all-important for the study of so complex a feeling. We have remarked many times how love is transformed into hate and not into indifference. We should explain why this is so.

Feelings tend to become chaotic: they are complicated and fragile organisms. Fear, that salutary reaction, torments by confusing and paralysing us. Sensitivity, which is akin to spirit, is converted into a morose delight in our suffering. Love becomes ennui or rather changes to an estrangement full of affinities after the fashion of Ovid's so-cruel verse:

Nec sine te nec tecum vivere possum.[1]

Let us, if possible, examine the mechanism of this paradoxical inversion. In the first place love is inverted through its own excess; gross indulgence ends in satiety and this, with fine natures, approaches bitterness. Then, too, love exhausts itself in a dismal repetition, in a sentimental comedy which it craves but which, like all insincerity, is apt to become wearisome. Add to this the fact that, since the choice has been his own, the victim cannot blame the other for his deception; he must there-fore confess that he has been mistaken upon the most vital of all

[1] I can neither live with thee nor without thee.

issues. It sometimes happens, too, that the suffering of love is enjoyed and unconsciously provoked.

In the same way dread arouses defensive reactions. But the defensive mechanism, once set in motion, is liable to be abandoned to the basest excitements and dread is seen to lead to self-paralysis. The paradox of it is that one can then take pleasure even in one's anguish: for those who make sensation their object and desire, above all, to feel, there is little difference between enjoyment and suffering. That is why, when those sufferings come from the heart, the pursuit of them is exacting. Since love is not to be won by any means which we can master and can only be maintained by the presence of another, it is almost unavoidable that there should be lack of harmony and, as is so aptly said, *dissensions*, between two persons thus associated. From the moment when the unification of our being by virtue of the other's idealised image of it no longer functions so powerfully (if we do not take heed to sublimate love and make it minister to a work more mighty), we become aware of petty discords which, till then, had not been perceived at all.

In all undertakings and engagements there is a bliss of ignorance, which means being anaesthetised to the difficulties or only perceiving them when one can no longer draw back. On the other hand, since love is maintained by the projection of the image, unless constantly renewed and that with a certain skill, continual presence is wont to arrest the process. The fact is, every feeling adapts a changing being to another who changes no less, and this adaptation must itself be capable of development. In order that love may remain unaltered and also that it may uplift and transcend itself, it is expedient that it should itself be amenable to changes of time and place, to the alternations of departure and return, to successive discoveries, even to harmless crises. This need is met at first by the daily round and also by coquetry.

A woman's instinct knows that, to attract, she must seem to evade; she must reject and then, like the Shulamite, cry "*Come back!''* The beauty of a face is nothing if not renewed and, to preserve it, art counsels change of appearance: it is only so that the smile and the glance keep their value. This is no less the case with conversation, and here man excels. That the life of feeling may be possible there should be every conceivable variety, provided that the unity remains intact. That is why love (human and divine) which, in the monotony of continual presence, is liable to grow lukewarm, always seems to be rejuvenated by separation. Apart from the fact that absence restores the ideal image and establishes the unity of purpose, the suffering caused by long separation becomes a common possession which no discord can disintegrate.

The chief joy of love is, in fact, not so much the unity of inner being as this constant sharing, this return of our thought to ourselves after passing through the consciousness of another, this circumincession the origin of which we cannot tell. But as soon as some incident, some grain of dust, some delay disturbs that return of our thought to us love falls into a state of torment, and the more so just because this dissonance derives from one with whom we are so intimate. The pain inflicted by a foe is sweet compared to that which a lover can cause: that is a wound for the spirit which seems almost irreparable, driving us to distrust love itself so that, like Virgil, we dub it *harsh* and *cruel*. It is a state which easily slips into one of loathing.

Moreover, when love and hate are compared, it is the latter which seems the more constant. It more easily remains in a state of intensity. And, since love sees people as they will never really be, hate is the more clear-sighted; hate often beholds them as, in secret and shame, they really are. Hate can justify itself more surely, for, with man, goodness is, as it were, in a germinal state of desire and struggle while, on the other hand, evil scores unmistakable signs upon our history. And just because we are glad to find absolution in self-accusation, it is more easy to believe the evil than the good. Thus the transition from love to hate is far more simple than the reverse.

The most frequent inversion of love is jealousy. Love being the image of the self projected by chance upon another person, the slightest doubt about that image is sufficient to make it seem foreign to us and still more to make us believe it to be the sole property of another person. Thus the torment of the jealous man is understandable. Since the projection is no longer successfully consummated it becomes impossible for him to refashion his own inner unity. Not only does he feel himself to be disintegrated but he has also the impression that the only thing which could have made him happy has been stolen from him by another. It is characteristic of this feeling that it causes its victim to revolve in a kind of circle from which he cannot extricate himself. For jealousy is nourished on the most trifling of details, and always finds plenty of them.

Of all the various kinds of jealousy that of envious jealousy is the most paradoxical. It might be called the complex of Cain. It is, at one and the same time, both admiring and destructive. And it is perhaps in some such jealousy that the most secret griefs are rooted. The evil which befalls us is less hateful than the unattainable good. It is not so much from others as from our own insufficiency that we suffer; at bottom it is ourselves that we loathe. Suppose I, a mere mediocrity, live with some person who is infinitely good. The very proofs of friendship which he offers me can seem like tacit reproaches. When we ourselves cannot rise to the same degree of goodness and love it is disturbing to receive goodness and love. Then, from spite, from despair, we are tempted to become tyrannical.

Apart from this jealousy incited by malice and infidelity, a jealousy born of virtue itself is also possible. Claudel has described this process in l'Annonce; consider the relation between Mara and Violaine. That is why within love (as, to-day, we say so knowingly) the traces of sadism and masochism are often discoverable; I refer to the morose craving to make the beloved suffer and, still more, to make oneself suffer. And, just as laughter is a petty cruelty curing us of real cruelty by a kind of vaccination, or weeping a slight nervous crisis saving us from a real one, or a kiss an innocuous embrace, so the coquetry so prevalent in love is also a form of purification. Woman pretends contempt, spite, separation without really believing in them and, indeed, making it quite clear that she does not. Like the Olympic rivalry between nations, she wages a fictitious, but avoids a real warfare. But it is a dangerous game; it must be remembered that love is unconsciously cruel. It is notable that as soon as they cease to love us for an instant, our lovers are quick to discover the precise remark which will wound us most deeply, the most winged and poisoned dart.

The attitudes which we have just described are mainly masculine. There are others which are more relevant to the woman: for example, that scorn of being loved which M. Gide has analysed so well in his *Ecole des Femmes*: it is the inverse aspect of esteem and admiration. Woman, less sensual and more sentimental, approaches man with a global esteem, an intense admiration, an almost absolute disinterestedness. Neither grave faults nor baseness prevent a woman from loving if, otherwise, the man preserves his prestige in her eyes, but rather a general mediocrity or the lack of those virile qualities which she expects. Woman is so fashioned that she endures a banal and mean man with difficulty.

But though nature has made woman maternal by instinct she has not endowed man with a radical heroism. Our male virtue is more a matter of will. Thus, when she compares man with herself, woman is tempted to find him petty. André Gide shows us a perfectly sincere woman who is astonished to encounter lack of loyalty in her husband. But, in one shape or another, a crisis of this kind can occur in all unions when, in petty daily affairs, reality is substituted for the ideal image. At that moment, as we shall soon see, all love needs a new incarnation. When this re-adaptation does not occur, two feelings are possible; the one is *scorn*, the other *pity*. But each of them destroys love at its roots; to have pity for him whom one loves is, perhaps, to uplift oneself, but, unless indeed this pity is analogous to the divine pity and is accompanied by a sense of redemption, it is no longer love.

A final deviation in love, also more frequent with woman, is the instinct of servitude and the unconscious desire to be dominated, which explains why, although one of the parties may suffer at the hands of the other, some couples are inseparable. It is not uncommon to see associations between two persons founded upon their complementary defects. He who unconsciously desires to beat will tend to marry one who desires to be beaten. Fools attract and bewitch each other. The tyrant loves the slave, the torturer seeks a victim. Inversely, those who relish being victims seek a torturer. That is why one sees the young lion espouse the ewe lamb, the serpent fascinate the dove and Alceste caught in the net of a coquette, as though they all strove to hurl themselves into their unhappiness.

We have now studied the psychical process of the appearance, exaltation and, at times, inversion of the phenomenon called love. But, as with all such explanations, the study of the mechanism is both veracious and misleading. It is especially so if it remains isolated, if it is not united with and, as it were, taken up into a higher hypothesis; if it is not related to all that is most fundamental in man, to his knowledge, to his destiny, to the tokens of his *essence*, this explanation by process is liable to become fallacious.

We shall realise all this if we note carefully that, whether it be 'Proustian' or 'Freudian', it is possible for the mechanism of love to exist without there being any real or abiding love; that it is possible for love to make its appearance with practically no mechanism at all and by a kind of grace; that, if it be of the most subtle kind, the explanation of love by mechanism is all the more true in that love is very near to passion and is then a caricature of itself; or, again, that this explanation by the process is all the more applicable to the love-passion when it is on the point of inversion. It is so whenever we interpret by means of the inferior factor, spirit by body, mind by the social factor, religion by the magical or sexual element; such interpretations are the more accurate in proportion to the counterfeit element in the object under consideration, that is to say, in proportion to the perversion of the mental phenomenon, the degeneration of the moral phenomenon, the corruption of the religious phenomenon.

When we think that we have explained a person by his *how* to the exclusion of his *why* (and every genetic explanation, since it explains the person by his history, is of this kind), we do not touch his real essence nor even his appearance, but rather what might be called his false essence, that is, what would be his essence if, instead of being engendered by nature or created by God, it were begotten by the spirit of man. Moreover, *mechanism* and *essence* are closely related. It is within the mechanism that essence is realised and revealed. However pure it may be, the essence depends upon the mechanism in some degree. More than this, the mechanism is a type, a symbol of the essence. In the realm of essences the spirit moves from illumination to illumination without interim or interruption, after the fashion of thought ascribed to the angels. If mechanism and essence are thus closely related a few of love's developments will serve our purpose.

★

The essence of love consists in the gift of the self to another, and no process can explain that donation. For the modern mind, to explain is to project a reality on to the plane of mechanism. When put into words the donation of love loses its essential characteristic, the knowledge that it is a gift. It appears as a subtle calculation, a sentimental satisfaction, a crystallisation like that of minerals, a romantic ecstasy, a physiological function, a sociological rite, a psychological cure, or as an existential disease; and though we may have reached the limit of such diminishing explanations, the list is not at all complete. Certainly, under some aspects, love is indeed all that, but it has each of these characteristics accidentally and in addition.

But what then is a gift? We are confronted with one of those words which are so primary that it is difficult to define it by reducing it to a more simple notion; we can at least clarify it by contrast.

A gift is an act which is completely disinterested, in which there is no return of the subject upon the subject; without this it is not a gift but a calculation. The gift is disinterested; it is free: it has set itself beyond all constraint, even beyond all reason, if reason ever were a constraint. On the other hand, the gift, when made by a human being, demands that that being deprive himself of what he possesses. There is no real gift without a certain sacrifice of self: in the gift of love there is necessarily loss of substance, privation of possession, mortification, as we see in nature in the case of those insects in which, for the male, love and death are the same thing.

Such a gift is certainly a gracious thing. It resounds upon every level of being, and every chord of our nature resounds to its note.

But, even in these joys, the essence of love is not in the joy; it consists in the idea that this joy is a symbol and an effect of love, that it is given with love and that it re-doubles in the joy of the other. The loftiest act of love is therefore not in receiving, but in giving. There, moreover, lies the difference between love and passion; the latter is nothing but love without sacrifice and consequently without gift. The second stage of love consists in the return of the beloved to the lover.

It is the essence of love to be reciprocal. The love which returns is not so much a *re-connaissance* as a *con-naissance* (mutual birth): we are born, we are reborn together from the same spark. Loving and being loved are one and the same act: the gift which is made includes the very being of the giver in its indivisible totality; it is the gift not so much of what *one has* as of what *one is*. This love, I say, contains all that is less than our being: life, sustenance, possessions, cares, abode, time, death, memory. And the gift received also includes all these. Thus one can see that in love the saying of St. John of the Cross is exemplified: "I have determined to lose and I have gained everything".

Love is essentially a substitute for possession. In the end, possessing all we had lost, we find ourselves again. But then, you will say, what is the difference? And of what use is it thus to substitute? The difference is infinite: for what we have henceforth we keep without egotism, since what once was *possessed* is now *given*. We give up, we yield this object and we find ourselves in possession of another identical object. For example, one gives a flower from one's garden and receives the same flower from the other's garden so that the gardener, passing on the morrow, sees no difference. For the outsider it comes to exactly the same thing; but for him who loves the very universe is transformed. Certainly, if the object were only a thing, there would be no difference; but, in the human order, the object is never simply a thing, it is also *relation*. For the spirit, the flower given and the flower received are different realities.

Moreover, those who love know that an object is worth more if it has been given to us, than if we possessed or acquired it. He who is clothed by love and all of whose garments are presents (like the child or the monk) is the most glorious of beings. The object given is then found to be purified from the bondage of possession which diminished its reality, since, for him who has it, each object at length becomes opaque. It is better to receive than to have.

Here too, in a special case, love reveals to us the law of all being. Goods have, without doubt, been bequeathed to man only in order, by their exchange, to increase love: there, had not greed spoiled everything, would be the profound meaning of commerce. "We only possess truly," says G. Thibon somewhere, "what we receive; and what we expect from the one who loves us, is that he should give us what we had already. For the repose of my soul, I need to receive it from thee as an alms." Would it perhaps be quite a good definition of being to say: *being is that which should be exchanged?*

Now, in the course of this exchange between the *amare* (to love) and the *amari* (to be loved) and through this very exchange, a third term appears which is the work of love. Love is not conceived without generation. It is necessary here to revive a very ancient idea, one long forgotten maybe, but which enables us to penetrate to the very foundations of this creative mystery. Plotinus had foreseen it when he said that action is a product and a weakened image of contemplation, that he who contemplates should not will the result of his contemplation, that this result proceeds naturally from the act of contemplating. A dancer thinks of nothing and yet his footsteps make patterns on the ground. It is in this sense that generation is not the *end* of love, but its result, its irradiation, its echo and its image. *When there are two there are three*; or rather *when the two become only one*, a third term is born. But, let us note, this third term appears in two manners and at two different levels: love *discovers* a third term which already existed and *creates* from it one which has not yet come into existence.

As soon as we love, we become aware that love demands a setting in which we can love one another. We only love truly if we love in a sphere which is superior to us, in a unity more lofty and more fulfilled, in a plenary term which assures the union of the other two.

Just as respiration supposes an atmosphere, so love calls for an *erosphere*. For those who have no religion at their disposal, this common term will be simply the personification of love; they will say that they love in their love. "Do that for the sake of our love." For others, the *erosphere* will be a common ideal: country, science. . . .

But the true and real term which unites the loves, which establishes them, without which they can neither understand each other nor expand, is that which men have named God. In fact the third term should be a being which is present in the two other beings, assuring their interchange in spite of space and time; it can only be so if it is itself superior to time, to space and is itself capable of love, let us even say, wholly defined by love. That is why, even for the unbeliever, love (if it is total) necessarily becomes religious; it passes beyond the mutual ecstasy with which it begins and rises to an unique adoration.

But the most evident middle term to be seen in the work of love is the child. In making the child the unconscious work of love and its concrete image still more than the mark and end of nuptial union, we might seem to depart from the traditional idea. In reality, as we shall soon see, we plumb to a greater depth with this very idea. Generation of children without love is indeed conceivable. Such would be the case with an Eastern potentate taking a slave in order to have descendants, or with a rich bourgeois making a marriage by arrangement to ensure himself an heir. On the other hand, one cannot conceive the absence of a generation according to the spirit; love is always fertile, if only in the transformation of those who love.

Yet the child is not the product of the father and mother but of their mutual affection, and much less of their definite purpose than of their nature. That is why the new-born child is always a surprise; it is never fully expected in the form it takes; in any case never in its sex. An only child should indeed suffice to close the circuit of love. In the most divine family known on earth, there was only one child, but this child was conceived by faith as one who gathered up all human differences in himself. And even if society had no need for numerous children and could be content with a simple substitution of two for two, the fact that from love there could emerge those similar, but unpredictable portraits which compose a family would remain a thing of beauty.

Moreover, every work of love has need of love in order to grow; the *opus amoris*[1] cannot be detached from love, it must remain in its ambit. If, in order to live its life apart from the

[1] Work of love.

outset, the work of love were detached from love, the *fertility* of love would not differ from the *spawning* of nature. The sunbeam does not remain in the sun. But the more one mounts in the scale of being the more one notices that the work remains hidden for a long time within the principles which have begotten it. All love educates. Still more, education can only take place within the ambit of love, and that is why it is proper that the most perfect work of love, which is the child, should long remain in the form of cell, of embryo, then of the new-born babe, of the little child, of the adolescent, and also that its maturity should be retarded for a long time. No doubt all love creates, but it is in two tempos; in the moment of its first ecstasy it produces an initial state; then, in the long duration of its labours and cares, it develops this beginning and fashions a freedom from it. That is what Plato divined when he said that love is an *educator* as well as a *generator*, the education being no other than the continued presence of love around its offspring.

Nevertheless, this educational rôle proper to love is not only accomplished in the physical order; it could even be said that generation after the flesh is only the symbol and ground of generation after the spirit. We are not the children of our parents because they have begotten us but because they have prolonged the process of generation by maintaining us for some score of years within the field of their mutual affection. That is why divorce, which seems the sign of human freedom, is so detrimental to the development of the free man.

Moreover, the educative rôle does not affect only the off-spring of love but also those who love each other. In addition to the external fertility of which we usually speak there is an inward fertility which brings it to pass that the first children of love are the parents themselves. The husband is the child of the wife; and perhaps, although less obviously, the reverse is also true. It is doubtless in order to distinguish the inward fertility essential to love from the outward and accidental fertility that the Creator permits occasional sterility, that is to say, love without apparent fertility. In that event the *opus amoris* remains within the scope of love; it is that which begets, rears, instructs, matures, expands those who love: it is enough.

★

Finally, let us consider the relation between the two planes of *mechanism* and *essence*.

The essence of love is very rarely attained in its plenitude. Perhaps, indeed, it never has been. In this world of ours, it is always associated with mechanism. For the greater part of the time, it is the mechanism which fills the field of consciousness. But a *minimum* of essence is enough to change the *meaning* of a mechanism. It is said that there is nothing in the reason which has not already existed in experience, except reason itself. And it could be said of love: *Nihil est in amore quod non prius fuerit in mecanismo amoris, nisi ipse amor.*[1] This maxim may even be yet more true of love than of reason, for love is an end transcending all the means which it promotes, all the acts and symbols which manifest it. It is far beyond the flesh, beyond even feeling, beyond all that presents or represents it: it is what we wished to signify by saying that it is a gift.

It is the function of the mechanism to place the essence within reach of the greatest number. The mechanism of love, so powerful, so regular, so total, so statistical (to such a degree that, in certain circumstances, it does not seem to matter what man loves what woman) causes the most rare of all experiences to be offered to the greater part of mankind, so that they are even tempted to believe that they have only to let nature have its way to be free of a realm which seems to be beyond nature. The blind law of great numbers here works in favour of the essences.

In the order of love we can waver between two hypotheses: we can say that everything happens as though each couple were the result of a fortuitous meeting between two monads having

---

[1] There is nothing in love which was not previously in the mechanism of love, except love itself.

the illusion of being made for one another, and we can equally well contend that everything happens as if those who love each other had, from all eternity, been predestined to love each other, although they may seem to have met by chance. These two hypotheses are both true, the second perhaps the more so, at least where love is really concerned.

Suppose that a demiurge wishes to give musical sense to beings drawn from the slime; suppose these beings to be very earthly and that it were impossible to make them participate in beauty by direct revelation; suppose finally that this demiurge were able to communicate movements to them; suppose in particular that he could constrain the fingers of his creature to play on the keys of a keyboard or on the stops of a flute so as to let the melody flow forth. This would be produced mechanically; but it would also happen that, from time to time, these elementary beings would attain to an almost pure musical emotion, that the mechanism would induce this aesthetic state which the demiurge could not arouse directly, because of their deficiency.

Observe, moreover, that all poetry and all religion proceed like this demiurge. The poetic and mystical states are always induced by mechanisms; the *mechanism* is everywhere necessary to sustain the *essence*, in order to supplement it at need and to summon it, when tardy, by a preliminary imitation. The relation of language (which is a mechanism) to thought (which is never such) is also elucidated in this way. We undoubtedly deceive ourselves when we believe that this chosen one was predestined for us and that we love her with a unique and inexplicable love. But the psychologist, who believes that, by reducing it to an hallucination, to a crystallisation or a sublimation, he has analysed love, deceives himself still more, for the mechanism, however perfect it may be, cannot itself arouse the least particle of essence.

It remains true that the essence of love cannot be produced nor even sustained by ourselves: it is out of time and we are in transit. It is pure and we are impure beings. It is disinterested and we calculate. On the other hand, the mechanism of love is so changeable that it can easily turn to loathing. Thus everything menaces love. The very means which sustain it can turn against it, the faith which animates it is too lofty for the inconstancy of our hearts. That is why, as we are about to see, society, custom, duration must come to the rescue of love.

5   The development of love

IN the preceding chapter we have studied the original crisis of love. We conceded the common illusion which consists in the observation and fixation of love in its moment of crisis alone. In contradistinction to other emotions love certainly begins with a state of violence and an almost morbid crisis. But, once this crisis has achieved the existence of the couple, a new reality comes into being, and, in course of time, develops. And the description of the fashion in which love manifests itself in the midst of duration is another subject for study, distinct from the first.

In the crisis we apprehended it chiefly in the state of action, of a quivering instant. In the course of duration we see it in the state of nature and custom, incarnate in life and society. In the last century Michelet understood how fallacious it was to study love in its opening phase alone and not to write its whole life history. "If love is no more than crisis," he said, "the Loire might equally well be termed a flood." And Michelet observed also that, if observation of the crisis induces us to lay the accent upon the fatality of love, the study of its history allows us to recognise in it the communal labour of two freedoms. Love is only human because it has a history, because we can imprint the seal of our personalities upon its activity.

The fact is that it is only through infinite new beginnings that the infinite enters time. And, in contrast to the notion normally held by our romantic societies with their libertarian conception of liberty, in love it is not the commencement (that so-ambiguous and disturbing commencement), but the continuity, the permanence, the continuation of the initial spark in a contained and gentle fire, with its inevitable cinders, that really matters. That is why earlier societies, taking their stand upon the sense of propriety, knowledge of circumstances and principles, the divination of durable and fertile affinities, were justified in directing the choice of the young. It is true that marriage is the fruit of love; it is still more true that love is the fruit of marriage. And the art of loving is not in the least merely a gathering of the fruits of voluptuousness as Ovid, Catullus and the libertine tradition supposed; it is rather the science of making the fleeting love of youth endure and multiply throughout the course of a long human life.

In spite of the deep identity which the vow of fidelity expresses, like every normal feeling, love is, in fact, in a state of continual transformation. It cannot continue without constant renewal, without perpetual variation. It is the adaptation of one changing being to another and the adaptation must itself be capable of change. In order not to be destroyed by the automatism which lies in wait for it, it needs change of time, of place, of structure, of the alternations of departure and return, of successive discoveries and of harmless crises. But fidelity consists in the integration of all these accidents and in profiting by them. Just as true identity is a live identity which incorporates changes and makes them work together for permanence, so true fidelity is inventive: it makes use of danger and vexation to weave from them a tough and solid web which has the splendour of natural things; like light, the glance and the smile this fidelity incessantly reveals itself and vanishes.

At the root of love there is, no doubt, an eternal repetition, an implacable monotony. The most absolute type of love is very much like that which Juliette Drouet devoted to Victor Hugo. She was the nun of profane love. She had no family or possessions or religion or occupation. Hugo's children were not hers and her child was not Hugo's. For fifty years she wrote the same letter twenty thousand times. But it is just such a love-fixation which, even if it does not become sin, approaches morbidity. Juliette's love was a transparent folly, without development, without rhythm, save that of jealousy; and, if the adoration of Juliette for Hugo had not been still stronger than her love, her passion would readily have become inverted.

Genuine mystical love knows development also, and the science of the love of God consists in part in knowing how to discern its stages. It is the same with human love: it lives, it develops because the monotonous repetition of gestures, sayings and situations nourishes it silently with the utmost variety. Whence come these variations? In the first place from the fruition of love; from, I would say, the children who, at each birth and above all at the first, create new situations and transform the very fibre of love by introducing into it the relationships of paternity and maternity. Love feeds upon the accidents of life, on crises, on mutual forgiveness, on trials overcome; it is modified in secret by the rhythm and the wane of desire; it is transformed by the death of one of the pair. Moreover, since personality varies with life's phases under the impact of profession, time and experience, this occurs imperceptibly. In this respect perhaps woman alters more than man; she changes from morning to evening. The association of love thus undergoes changes more profound than any other. Friendship is, indeed, less subject to modification; when your friend grows old he gives you the same kind of succour. But an old woman and a young woman do not give the same kind of love.

Society, which reckons with these metamorphoses, seeks to safeguard love against itself. In the country, it surprises the couple behind the hedge; it hales them to the registry office, it enforces marriage. It deprecates free love; it honours the public alliance, and makes its rupture difficult. As Montaigne advises, it wishes to marry the two persons according to the most abiding principles: patrimony, tradition, propriety, expediency. But, still more than this external or social obligation, however potent, what maintains love in the course of its duration is the internal process of conservation and fulfilment; it is this that preserves its identity in spite of obstacles, this that matures it, and, at life's end, leaves it still young and incomplete and ready, so it seems, for an eternal progress. And nowhere is the character of a development better perceived than in the history of the couple, when it proceeds according to the law of reason and not according to the eruptions of passion. The first crisis supplies the germ, but the development ensures that the germ shall maintain its identity in infinitely varied circumstances.

Thus, not only is the identity preserved (which, in the final reckoning, would be a small matter) but it lives, that is to say it manifests itself in unpredictable and richer forms, since, in a normal development, all the past is integrated in the future. Nothing is lost, everything is recreated.

There, in a new age, is to be found the constant and fundamental law of love, so well stated but so ill comprehended by Freud: the *sublimation*. Married love cannot exist without surpassing itself, without surmounting itself, without 'sublimating' itself, as I will demonstrate in the next chapter. But sublimation is in no way the renouncement or repudiation of the principle of love; to *sublimate* is not to *deny* but to *assume*; it is not to destroy but to restore upon a higher level; not to condemn but to glorify. That is why Platonism is false, for it sundered the bonds of the real with the ideal. Sublimation is a peaceful effort to achieve nature's work in us, that of perpetually raising up the lower by causing it to participate in the higher life. It is then quite understandable why all who have spoken of love with profundity have distinguished its states, phases or, as St. Teresa said, 'mansions'. And here again we see how the analysis of mystical can clarify ordinary experiences for, without doubt, there is but one love. The law of love is thus that of deepening to the essence. And, just as in climbing to the top of a mountain the continual ascent takes us through zones of different vegetation, so it is with this development of love. When consummated, it is found to have passed through quite distinct stages analogous to the 'mansions' of the 'castle' of the soul.

Nevertheless, before studying this development, it should be noted that this is a *double* development, and, in this respect, differs profoundly from mystical development. Every human development involves an inward testing. And if the test proper to the development of mystical love is that of solitude and the impossibility of experiencing without uncertainty the presence of the divine guest, the difficulty in the development of human love consists, on the contrary, in the presence of another being different in nature from yourself whose development does not follow the same phases. That is one of love's crosses. It is necessary too, before studying this development, to give our attention to a fundamental problem, that of the difference in nature between man and woman.

★

We have already encountered this difficulty in the preceding chapter while studying the beginnings of love. But, at the moment of the original crisis and in the instant of the discovery which man makes of woman and woman of man, it is the *image* or the *senses* which are the instruments of knowledge: very imperfect instruments. If we examine the life of the couple throughout its course it is a very different matter; each takes cognisance of the other, not in the moment of exaltation, but throughout the whole period. Then each perceives not the *accidental* but the *natural* in the other, the nature being that which subsists through the variations. And the nature of man is not at all the same as that of woman.

The difference between the two natures is difficult to grasp, due primarily to the fact that the philosophy of woman has been written by men. Generally speaking, such philosophy is the work of celibates or misogynists and, when man speaks about woman, it is usually under the aspect of pleasure, passion or the housewife's function. The books which women have written about themselves (such as those of Marcelle Tinayre, Gina Lombroso, Colette) are rather special pleading than analysis. For Michelet, woman is essentially a sick soul who must therefore be defended; thus, amongst masculine studies, his are perhaps the most sympathetic, though they still partake of such special pleading. Woman remains for man an unexplored domain, though nigh—too nigh, no doubt, to stimulate the wish for understanding.

There is a saying in the Bible which we should consider here. The author of *Genesis* does not say "God made man and woman" but "God created them male and female", which suggests that God imprinted His image and likeness upon two different planes of being and, probably, after two inverse patterns. Thus the two errors into which analysis tends to fall are promoted. Soon (as with certain poets such as Edgar Poë and Novalis) woman will be shown as a strange and unreal being, an angel stranded in this world, terrestrial only in appearance. Then, and more generally, woman will be conceived as a variation of man, *mas occasionatus*, as the Middle Ages put it. The normal psychology of man is taken and modified in certain respects to fit the feminine nature. Thus woman is conceived as a particularly capricious 'man', a 'man' particularly devoted. Since these different states have been studied in the first place with reference to masculine being, it was almost inevitable that certain characteristics more typical of the noble sex should become inserted into the notion of intelligence and will; it is for that reason that the examination of the differences between man and woman is not yet concluded.

I would prefer to start from the assumption that man and

woman differ in essence. That does not imply that they are
mutually exclusive; we believe that there is a feminine nimbus
in all masculine being just as there is a presence, a virile
potentiality in the woman. On the plane of forms and physiology
Marañon has shown that a feminoid phase is to be found, at
adolescence, in all masculine development, and a long phase of
masculinity, lasting from the menopause to the end, in feminine
development. Thus each sex would seem to imitate the other
even on the physical level and woman for a longer period than
man.

Whatever there may be in such theories of inter-sexual states
there can be no doubt that the genius is one who, together with
his own sex-character, manifests an harmonic of the other sex:
and for woman, who makes her mark in history only in so far as
she resembles man, that is still more true.

What now is the fundamental difference between the two types
of personality? The psychical man (by which I mean man in so
far as he differs from woman) is rather *act*. His psychical nature
is oriented towards action, that is, towards conquest and adminis-
tration, towards the discovery of tools permitting him to extend
the use of his members, towards the domination of society and
matter. To build, to make war, to destroy, to criticise—these
are his activities: they make history. That supposes a faculty
in man permitting him at any time to disassemble and reassemble
the object: we call it intelligence. And in the same way,
where the realisation of ideas is concerned, it is a faculty which
enables him, having set himself a distant mark, to descend by
degrees, the last of which is the present, in order to bridge
the gap between idea and deed: this is the human will. Male
intelligence and will are very efficacious for the utilisation of
objects, but much less so for their enjoyment and not always
for understanding them. Thus man knows how to *utilise* time,
but he rarely knows how to *enjoy* it.

It may be said that, with man, it is through the senses and not
through the intelligence that enjoyment comes. I reply that,

with the male, the senses themselves retain something of the masculine mould of the intelligence. Man does not penetrate into the inwardness of an object; or, if he does, only fleetingly. That is why the male is greedy, gluttonous, ferocious in his voluptuousness, to such a degree that he has to learn to curb his pleasure. If he lets himself go he spoils everything. At all events when man enters into relation with an object he transforms it according to his own pattern and *represents* it to himself. He empties it of its substance, its sap, its nature so as to reduce it to his measure; in this respect Kant is the most masculine genius of all. In the domain of feeling it is the same. Even the most voluptuous man, in so far as the voluptuousness of masculine intelligence is concerned, remains enclosed in himself. From this point of view M. Gide is a masculine genius.

While man is thus essentially *act*, woman is essentially *nature*. Her intelligence does not work like that of a man. Woman has certainly an admirable faculty for mimicry and, since our civilisation is entirely masculine, she mimics masculine methods with a curious facility. That does not alter the fact that, if left to itself, her intelligence would not work like ours. Instead of disassembling and reassembling an object she would immediately place herself in a central and vital point, in the concrete relation which the object has for her own life. We interpret that in our language by saying that she is intuitive and understands with her heart. Proofs have little interest for her and it is very difficult to convince her that she is mistaken.

The process is more striking still in the will. Woman does not proceed naturally from the means to the end. She places herself immediately, like Joan of Arc, in the end which she imagines as realised and thinks that, immediately the problem is resolved for her, it has also disappeared for others. That is why to man woman seems obstinate. "What woman wills, God wills," says the proverb. Just as arguments contrary to her views do not trouble her, so checks and denials scarcely influence her. It is possible that the use of her senses is different from ours. Touch, in particular, keeps her at the heart of the object, as can be seen when she handles a little child; in the order of love, she seeks fusion rather than pleasure.

In every way she is much more in accord with nature, and that is why, like nature, she has a soothing effect upon man, the restless creature who is all *act*. She is also more *species* than man; thus in each woman the 'eternal woman' is much more discernible than is the 'man in himself' in man. It has been remarked that diversity of temperament is much less obvious with women than with men.

It must also be noted that woman is much more highly sexed than man, in the sense that the sex of man is concentrated, like an army battering against one isolated point of the frontiers; disengage it and you still have a man who is, at least physically, complete. On the contrary, with woman, sex is more diffused, expansive and ubiquitous. Man has sexual organs; woman possesses what is rather in the nature of an organic sex: the rhythms of the seasons, months and days are engraved in the body of woman whereas man remains somewhat indifferent to them. Puberty and menopause transform her. Therefore she is much more a part of the cosmos and its respiration than we are.

We now see how curiously these two essences, masculine and feminine, complement each other. The masculine essence occupies a median zone, while the feminine encompasses that zone at its loftiest and lowest levels. Woman is, in a sense, *amphibious*; she inhabits two natures and two worlds, the most lowly and material and the most lofty and spiritual. She is, by nature, made either for housekeeping and domestic tasks or for the practice of pure love and devotion, and we are not surprised to see her passing from the one to the other. Man, on the other hand, has compartments, sectors and cells in his mind: he likes to have things segregated each in its own category. Although there are sublime exceptions, he is made for the world of calculation, of combination, of art and science; he is ill at ease in domesticity and very much so in mysticism and still more with a combination of these two contraries.

Like life, which is always dual, more lofty and more low than we suppose, woman is ambiguous. That is why she is ill at ease in the intermediary zone of *honesty* and *mediocrity*; she is *saint* or *sinner*, angel or devil, just as a drunk woman is a more monstrous exhibition than a drunk man. Whatever she does she must *dedicate* herself whether to good or evil. Her situations are states, such as those of virgin, wife, mother, widow and even those of courtesan and daughter. No one would dream of depicting man in corresponding terms for, to say the least, they would be inadequate. That is why dress, which symbolises a state of mind, is so bound up with the feminine nature. Woman is more dependent upon her clothing for it manifests her mystery; that is why the toilet is symbolic.

As analyst, dissector, calculator, arbitrator, justiciary, man is *mind*. He has the necessary capacity for domination, whether in the city or the home; but here, as has often been remarked, though man governs, woman reigns. Woman craves support, control, a master; nevertheless it is from her that stimulus, élan, foresight, dismissal of the past and courage to confront the risks of life most often come. *Action* fulfils her nature, but it is nature that impels action.

It is thus that a harmony between man and woman is effected. Consider, for example, how quiet and disquiet, those two tides of the soul, are distributed between the two natures. Man, the master, is more serene than woman with her many agitations. Yet if we penetrate to the depths of the masculine certitude we find that it conceals much anxiety, regret and remorse.

In tragedies it is man who is the great waverer. Virgil, telling of Vulcan in the bed of Venus, shows him full of doubts. It has been said of man that he is strong when faced with fact but weak when confronted by himself; that he is not at ease or at home in the universe. Pessimism and scepticism, the taste for nihilism, come from man. Were he to pursue his thoughts to their conclusion he would become gloomy and savage. His very achievements compel man to dissipate himself. For all their brilliance and splendour, they seem meagre and ineffectual by themselves; they need an unknown quantity to connect and complete them. Woman is that which redeems and, so to speak, compensates for circumstances.

It is said, moreover, that woman is more emotional than man. Here too there is room for qualification. It is to be noted that, at an unexpected explosion, woman starts less violently than man.

Curiously enough, women have rarely produced works demanding intense sensibility such as those of music, painting, poetry and, in spite of the paradox, it might perhaps be added, philosophy. Mme de Staël, George Sand, Anna de Noailles are rich in sentiment and vitality, but delicacy of touch and poetic rhythm, the precise nuance of tenderness, and sensitivity of spirit must be sought from male minds.

It is well known that, when abandoned to passion, woman is more fierce. In the most profound emotions such as anger, remorse, hate, women are less submissive. Confronted with sorrow they are not so soft as we are. Are they perhaps also less sensitive? They endure without complaint, are less agitated by first symptoms, less prone to fall ill. It is not that they are more courageous than men; no doubt they have less to overcome for, with them, there is less of a schism between duty and nature.

Mind is distinguished from *nature* by a hiatus between the sensitive subject and the sensation, between sufferer and suffering. In *nature*, on the contrary, subject and sensation, form and matter, sufferer and suffering tend to become one. Man *has* a sentiment, a sensation; woman *is* sentiment, sensation, sorrow, love. Man gives; woman is gift. That is why man rather suggests the animal, whereas woman is sometimes compared to the vegetable world. Novalis said that woman is like the plant or the flower. Like vegetable nature she is calm, serene and

sure, rooted and celestial, while man is agitated, he argues, he
seeks his prey. Moreover, as once Goethe and now M.
Bachelard have remarked, woman resembles *water* and *earth*.
Man is more like flame. Man is moved to make history; he is
eccentric. He typifies time while woman typifies the presence
of eternity in time.

Beside the act which is usually called effort, a concentration
and girding of soul, there is also an act which is less obvious—
the return of the psyche to its sources in quest of a fuller self-
possession, while ceasing all partial activities which prevent a
total endeavour. It is clear that every achievement stems from
this preliminary repose and, too, that it symbolises what we
wish to contemplate in nature, what art, in its turn, wants to
produce, what love desires and even what it is. Now woman
participates more fully than man in this repose, and she has also
the capacity to communicate it. *In omnibus requiem quaesivi*,[1]
says Wisdom.

★

These considerations may seem to divert us from our theme,
the development of love. But, as we are about to see, in this
development of a symbiosis, each lends to the other what it
lacks for the reconstitution of a more harmonious unity.

It is characteristic of the development of love that it falls into
phases. But since it is a *coupled* development its phases are
different for each of the two persons engaged in a common
destiny. The accord is always a dissonance; one sounds this
note, the other that; one is ahead, the other behind. Even in
the state of matrimony the love of the couple is like an adventure,
in the sense that it leads towards ever new horizons, drawing us
where we would not go. The appearance of the child, not
always wanted but accepted and discovered with a delighted
surprise by the couple, is typical of this mechanism. At each
period in love's development the crust cracks and new situations
appear. The mere pleasure of loving, which was perhaps the

[1] In all things I sought repose.

primary object, is now at an end and the procession of duties is revealed. Thus, with incessant transformations and renunciations, love moves on beyond its immediate desire but in conformity with its profound purpose.

★

There is a danger that the following pages may discuss what seems common knowledge. I beg the reader to observe human behaviour as though he were not man, as Fabre was able to describe the praying mantis or, still better, as Huxley, in the *Brave New World*, showed us the picture of a paradoxical world in which both family and love were suppressed. Our concern is only to see, to say and to justify.

★

The first phase of love is one of initiation, surprise and mystery; it is the nuptial phase, a phase of consecration, so to speak, concerning which men are silent even in their books. It is essential that it should be preceded by the test of absence or, at all events, by preparatory stages. We see how, at all times and in every place, society has multiplied obstacles and delays, weaving that web of propriety and impropriety which retards the natural attraction of lovers to each other.

In our day, under the influence of the Far West, there is a tendency to suppress these obstacles, to reduce these rites of initiation to a minimum and even to legitimate an experiment of marriage before marriage. But it is very probable that, in so doing, our contemporaries strike at a fundamental law in the development of love. That it may be rooted in duration, this love must experience a long-awaited initial moment, and the ceremony of the wedding-feast, in which joy and solemnity mingle, should symbolise something ineffably august and solemn and associate the nuptial rite with that of death.

It is a common notion that the fulness and perfection of love last no longer than a month. One thinks of the harmony of bodies as a mechanical and instinctive affair although, with man, the most physical of functions is always troubled by the spirit and the more so in so far as intelligence keeps pace with instinct. It is an error to imagine that the more animal a function seems, the more one should imitate the animal in order to accomplish it. The difference between man and woman, already outlined in the case of animals and notably in the mammals, can be observed here again: the male partner is to some extent more savage, the other more passive and patient. Acquiescence can by no means be brought about by surprise or violence as fruit can be mastered by the teeth. Time, respect and the yielding of strength to gentleness are needed and, in the first beginnings of love, it is already to be observed that there is also implicit a complete ethic.

In order that the act of union may also be a true bond of unity, neither of the two persons should experience states of feeling too much at variance with the other; what is joy for the one must not be pain or humiliation for the other. It is obvious that this can only be brought to pass by a delicacy touched with sacrifice which is itself a fruit of love. The physical unity of the couple is thus rather the result than the cause of love. In any case, the first act is the golden nail upon which hangs the mantle of destiny and it is strange to observe how, after so many centuries, at this point intelligence has come to a halt and can merely smile.

The first phase of love differs in man and woman. It is a fact which man never really understands; thence arises a first division, a first cause of estrangement. For the life of love does not affect man's bodily equilibrium. Moreover, marriage has not much changed his outer life. With woman, on the other hand, the change is radical, and much more so in our civilised than in primitive societies in which she remained at home. With woman the change is at once social and physiological. From being a subject and dependent she becomes mistress; in a moment what had been forbidden becomes an obligation, what had been hardly conceivable a duty. At the same time, and most of all where her mother is concerned, her life becomes one of liberation. From the moment when she knows that she has conceived her very being changes and she enters upon a cycle of expectation and weariness; before her mirror she seems another person; she faces great sufferings and great risks. In all this man can share only in sympathy, watching these changes which he himself has set in motion. He feels himself to be the founder of a family and is anxious. He is responsible for another being and therefore for himself.

Thus, from the beginning, love is transfigured. It is now no longer a problem to be resolved and thereby it inevitably loses some of its charm. The serious side of life, the thought of a task to fulfil in this world, the expectation of that great unknown which the child will be, social relationships, the very silence which falls after the wedding tumult, the more rigorous control and opposition of the two families, all add to the first gravity of love and give to it the character of an historical event. While, in the first phase, love seemed an end in itself, it seems now to become a means to an end beyond itself—the family, upon which it risks being immolated.

During the whole first phase it can be said that love heals: this is love the physician, love the psychiatrist. As I have said, the peril of adolescence consists in its solitude, in the impossibility of overcoming the complexes of early infancy, of proving to oneself that superiority over them which it demands, of compensating for the rebuffs of life or the humiliations inflicted upon us by adults. That turmoil is dissipated by the complete unity of the couple, offering, in this first phase, its daily wonders. Thenceforward the painful monologue of the dawn of life becomes a dialogue. All that, for the adolescent, was confused is bound to become clarified in recital, in confidences, from the necessity for accounting to each other for each change of expression. The woman reassures the man with her good sense and sweetness; the man reassures the woman with his knowledge, his decisions in practical matters, his richer vocabulary with which he can express almost everything. The scruples and dreads which are so characteristic of modern society are, for the first time, alleviated by a life in common. Instead of remaining an inner mentor, the moral conscience is incarnate in the beloved and she is more indulgent than our own. The vague fear left with us from our scolded childhood is found to be cured.

This mutual inspection of thoughts and dreams certainly has its inconveniences. It is impossible that differences and nascent quarrels should not arise but, in this first phase, the signs of possible disagreement are recognised at once and dissipated by a mere look of love and by its redoubling, so that everything contributes to love. It is true that love detaches us from our home. It is a disturbing factor in family society; that is why parents both dread and desire it. But it is good that children should leave their home, even if only so as to appreciate it by comparison, which is the best way to knowledge. Whereas formerly, being either over-indulgent or over-critical, man was content simply to live in his home, now he puts it to the test. Since it must now be extended to another the sensitivity of the heart expands. Thus, and especially with the husband, the capacity for compassion is born; he becomes sensitive to the inner feelings of someone other than himself.

Love also enlarges feeling since it obliges one to love another family. This is not at all how one generally loves. How can one love those who see you come as a ravisher, who, in spite of conventional sentiments, often love you only from a sense of duty, who, in spite of protestations, do not assimilate you easily, for whom you are not so much a new son as the possible father of the grandson? You feel a certain aversion to treating a woman unknown a year ago as a mother; instinct rather impels you to fly from the parents of the beloved who are your competitors in her heart. But here love comes to pass by refraction. If the parents-in-law are not always loved with a tender affection, you respect your wife's love for her parents and their image in her eyes. And, in this way, when love for our own parents diminishes in intensity, participation in the affections of another increases our own power of loving.

It is in this first environment that, after a tedious and tranquil pre-history, the child appears. Here uncertainty is a stronger bond than certainty. The fact that the husband who has occasioned the life runs no risk of perishing through the birth arouses in him a feeling of gratitude towards his wife by which he redeems himself. This unknown child, for whom one has to prepare two names, two countenances, this being, uncertain up to the last moment—who, however much it may be expected, comes like a thief—this newcomer born of our blood yet not at all like us, this child cannot but modify love profoundly. Through its presence it recreates, legitimises and makes love incarnate.

Before the advent of the child, the marriage ought to be established by an oath; its fabric is fragile, since it is poised upon a double will. We have seen how easily love is inverted. At the moment when the life of the couple runs the risk of being spoiled (whether the pair come to the point of clinging to each other in adoration or whether they begin to drift apart towards someone else), after almost completing the circuit of the heavens, love reappears through the child in the form of a being sprung from love. This child, it is true, is only a bundle of wants, a kind of little domestic animal, but it is all the better for love than if it were already 'a thinking reed', for its constant needs, rhythmic as nature, its frailty, its lack of real existence, the sublime detachment which gives it an angelic air, its crises, its trivial and serious maladies, all these constitute a source of shared emotions.

We know how suffering is a stronger bond than pleasure. The child is, no doubt, the effect of pleasure but much more is it the fruit of suffering; it makes love still more real.

The child is a third term, but inasmuch as it does not yet speak (*infans*), it does not enter the society of the parents; moreover it will only enter it very tardily and always imperfectly. Whatever its age, the parents' love will always remain a forbidden subject. The knowledge of the mystery which has caused it to be born will be concealed from it; no one has ever known the history of his conception nor explored his origin, which is almost as obscure as his agony and his end.

From the time when the child makes his appearance the future enters in, that is to say, fear and hope—all the fears, all the hopes at the same time—and these interchanges of contrary feelings so occupy the field that, if they still leave room for love, it is in quite a different sense. In truth, since the child, conveying the *relation,* makes the husband a father and the wife a mother, he changes everything. Although this last comer is powerless, it is he who is now the centre and consecrator. In particular he reunites the married pair to their ancestors. "A man shall leave father and mother," says the Bible, "and shall cleave to his wife." No doubt, but from the time when the child appears, the father and mother of the father and mother return and scarcely leave you again. The family unity, always a little sundered by the wedding festival, is reconstituted around the cradle, and one then sees the family like a pyramid inverted on its point.

The danger is lest the mother-child couple should put an end to the affection of husband and wife. This couple (above all if it is a mother-son couple) is more natural still than that which makes man and woman one flesh. It demands no efforts of mutual adaptation. At first the carnal bond is so vital that the child is like a prolongation of the body of its mother from which it has issued and which it has wounded. At this point, the child has no connection with the body of its father who cannot comprehend the relation of this flesh with his flesh and is amazed at the resemblance as though at a miracle. And, for the child, the father is a stranger whose presence is incomprehensible since he has no need for it at all. And since the sexual life of woman is often backward it may be that a mother may concentrate her affection upon her child, especially if the first experiences of love have disappointed her. She is then seen to impose premature sacrifices upon her husband, in the guise of a duty which for her is a very mild one. That is why, in the shape of that notorious Oedipus complex, the morbid forms of which Freud has studied, lurks an almost inevitable crisis in the history of love, partaking of the differences of sex and function. But there too nature has set the cure beside the ill.

The remedy for the ills caused by love is a summons to progress in love. In other terms, love can cure the wounds it inflicts on condition that it rises to greater heights. If the love-instinct led to monogenesis the mother-child couple might conflict with the husband-wife couple since, in itself, it is beautiful and perfect. There is perhaps nothing which suggests simplicity and sublimity more perfectly than this community formed by the mother and the male child, where the contraries are admirably associated: the masculine form in infant frailty and feminine grace (still almost virginal) in the maternal form. The absence of the husband, seemingly no more than a useless protector, is no loss. The virgin and the child form a complete universe: there God takes His rest.

But the child, when an only child, is of one sex alone; he would not know what to make of the harmonious dissonances of love. That these may be renewed in the future both parents must be able to rediscover the sex opposite to their own in their offspring. They must be able to love the other's sex in an image of themselves which is free of all desire, however sub-limated. That love may leave its completed image it is at least necessary that the father should have his daughter and the mother her son.

Thus the first paternity naturally calls for another. The pains of child-bearing are effaced from the mother's memory so that only the joy of having brought a man into the world remains. Never sufficient, never completed, it is only for reasons of health, of status, of economy that the family is limited. Then, even though the propagative instinct be appeased, a generous urge impels towards the multiplication of beings. In this domain the law of economy is checkmated. Affective energy should be enfeebled by propagation and each successive child be less loved. But we know that, in fact, this is not so at all. See how the mothers are rejuvenated at each birth and how their capacity for loving is augmented!

★

Let us now examine the second phase of the development of love which is its crisis. Like every life-process, the development of love generally goes through a critical phase which is, no doubt, necessary in order that it may attain maturity. Allendy says that the crisis nearly always occurs after the tenth year. It is due to complex causes, both physical and psychical. Discovery, the law of nascent love, cannot be prolonged. When two persons live a common life in which no self-communion and no privacy are possible there comes a time when they can no longer ignore themselves. Inversion comes into play. This perspicacity, instead of discovering secret grandeurs, brings to light defects, idiosyncrasies, deformities, everything that, in the first phase, has been necessarily hidden and is now all the more obvious. These are, however, petty defects, mediocrities, insincerities, rather than great faults or vices. Brief is the perfect bloom of all virtue and of all existence.

This is also the moment when the woman seems less beautiful because so familiar (beauty consists in part of surprise), because of her sickness and her confinements, and also because she feels herself less tenderly beloved (beauty consists in part in the idea that one is loved). Renewal is no longer possible. Your vows and society have caught you for ever. *For ever, for always . . .* how harsh are these words for her who has almost her whole life in front of her! Could not one choose afresh and, as they say, 'make a new start in life'? Is it a duty to renounce one's happiness for ever? The sense of the irreparable leads to self-accusations, which are always more difficult to endure than accusations from others. "You say that I am not what you thought," says Robert to Evelyn in the *Ecole des Femmes*, "but then you yourself are not what I thought." And Evelyn: "All that is left for me to do is to put myself at the disposal of a person whom I no longer love nor respect . . . of a puppet whose wife I am; that is my lot, my reason for being, my goal, and I have no other horizon in the world.''

This crisis comes in a different form to man and to woman. On the occasion of his first infidelities the man feels his potential polygamy arousing; his instinct is more vigorous, more diversified, less fixed upon a single person than that of the woman. Physically, even, the woman is more faithful; being impregnated by a man she remains his possession. It is from affection that she turns to adultery and from a great boredom rather than from sensuality. It sometimes happens that, with woman, a second sexuality tardily awakens. The doctors and psychiatrists of our time tell us clearly things of which formerly only novelists warned us. It sometimes happens that woman does not know the awakening of the senses till several years after her marriage and even after her maternities. Then what, till then, had been easy becomes hard for her. If, at that juncture, she meets in her home a person who focuses her new sensibility, an almost incurable wound can be inflicted on her soul, as Balzac has so admirably shown in his *Lys* where the kiss of an adolescent troubles the pure Henriette for the rest of her life. It may be said that the more inoffensive the person who appears in the home—young man, boy, valet, priest—the more dangerous he is; for the first stirrings of infidelity disguise themselves as devotion and the woman is caught in the trap of pity. The man too, at times, as may be seen in the *Symphonie Pastorale*.

At this juncture the profound law enclosing the home within itself and forcing it to set a seal upon its secret must be observed. It has joys and sorrows for its portion which should remain for ever private and almost unexpressed even by those who experience them. This conjugal mystery, whether it be one of distress or of satisfaction, and even if it implies drastic deceptions, is one which, since that would be a breach of confidence, should not be noised abroad. Nevertheless, since the couple do not live on a desert island but surrounded by prying eyes, since people are frivolous, curious or jealous, this closely guarded sorrow incurs the risk of publicity. With the poor it is the neighbours, with the rich, the servants who seize upon the slightest rumours of a breach. Even the parents work against them in this second phase of love, when the mother would be glad to regain her daughter's comradeship and the husband's mother again becomes maternal. And if one of the two succumbs to a confession against the other, they soon become entangled in suspicious alliances destructive to the unity of love. The home is not designed for the habitual presence of a third person. It would need an angelic art (uncles and aunts formerly attained to it) to live in a family without introducing the least friction into it. The protracted intrusion of a third person into conjugal society cannot occur without danger. The constant presence of a third person modifies the relationship of the other two and usually disintegrates it, for new affinities and detrimental comparisons make their appearance. Goethe says so; Sainte-Beuve and Victor Hugo afterwards experienced it. This crisis of love is the subject of modern drama. Since the *Princesse de Clèves* the majority of novels have taken it as the centre of interest; and nothing is in fact more dramatic than this almost involuntary dissociation of an eternal affection. Nothing suggests better the idea of fatality.

Here again we see clearly that difference in timing in the phases of life which always prevents man and woman from being at the same point in its rhythm.

We might say that maternity should be rejuvenating and woman grow in peace and majesty every time she brings a man into the world. Formerly, when we knew how to respect the hard and simple laws of life, that was not exceptional. But, in our inconsequent civilisations, in which, in spite of hygiene and sometimes because of it, so many natural rules of morality and life are violated, it comes to pass that, after her first experience of maternity, the woman finds inherited maladies making their appearance while the man, on the contrary, is in his prime. He achieves recognition between the ages of forty and fifty. His career helps him to keep young while the woman's tasks make her old before her time.

This dislocation is less perceptible in the bourgeois world of towns owing to the artifices of fashion and of town life. But it is very evident in the country where woman so soon looks her age; where formerly, at about thirty years of age, she took from her cupboard the head-dress which she must wear till death; where thenceforward, being no more than her master's principal servant, she renounced all pretensions to good looks. Joubert said of his wife in such a case: "I knew her worth and her graces; she has lost her graces, but she has kept her worth." It is true that man also loses some of his first beauty. His work brings him wrinkles and stiffness. Specialisation develops one of his faculties; it deadens all the others. Michelet contrasts modern with ancient man who kept himself in good form: Penelope recognised Ulysses by his beauty which his trials and voyages had not changed.

Quite apart from the crises which shatter love for ever and so easily arise at this moment in its development (for the notion of a possible new beginning with another person is all the more tempting when life has been disappointing and there is still time to *remake* it), we are then at the age when nearly all loves, being subject to the law of duration, experience inevitable testing. It is so tempting to resolve the problem by transforming love into comradeship, union into juxtaposition, the household into an aggregation of interests great and small, the mating into a frank friendship of two former lovers united by habit alone. It is the time when a separation of egoisms and devotions recurs. The husband proceeds on his 'affairs', the wife to her 'works'; the husband to his task, his profession; the woman to her fashions, her preserves, the husband to his 'club', the wife to her 'salon', and love languishes and perishes all the more easily in that it is replaced by a condition which resembles it in appearance.

Sainte-Beuve described this hardening of our personalities very well when he said: "At certain points one hardens, at others one rots, one does not ripen." Many maturities are in fact false maturities which exist only outwardly and in semblance. How many men, whom we call mature, and who may think themselves so, are only adolescents in the guise of precocious old men, according to the law which causes each phase of development to tend to be prolonged into the next. This prolongation of adolescence, of its fervour, fire and intractability during the second phase of life may be expedient for success in art, politics or pleasure, but the fact that corruption or fermentation may be accidentally profitable does not change its nature. To become mature means to let duration fulfil its work in us, to recover youth through engagement with existence.

From the point of view of love, maturity should be less a transformation than a fulfilment. It is sometimes said that love is transmuted in affection; in that case, in its essence, it would lack what had been lost. The difficulty is to achieve a transformation into affection which does not cease to be love. How many unions there are which are no more than comradeship where two persons who have or think they have loved each other survive this first heart-state, celebrate or bury it! There it is that the deep difference between passion and sensibility is to be seen. Joubert remarked that all his passions were quickly spent while all his feelings left permanent roots in him.

Love opens with an emotional phase; it is only after long duration that it can be transformed into sensibility. This sensibility is a habit of the soul, but it must be remembered that there are two kinds of habit: one which is simply mechanical and automatic, the other which is a quality always alert, a disposition ever more constant, a kind of ever-increasing awareness of spirit, an awakening of obscure potentialities in the soul.

This quality is not far from being a definition of sensibility. Sensibility exists in us without our always being conscious of it; but, at the least provocation, it shows itself in the guise of a tender emotion, at once very gentle and poignant. Instead of sweeping our personality beyond itself, as in passion or in nascent love, it restores it to itself.

In this second phase love which has become sensibility has little need of external manifestation; it abides less in the body than in the conjunction of soul and body. During the first phase of love each clung to the angelic element in the other or at least imagined an angel in the other. Love cannot be redeemed until it becomes love of the person in the flesh and with all his lapses, deformities and pettinesses. It is not necessary for each to love the other's defects, but rather to love the other so that their defects are seen as an almost negligible result of their existence.

In the first phase of love, the joys, the journeys, the pleasures, the presents, the festivals and all the magic of life were necessary in order to weave the fabric. Now it is rather the illnesses, the obstacles, the sorrows, the bitternesses which become the material of union and the secret nurture of sensibility. We know well enough that pain conduces more to a realisation of existence and to unity than does pleasure. It should also be noted that this renascence, or rather this metamorphosis of love, is facilitated by the shared conception of success or glory. Pascal says in his *Discours* that a life, when it begins, is lovely because of love, and that it ends because of ambition. But he is over-critical, for all love develops when a great ambition is shared.

The history of Héloïse and Abélard reveals Héloïse as more jealous of Abélard's glory than Abélard himself. This is often woman's instinctive reaction. At this juncture in the life of love she is often to be seen making of her man a fine puppet which she pushes in the world, whose career she assures: for at this age man is slothful and she is ambitious for him. He would be satisfied to remain a colonel, she wants him to be a general. It is the moment when, in return, the husband discovers the merit of the vanished concord and publicly sings the praises of his capable wife. Then new bonds are woven, mutual esteem and love blossom afresh. That there were something to forgive would but forge a fresh bond.

Thus this law of development is again to be seen: whenever the nature of things militates against the duration of love, by a form of compensation this same nature at once refashions what it has undone and creates unity out of discord. Love deepens just because it has survived a crisis in which it might possibly have perished.

★

We pass now to the third phase of the development, that of old age. At this age is love still possible? Has it not become something quite different? Victor Hugo's saying will sustain us: "In love, to grow old is to become identified."

We would fain picture the development of love as corresponding to this design:

The development of love, like nature itself, has the characteristic of being bi-polar. If we call the vital pole V, that by means of which we are connected with the world of living beings, and where what Schopenhauer called the genius of the species and Freud the *libido* vibrates, we shall name the spiritual pole S the inverse pole, around which the life of the soul is concentrated. It is certain that these two poles are closely related. In our most fundamental states, even the most bestial, there is always a hormone of spirit sufficient to differentiate these states from their animal counterparts. Inversely, in our most exalted, most spiritual states there is, maybe at the lowest level, a sensuous stimulus.

The most imperceptible dose of spirit communicated to the flesh, the most subtle dose of the sensuous insinuated into the spirit is enough totally to transform both spirit and flesh. We shall emphasise this point shortly.   When the spiritualists speak of sensuality, they envisage it as a gross, cloying or savage influence.   They forget that homeopathic doses often act best and that a room can be transformed by a scent: a centigram of fuchsine colours a lake.   In the love-states which we are now about to examine, vitality loses its magnetism and the edge of sensuality is blunted by age and custom.   In return spirituality increases, for it is a characteristic of the development of man that old age attains to spirit only by accident: the finest works of the artist are often his final flashes of genius.   At all events the inmost mind is ageless.

In the third stage love continues that of the two preceding stages which it fulfils; it is not a metamorphosis but an assumption. At this juncture a kind of symbiosis between the two partners is often noticeable.   Whether because age obliterates the sex differences in their faces, or by a kind of mimicry and, perhaps, accord, they end by almost resembling each other.   Just as the autumn leaves are more apparent than those of spring (when the vigour of the sap is exhausted the fibres are similar) so it is in the last phase that this resemblance of the wife to the mother, to our own mother, becomes more apparent.   Grand-paternity and grand-maternity are very different from the first.   This point, which the identity of the words (father, grandfather, mother, grandmother) disguises, has not perhaps been sufficiently emphasised.

The object of paternity is the being sprung from your blood and the labour of your love.   It is immediate, it is carnal, it is somewhat limited.   Grand-paternity is of quite a different kind, for the grandson owes nothing to the labour of the grand-father who has no more conceived than the grandmother has begotten him.   The grandson is apparently more remote than the son: he is the child of the stranger; but the love which the grandfather bears towards him is more disinterested.   This child has both his and a different blood: four ancestors, with as many strains, are to be found in him.   We expect him to bring to life again fourteen remembered faces. . . . And the love of the grandfather, attached to this potential being (all the more in that he will not see him mature), becomes detached, extended, sublimated. He loves less severely, less proudly. The shortening of the time still left to him, the notion that, in its entirety, life is very brief and that childhood is the time when it should be most enjoyed, the recollections of early childhood which return with the last phase, perhaps also the wish to leave behind him a more genial portrait than that bequeathed to his children, somewhat more harsh because of his strictness, all conspire to constrain the grandfather towards a pure kindliness in which his paternity approximates to that of God. It only remains to him to make his testament, that is to say to bear testimony to what he wished to effect and has not been able to fulfil, leaving to others the task of pursuing it. This state of serenity, of indifference and of illumination is favourable for love, in any case for that love of kindness, peace and oblation which foreshadows rest.

In this perspective nuptial love may be reborn in an unknown form. We do not find old folk becoming divorced and we do find in them for the most part an almost physical need of the other's presence. Old age brings us back to our consort. A comradeship stronger than of old is then, of necessity, to be found, owing to the removal of the children which so often happens in our individualistic civilisation, to the infirmities which make us crave the other's support, and to the almost animal habit of being together. In this third state, love is without passion; it is not even, properly speaking, a feeling but a kind of state. It assumes something sacred, I will dare to say *sacral*, because time that has fled, maturity accomplished, the impossibility of experiencing any further growth, the approach of the end give it a character of fixity. It repeats itself, it rediscovers itself, it recollects itself. Nothing can excite it but also nothing can assault it. We are beyond the flux and almost out of time. At this moment love approximates to religion.

In the eyes of outside observers the couple seems priestly, priestly at all events in the primitive religion of hearth and home. It is true that, in order that love may attain this elevation and be more than a solitary sacrifice, death must intervene. It is the moment for establishing the relation between love and death; it is fundamental, for love is nature's device for the conquest of death.

In the ordinary course of affairs, that relation is violated by social deceit, mutual illusion, silence. Whenever a mortal menace hovers over the couple (as happens at every birth), love closes its ranks. But love must come to a final reckoning with death. In the normal course of destiny it seems that it is the man who must first depart. The custom that the man should be the elder is connected with this idea. Woman is made to mourn the man and not vice versa. Death is doubtless necessary so that love may become a cult and make manifest its latent character of adoration. When death appears on the scene a career is suddenly closed and the life of the deceased is seen adorned with the beauty of a work of art to which only meaning and symbols can be added, but which is complete and immutable.

Just as we can only become conscious of what is fully accomplished, so it is only after the death of one partner that the other has a full consciousness of love. This mechanism is already to be seen in the absence which foreshadows death, but absence is adulterated by the idea of return. After death, which is a final absence, all history becomes legend. Only *what should be said* concerning the other is remembered, what is noble, what, deserves to be told. The daily ennuis, the domestic frenzies, the family quarrels, the wounding words are not recollected, but only the oldest memories, sometimes the most fabulous, one would not say the most false, because the reality of a man is not in his moods nor is his history in the daily round. Indeed, this good, brave, devoted lover, whose picture the other preserves in her breast, is not my true portrait. But it is my ideal image, that towards which I strove, that which I wanted to preserve, that which should be preserved by those who love and survive me. That is why the dead are more beautiful than the living. Just as the memory which the child keeps of his dead father is full of regret and remorse for not having understood him in time, so the image which, in love, the widow retains, is more real than the confused impression of him which she had during their life together.

In the absence of a visible object, in the impossibility henceforward of bestowing our care and concern upon the other and receiving a response, love is lifted up to the level of sacrifice. Around the tombstone, before the unimaginable relics, the mind remakes a divine image. For the life of love it is stronger than this bodily separation. Since the essence of love consists in constant communication, one would suppose that absolute absence would be a dreadful thing. But here again nature has prepared a compensatory mechanism. Bodily contact effects not only fecundation but also impregnation, that is to say it causes all the elements of our being to penetrate and propagate in another human being. Bodily impregnation can easily be only the medium for a psychical, moral, even mystical impregnation. Thence derives the impression and, maybe, the reality of an indwelling of the one in the other, of a kind of presence of the one in the other which is not sundered by absence and can be the more vivid as the physical life abates and its haven draws near. Victor Hugo, in that poem concerning the love of Old Folk called *Booz endormi*, gives this speech to Boaz:

> How long it is since she with whom I lay,
> O Lord, has left for thine my widowed bed;
> Yet still our spirits mingle, as our clay,
> And she half living yet, and I half dead.

On this last level love is already dissociated, decomposed by death; there is no sense of completion, but only of preparation for a new state. What does this common notion of an eternal reunion amount to for philosophy?

The Christian religion has given no precise reply to that question. It teaches the immortality of the soul, or rather the resurrection of the whole being, but not the eternity of the couple, doubtless because it is respectful before the unknowable. Immortality is a dogma; the idea that we shall see each other again is a matter of piety. Yet the couple (at least if they have passed their life in time in perfecting the relation between them) seems more imperishable than the separate soul. On the other hand, could the being of the one, in a lonely immortality, find beatitude away from the other? Such are the intuitions of the heart. Do they justify any hope?

The Catholic religion is full of shadow, silence and reserve concerning the after-death state. No doubt that is so because from the very first it has had to resist this craving to imagine the after-life as a continuation of this earthly existence. It seems difficult to imagine that if, after death, there is a conscious life for the spirit, human love will be wholly foreign to it. To conceive the permanence of the *I* without a permanence of the *we* seems difficult without supposing metamorphoses or annihilations, substitutions of being which would result in our loss of personal identity. On the other hand, if God is essentially love, even if, as faith conceives, His infinite life is a gift, it would be hard to admit that God extinguishes for ever this faculty for love in us, the most profound resemblance to Him which we have. We confront here the so-vexed question of the persistence of time in eternity.

It is inconceivable that time, as it is, should continue in eternity without rendering eternity temporal. But it is difficult to imagine eternity absorbing into itself the whole essence of time, for that would be to submerge the person in God. It cannot indeed be held that the love of the couple continues in the beyond in its terrestrial form, however sublimated. Would not that be the very definition of torment such as Dante suggests for Francesca de Rimini? On the other hand, it cannot be that the conditions of eternal life are so novel, so radically distinct from ours that they should abolish all pursuit and every memory of a profound love, above all if that love were a preparation for it.

But the analysis which we have made of the successive metamorphoses of love in the course of time can doubtless shed some light here. What, in short, have we said if not that love can change in form without changing in essence? It is possible that the metamorphoses of time may be only the symbol of a radical metamorphosis effecting the translation of love into another dimension. In this new and eternal state love is profoundly transformed; it is in God that those who love each other will love thenceforth, and we are incapable of imagining, of conceiving and even of comprehending the effects of this final transformation. Thenceforth God plays upon the instrument and holds the bow: human beings can only modulate the notes. If the couple continue to exist in some sublime fashion, it is but to serve as the vehicle of an absolute love which has no limits. And here again we find the idea that love, although it appears as a dyad, contains a latent triad: if it seems to man that there are two and only two in the act of loving, in reality, in order that love may live, the two must love in a third: it is through this third being, love's foundation, that its eternity is already present in time.

★

There then is set forth the line of love's development. We have tried to show it as heroic yet familiar, noble yet diurnal, lovely yet nevertheless commonplace. Our concern to depict love in its full development has constrained us to apprehend it through the institution of marriage. But is there not a great gulf between love and marriage? Are not these two essences so mutually exclusive that when the one is present the other dissolves? It is to be noted that heroes and saints have rarely been married or passionate persons, nor those who have spoken well of love, not Kierkegaard nor, in the main, Goethe. The Church, which has made an institution of marriage, has set divine love above marriage.

Kierkegaard has noted the eternal contradiction of which marriage is the prey. Marriage is, apparently, the mortal enemy of love. And, in the first place, it is to be remarked that community of spirit with a woman is reduced by a liking for the voluptuous daily proximity, by the impossibility of bringing two spiritual lives into accord, by the law which brings it to pass that in dual life the weaker personality is absorbed. Rare is the woman who aids a man to remain faithful to himself, for that would mean acting against her own interests. When the virgin of first love and the wife of the wedding disappear to give place to the comrade, man is already in the toils. Like the praying mantis, woman, so Kierkegaard says, devours the brain. On the other hand, marriage, from the philosophic point of view, runs the risk of repetition and custom; it brings absolute uniformity, total familiarity, perpetual intimacy, all of them conditions least favourable for love which thrives on conquests and surprises. The misfortune of marriage is the proximity of the fruit, its superabundance, as may be seen when one compares it to the romantic love in which the knight labours for ten years for a kiss which may not be granted to him.

Finally, is there not a contradiction in the fact that *love* should be a *duty*? Kierkegaard has told of the tribe in Paraguay found by the Jesuits who were so indolent that they were obliged to sound the bells at midnight to recall the married to their task. It is a picture of the state of marriage which, by transforming love into an obligation, robs it of its very essence. Such are the thoughts of the seducer. But the seducer knows too that he no longer attains what he seeks since he cannot prolong the miraculous moment and, after the night of love, writes: "All is over and I do not wish to see her any more; a young girl is a feeble creature and when she has given all she has lost all." The punishment of the seducer is that in no way can he make the moment last and that he is condemned to a repetition still more wearisome than that of marriage.

For Kierkegaard, the horror of habit, inevitable in marriage, is the horror of duration, of history; the fact is that he wants to perpetuate eternity in the instant. Romantic love is faithful in that it serves its apprenticeship through fifteen years of conflict with lion and ogre; but conjugal love contends with a foe still more dangerous: time. Kierkegaard mentions too that the qualities ascribed to this love all determine the person from within—faithful, constant, humble, patient, magnanimous, indulgent, sincere, sober, vigilant, assiduous, submissive, happy. He says profoundly that these qualities are determinations of time, for their reality does not consist in the fact that they exist forever.

That is why this kind of love is so closely related to history, the essence of which is that it is an increasing progression in the course of which the original factor is multiplied: the silver wedding foretells the golden. And if we are astonished that love should be a labour, it is because we forget that it is a duty: not an intruder, not impertinent, but a friend, an accomplice. In the case of married people the course which they delight to follow is not only permitted, it is imposed upon them. And, far from its being not so good to say "you ought" as to say "it is permissible for you", there is more in duty than permission; for duty realises the synthesis of spontaneity and necessity, in which abides the bond of perfection. Moreover, for Kierkegaard, even though he does not enter into it, the institution of marriage is related to love; it safeguards it by preventing it from dissipating itself in a false infinity of the instant in order to become incarnate in human duration.

★

As I have said, marriage and love are closely related. But if, from within marriage and after a long interval, a person finds that he is linked in love to someone other than his wife, which attachment should be given precedence over the other? How then is one to choose between the truth of feeling and social expediency? In fact, it comes to this, that love is reborn outside its former limits and he who once pledged his life perceives that he has been mistaken; however, nothing is lost, for one can *begin again*. If the law of love is a law of liberty why should love agree to a perpetual engagement? If a man asserts his liberty 'by leaving his father and his mother' why should he not assert it again by leaving his wife? Can love live with hypocrisy?

The problem of divorce, that is to say of a violent change of direction in love, must inevitably challenge the mind. The horror engendered by the daily round, doubt, suspicion, regret for vows, the craving for experience, all conspire to cause the birth of a second love upon the circumference of the first. And social inhibitions concur in giving to adultery that savour of forbidden things which seems to magnify liberty. In order to represent the problem in its most elevated form, I leave on one side divorces which are evidently due to weakness. But is it not possible to ask, like Goethe, if there are not separations which are an ascent and if a first love cannot be abandoned for a second yet more perfect, more intimate and the only eternal one; and if the very law of development does not lead it to some form of divorce as a means of elevation?

In his *Elective Affinities* Goethe puts the problem as clearly as possible. He shows us a happy ménage which, by chance, encounters two other persons; and both parties of the marriage have the impression that they would find their happiness in union with one of these two persons, so that the breaking of the conjugal bond would assure the happiness of four destinies. Must these four destinies be sacrificed to a precarious promise and to respect for convention? Goethe's solution is well known: he represents Odile, the young girl loved by the husband, as a predestined virgin and their love as a mystic love. In order to escape blame Odile lets herself die. And, although Goethe deems the affinity between Edward and Odile to be essentially pure he condemns its earthly realisation. Thus he returns by the way of wisdom to the saying of the Evangelist: "Whosoever looketh on a woman to lust after her hath committed adultery with her already in his heart." He sets the social contract above love, or rather he does not admit that there is a true earthly love outside the love consecrated by the law.

It is not that Goethe denies the reality of Edward's love for Odile; why disapprove of a feeling in which personal liberty counts for nothing? The expression of his love can be prevented but he cannot prevent himself from loving. Goethe does not condemn this union of spirit: he dismisses it to eternity. He gives it no place in the sphere of earthly and possible things, he devotes it to total sacrifice. This is also the solution of Balzac in the *Lys* and of Claudel in the *Soulier de Satin*.

When the problem of love is pushed to its limit we find the final law which ordains that the real questions are insoluble or rather that their solution has the pattern of the Cross. In the last resort we find the paradox, the irrational, the absurd in ourselves, what others will call oblation, sacrifice, consumma- tion. It is this that the partisans of divorce never understand: they aim at suppressing these paradoxes, although they are part of the very stuff of existence. The field of honour is sometimes absurd; so is the martyr and often enough his fidelity. It is inconceivable that love should not have its victims since, of all human sentiments, it tends most towards oblation. The immo- lation of a first love in order to begin a second, even by mutual consent, is maybe a deed which conforms to personal wishes, to what man calls happiness; it is not a deed of love. That is doubtless why the Christ, indulgent to frailty, is severe towards the adulterer. Sacrifice remains the solution of that which has no solution.

★

Development is manifested in its highest degree in the history of love since there we behold an originally potent germ main- taining itself intact and experiencing its phases in an ascending order. It can never be sufficiently emphasised that the really strange thing about it is the fact that the subject of love is not the master of this development either at its beginning or during its whole course. Hence the impression of an order *already given* which comes almost with a sense of fatality to those who reflect upon their love, who rehearse its stages, some happy, some sad, but most of them united in feeling. Were the sources of this impression to be sought it would be seen that the gap between the *aims* proposed by the consciousness and the *end* imposed by the nature of things is nowhere more apparent than here. It could even be said that this discrepancy between aims and ends is an essential element in human love, since instinct after all only seeks a connection while nature desires the permanence of the rational being. Such is the case when individuals desire only a titillation of the senses while creation labours to bring to birth a hero or a saint able to transform the lives of multitudes of men. What disproportion! On the one hand a life so substantial that we deem it to be immortal and, on the other, a most obscure sensation.

This difference inherent in the very principle of love continues throughout its whole course. The desire for a savoury soup, for a warm bed and domestic comfort, in the woman for independence from her mother, for nice clothes and a home of her own, later, anxiety for daily bread, the tedium of life, the children's teeth and their mischief, their amusements, their maladies, their success, their establishment in life; it is these that make up the normal world. There does not remain much room for what is called love, which is found to be dissolved or at least refracted in a mass of dull daily tasks.

However, running through this banal story, animating and sublimating it, are two other stories which seem to have no relation to it. It is, at first sight, the story of a species which propagates itself after the fashion of the animal kind by the sowing of seeds; it is the story of a race, a country, the story of one or rather of many families. But also and more profoundly (for all the preceding elements are mortal and know it), it is the story of a human *dyad*, that of two intermingled destinies which assuredly together form a single destiny. But these destinies are woven and interlaced, perpetually outdistancing each other in flights which are involuntary but nevertheless by mutual consent, in a succession of discoveries which, if the mind were not absorbed in its duties, should cause astonishment.

In truth, although all love begins with tender emotions, the lover finds himself caught up in a great machine. As this story unfolds it is less and less related to its origins. In so far as he is carried away by love the lover has less and less time for loving. And he is compelled to exercise virtues which seem altogether foreign to love. Thus love seems almost like a ruse of nature to gain her ends. A ruse, I said, for, from the external point of view, love is a contrivance for inducing man to perform voluntarily what is most repugnant to him, to know self-sacrifice, nay even, in the end, the sacrifice of love, since it is through absence that all love settles its account. Here we approach the ideas which we will consider in another chapter; love and oblation are essentially akin.

6 *Love as oblation*

WHEN we study the history of love, we see it gradually freeing itself from the organic elements which have engendered it in order to become a sentiment of custom and affection based upon mutual devotion with a view to a family and social end; when it has run its course, it rests in a kind of tranquil sacrifice. The normal development of love is, indeed, very rare, even in the happiest of unions. It experiences checks, rifts, revulsions and also periods of slumber and languor. It is possible to suppose that all these maladies may stem from the fact that, instead of accepting the law of renunciation which is essential to it, love tends towards egoism. Here then we encounter once again this basic problem of assessing the element of self-love in love for others.

When love, in so far as it is founded upon sexuality, is analysed, as we have just been doing at length, it is impossible not to recognise that love is always, in some degree, self-love and that it is in this that it differs from friendship, which is capable of disinterestedness.

In contrast to friendship, love touches us to the quick and in the flesh itself. Above all, the wounds of love are sweet (except in the case of jealousy), whereas friendship can neither heal nor assume its wounds. In love there is a blend of bitter and sweet which caused the author of the *Imitation* to say: *Sine dolore, non vivitur in amore*.[1] A true egoism feeds even upon suffering so that the lover, poor, yet at the same time rich, like every creator, finds satisfaction in his very agonies. We are dealing with a self-love of a peculiar kind: for it is a self-love which is also self-donation, a donation which, in the course of time, can and should purify itself and, in some fashion, always does purify itself because of the tasks imposed by love and the labours which it compels us to perform.

Dr. Allendy divides the history of love into three stages which he calls the assimilative, the reciprocal and the oblative stages. Like all triple categories applied to a development in time, it is not false but should not be carried too far. How could the transition from one stage to another occur without a break and in silent growth, if the further stage were not already contained in the former, as a presence and as first-fruits? How could that which is new be manifested were it not already latent in the old? In reality these three phases are rather three aspects of love. It is the prominence of these aspects which varies with the course of time. In all development the advanced, completed and final stage only brings to light the urge and germ latent in the beginnings; we must therefore return to the conception that oblation is an original element in love, even in the egoistic joy, even in the reciprocity.

★

But, amongst these oblative forms of love, there are paradoxical features which call for more precise consideration. We have in mind the attitude which is called virginity or continence. With men it is rather continence and with women virginity, for one can scarcely speak of a continent woman or of a masculine virgin, a fact which already indicates that the problem differs according to sex.

---

[1] There is no love-life without sorrow.

Continence, a mode of behaviour proper to man, of which the animal, unless compelled, is incapable, ought not to be conceived as a state concerned only with the body. For primitive mentality, feminine chastity is no more than a material and established fact. And that is, in part, due to the fact that this ordeal is only possible for woman, that society attaches a greater value to virginity in woman than in man. For the thinking man virginity has nothing to do with these signs and accidents. It can only be understood as a free and inward act by which a spiritual being, in complete awareness, renounces the enjoyment of sex for a time or for ever.

It is to be noted that this act has no moral value if its motive is only fear of the flesh, fear of the responsibilities which accompany love and, with woman, horror of man and of maternity. And it is already understandable how there may be abnormal forms of virginity; less numerous than the deformities of love, they are perhaps more insidious because of the veil of purity under which they conceal themselves from sight. Sins against love are obvious to the sinner and also often enough to those who surround him: but sins against the enforced chastity which masquerades under the name of virginity attract respect, above all in societies of the Christian type where virginity tends to be honoured for its own sake without regard to its inward significance, or to the condemnations of Jesus of the foolish virgins who had no oil of good works in their lamps.

It is the being in a *state of oblation* which is the essence of the vocation of virginity. It is not the fact of not knowing a man which makes the virgin, but the firm intention of not wishing to know with a view to being able to give oneself up more fully to a spiritual life, to infantile and suffering humanity, to the adoration of infinite Being. In a way the Romans already understood this: in the Vestal they honoured not so much the virgin as the priestess. With us the elderly spinster is even a cause for complaint; she is never reverenced, as though it were supposed that she remained so out of spite, through ill-luck and lack of opportunity.

We do not, therefore, at this point, approach the study of virginity as a condition contrary to love, nor even, properly speaking, as a state of pure renunciation, as the ascetic tradition sometimes suggests. We are inclined to consider it as a condition into which love ought to enter, if it is true that, both in its origin and its end, human love implies oblation. There should, then, be a relation between continence and love, even though appearances are to the contrary. And, in our day, it is not unusual to see the establishment of new affinities between the spiritual aspect of virginity and that of marriage; each of them, by a kind of osmosis, becomes permeated with the properties of the other. I remember how, during a conversation in our prisoners' camp, a married man told a priest how valuable was the priestly ideal for an understanding of the meaning of marriage, and the abbé replied that he had never understood the love of God more fully than from the relation of husband and wife. It is a sign of our times that such former opposites seem now to become co-ordinated, at all events at their summits.

As for the renunciation which is a fundamental factor in the state of continence, it is somewhat different from the renunciations implied in the very servitude of sexual love which are called mutual service, condescension, temporary absence, support, paternity, maternity, widowhood. That is so firstly because these renunciations are provisory, except in the last case, but above all because such renunciations are involved in the very mechanism of love and in that inevitable gearing of which we have spoken.

In virginity, on the other hand (and that is, perhaps, why it is liable to be so acutely criticised from the existential point of view), the person, often a young and adolescent person, re-nounces the extraordinary adventure of love, and also all the circumstances which accompany it, in advance and completely.

She withdraws from the stage, and pledges herself to a state which is more nearly that of eternity than of time, since the most realistic imagination cannot contend that sexual love and generation continue in eternity. Christian authors have often reminded us that virgins enter into eternal life in time, while mothers continue the life of the flesh. And the whole Encratic philosophy is based upon this metaphysical conception which makes of virginity, not only a practical preparation for eternity by mitigation of the cares of the flesh, but also a real commencement of eternity on earth by renunciation of this function of generation which perpetuates time.

Thus the virgin, by total sacrifice, seems to evade the small change of sacrifice. Is not this initial and total holocaust (in other respects quite free since the subject chooses it both in matter and form), an easier matter than the acceptance of a conjugal life which is not wanted? Nevertheless, in its very essence virginity certainly seems superior to marriage. Here is to be found the idea of dedication. In the Christian perspective, virginity is generally accompanied by a *votum* (vow), that is to say by an undertaking binding the person for the future. From this aspect of consecration, it is true that the state of virginity is existentially very different from that of marriage, at least as marriage appears to be with the majority of couples.

The evolution of conceptions of virginity has followed the same curve as that of other moral concepts; it has become precise, humanised. At first virginity is observed only in woman. For it is there alone that its physical foundation, its often proved guarantees, its often tragic violation are found. Virginity is consequently conceived as, above all, preservation from taint, from contact with the male principle, from any kind of aggression or violence. The virgin is a *tabu* person over whom the demonic element has no hold, whom the vital principle (almost the principle of evil for many mentalities) has not deflowered. The virgin is a being *enclosed* from all contacts, preserved from all infection and corruption, and possessing that character of integrity which makes of her a victim agreeable to the gods and set apart for their service.

It is readily comprehensible how, for this first mentality, the virgin has been conceived as having a special relation towards divinity, and this precisely because she has none at all with humanity. And it is also comprehensible how the notion of a Messiah born of a virgin should occur to the Jews. None the less, it is only quite late that, even in Israel, the idea of a spiritual value peculiar to virginity is seen to emerge. This idea, even if it was ever envisaged, was countered in antiquity by the far stronger idea that, since it ensured the permanence of the family, the nation and of that cult without which the dead would be deprived of care, the generative act was obligatory.

It is to be noted, moreover, as regard the Jews, that the divine promises made to Abraham concerned the continuance of his posterity, that they therefore implied the duty of multiplying the race. The admission of the moral value of an act by which this essential duty of generation was renounced required something of an innovation. Even in Israel this innovation was *a priori* most improbable: the God of the Old Testament willed the propagation of the stock of Adam and to this virginity was essentially opposed. It is Christian beliefs which have carried this ideal of virginity to its highest pitch; it was formerly almost unknown to mankind, and then only concerned the feminine sex, probably as a temporary measure, as may be seen in the case of the Vestals.

The relation of Christianity to virginity should be carefully defined; for it is not easily perceived. I remember Bergson's saying that the God of the Christians had, so to speak, abolished the ancient precept of the Creator: 'create and multiply' in favour of a more lofty and more inward admonition of pure love. But is it in fact correct to see in the religion of Jesus a repudiation of generation according to the flesh? Primitive Christianity certainly did not repeat this formula of growth and multiplication which was so essential for a former age. Men lived in a world which they thought about to be abolished; and the Christian of this first period could scarcely be interested in a high birth-rate. In the *First Epistle to the Corinthians* one might almost say that St. Paul is preaching a certain *birth-control* which, in his view, could be based on continence alone. The Christ limited Himself to recalling marriage to its original institution by the Creator of all flesh, re-affirming the ancient and mysterious axiom *erunt duo in carne una*[1] which is certainly not exclusive of generation.

Among Biblical precepts that of virginity is not to be found: the Jewish spirit would not have endured it. But, if the ethical code does not permit it, the example of individuals suggests it. The Founder of the new religion seemed as though detached from the works of the flesh: if He does not fulfil them it is due to a more lofty vocation, to an absolute intimacy with the divine, and certainly not because of a too precocious death. This impression produced by the personality of Jesus was so profound that the mother of Jesus could never be conceived by the primitive communities except as a virgin (a conception later to be defined), *before, after and during* the birth.

When Jesus spoke of virginity, He represented it as a way of life which could only be comprehended by those who already understood it; and that is tantamount to abstracting it from normal existence and even, in some sense, from doctrine, in order to leave it to inspiration. But, for Jesus, it was altogether impossible that His history should not be related to the life of men. Beyond the precept there is the teaching; beyond the teaching there is the example. And, for tender consciences, the 'I do it but I do not oblige you to imitate me', when uttered by a being who is silently admired, is more imperative than a command.

[1] The twain shall be one flesh.

Christianity thus suggested the vocation of virginity without obligation to adopt it: and the Western Church, favouring vows of celibacy and later making the state of celibacy the pre-condition of priesthood, has authorised souls to take this flight; she has consecrated and regulated it. *En passant*, we find there a singular example of the influence of morality upon biology. We behold a pure idea transforming a vital function by con-demning it to disuse, without in the least degree diminishing the biological potentiality of the species nor even that of the individual. If an impartial observer were to come to our earth and study human behaviour, he would be struck by this anti-biological class of people composed of both sexes, constituting a paradoxical exception at the heart of humanity, which is nevertheless appropriate, felicitous, and gracious. Even if this visitor were disposed to be doubtful about mankind, if he felt himself to be a stranger in a rebellious planet, he would be able to conclude from this fact alone that humanity is not as impermeable to spirit as might otherwise have been supposed.

This aspect of continence inevitably arouses innumerable criticisms. The first come from the hygienists, doctors and biologists who make the point that abstinence may be prejudicial to the organism, especially in the case of the woman whose organism is only fulfilled in maternity. But, however pertinent this view may be, it is countered by the fact that, even with women, continence can exist without effect upon psychical poise, though always upon the express condition that it is consecrated and devoted. Such a theory will, no doubt, always be maintained by unbalanced minds and it will be contended that the continent only appear healthy, or, that, if they are really in good health, they are hypocritical in their way of life, as the common man supposes. But such reasoning, where the reason is convinced that it is never wrong, invites error: the denigration of Pascal by his adversaries ever since his experience of the gulf, comes to mind in this connection.

Moreover, knowledge of the mechanism of internal secretion gives us grounds for discounting to some extent the objection based upon non-usage and even permits us to distinguish *continence*, which is innocuous for the human equilibrium, from *castration*, which is prejudicial to it, as was supposed from the very beginning.

An organ is rarely restricted to a single use. It is nature's art to give to all things several meanings and several purposes: in that respect she already, in some measure, imitates spirit. She also has the art of supplying and repairing where there is a defect. It might be thought that the equilibrium of woman, manifestly made to bear and nurture the child, would be upset when she cannot satisfy that need. And yet it is well known that feminine nature is more capable of self-sufficiency than that of man; that woman, as we shall soon see, adapts herself more readily to independence and even to a premature widowhood.

Critics concerned with the psychical aspect are more profound. As I have shown, sexual functions have the characteristic of vibrating along the whole nervous system, of associating themselves with a great number of other reactions, of causing profound modifications in the consciousness of the individual. These effects of the sexual hormone upon our nature are not disturbing: they seem to be necessary for the inner poise, for the intelligence, for the fulfilment of the male and female species. Moreover, these sexual functions are so ramified, so dynamic that nature does not easily obey the order to ignore or cease to value them, even were it possible to do so. We can, indeed, by discipline, prevent tendencies from crossing the threshold of consciousness. Let us even admit that, by a fundamental renunciation, we might be able to eradicate these tendencies and transform them into temptations clamouring at but not penetrating the portal of our being. Would it be so desirable, this introduction of disunity into the core of our personality, this constant struggle with a force so persistent that it cannot be overcome at one point without breaking out more vigorously at another?

Yet, even though we were to achieve our ends and these tendencies came to be neither perceived nor experienced, would they cease to exist? And does not the effort we have made to repress them tend to cause their revival in an insidious form? Hunted from the conscious zones of our soul, they proceed to establish themselves in secret regions, undergoing metamorphoses over which we have no control at all. It may be questioned whether continence does not diminish the radical virtue of man by removing the opportunity for an act of value for his psychical development and maturity. It may even be asked whether the practice of sexuality does not bestow a kind of understanding, as seems to be suggested by the tale of Adam's and Eve's imperfections after the Fall. It may be questioned whether virginity does not keep man in a state of infancy; if the understanding of the chaste is not too sentimental, too subtle or too austere, as the works of mystics and clerics seem to suggest: and those of Kant and Spinoza would not be excluded from this category. It may be asked, finally, whether the result of virginity is not a kind of suppression and so of diffused neurosis.

A second and more inward objection is that which Charles Morgan, the author of the essay *On Singleness of Mind*, has described. "The splendour of celibacy," he says, "is a desperate splendour; its denials are wounds; to support it without spiritual pride requires a genius of humility." The fact is that virginity is so exceptional a state that it cannot fail to encourage a return of self-love. It has this in common with the majority of heroic states; its greatest difficulty consists in the initial venture and, once embraced, it is far less exacting in practice than outsiders suppose. Like all heroism, it is somewhat over-estimated. It never fails to give a feeling of pride to its possessor: "Lord, I am not as other men are."

To virgins others often seem enslaved by the flesh, or at the least a mediocre and subordinate race. Moreover, **it induces** an illusion in their spirituality. The experiences of sexual love of even the most legitimate kind, once they have been looked at from the point of view of virginity and regarded from that lofty level, seem much more sensual and animal than they really are. The fact is that, having no actual experience of these matters and knowing them only in the guise of prohibitions or his own temptations, it is not easy for the ascetic to understand that spirit and flesh, love and sexuality, self-donation and the physical act may form a unity not easily dissolved. For the virgin mind, the notion of something base is sometimes associated with sexual behaviour.

Since the majority of writings on morals are the work of celibates, the idea is often to be found in them that the *opus carnis*[1] is, in itself, distinct from *amor*[2] and that this *opus*, even with man, remains animal and even worse than animal. Thence derives the note of defilement and inferiority and a morality which often stigmatises even legitimate sexuality, as is to be seen, for example, in Bossuet's *Traité de la Concupiscence*. We know how the consciousness of a privilege, when not accompanied by a corresponding duty, tends towards severity. That virginity develops spirituality, purity, detachment, is manifest. But it also magnifies the spirit of integrity, which is not far from that of intransigence and not always very far from that of intolerance. Virginity could thus be a somewhat inhuman spirit tending to deprive man of self-knowledge and travesty him with a false excellence.

These criticisms raise the very delicate problem of *abuse* and *use*. It should be recognised, we believe, that there are two very different kinds of *abuse*: there is an abuse which is a real corruption of essence, as a corpse is an abuse of the living man, as tyranny is an abuse of authority, presumption an abuse of courage. Then, for one essence, another which only looks like it is seen to be substituted.

[1] Work of the flesh.   [2] **Love.**

But there is also another abuse which is the natural consequence, the fatal excess and, if it may so be expressed, the
effluence of the essence. Thus, a certain authoritarianism is
necessary for the exercise of authority, a certain pride for the
exercise of courage, a softness for the exercise of mercy. It
would certainly be preferable if this second abuse did not exist.
It cannot easily be disputed that, by offering a field for its bacilli,
it prepares the way for the other. But this abuse is of quite a
different kind since it is allied to the actual doing of good
when occasion offers in an imperfect universe. Moreover, to
indulge in criticism of this second kind of abuse would be to
annihilate every man and every human institution. This second
abuse is, properly speaking, the excess of a quality and therefore
the germ of a defect, but it is something very different from
vice.

In so far as virginity is concerned, the problem is that of
knowing if the disadvantages which we have noted come from
the essence of continence or simply from its exercise. It is
difficult to give an answer to this question; for if the defect is
not attached to the essence at all, it is more nearly inseparable
than in other cases from the exercise of the virtue—unless,
however, the subject recognises and represses the effects of
suppression. It is evident that, if the instinct is repressed
without being subsumed, if it is mortified without being
sublimated, if it remains undefeated and clamorous, it gives
rise either to an arduous restraint which enervates the will,
or to disguises and metamorphoses. And it is equally clear
that the sexual instinct is so lively in the human species,
the sublimation so rare that this instinct is never completely
vanquished.

But this struggle of spirit and flesh of which we have spoken
characterises all conditions of human existence; it could even
be reasonably maintained that it is the continent man who is
least aware of it. For he has solved the problem at one stroke,
he has got the sensual fires under control and does not see them

blaze up at every spark. It must be recognised also that it is impossible to conceive of virginity apart from a congeries of conditions. The first is freedom. And it is a *total freedom* which is involved. This freedom requires awareness, for without knowledge one cannot be free. The problem here is a delicate one since our ascetic has very often not known what it is that he renounces and, on the other hand, often enters upon this way of life at an age when ignorance of life misleads him into thinking it easy. It may happen that knowledge awakens later and that, like the abbess of Jouarre, he finds that his vow has betrayed his nature. But during adolescence the experience of divine love and realisation that it is of another order may occur, without his having to test a proposition which dazzles the mind's eyes.

The beauty of virginity consists in its spontaneity. It is in this respect that the tokens of freedom are apt to be confused with the grace of the act, with, we would suggest, a facile amenability, with the joy and gaiety of it. And that is true of every exceptional state; since the fulfilment of our intention is not inevitable, mediocrity is better than an imperfect perfection and still more so than a gloomy perfection. After freedom the other precondition of virginity is that generosity of which Descartes spoke, comparing it to a virtuous humility. Virginity is only conceivable as a donation, as service, as responsibility towards others and not as some isolated glory.

It is, moreover, also a catharsis of the spirit. We know how the sexual function in man is misled by imagination. Sexual *need* is a small matter in comparison with sexual *desire* which is limitless and renewed by the slightest stimulus. All society is aphrodisiac: it multiplies desire. Under these conditions virginity is only possible when the individual creates a mental and social universe which subdues the turmoil of imagination, or rather directs it towards sublime ends. Virginity is not possible without what I would like to call a *parthenosphere*; and, since this *parthenosphere* demands almost the separation of the sexes (since cohabitation risks the stimulation of the image), it is necessarily duplicated in so far as it concerns man or woman.

Here, by way of dialectic, we rediscover the conventual conception; and that is why, if purely lay convents can be imagined, it is almost inevitable that such hetaera-societies should develop in a mystic milieu. It was so also with the Russian Communists, when, at the beginning of the first revolution, setting comradeship above love, they separated the sexes. Moreover, virginity and religion, although they have no intrinsic connection, seem to sustain each other; and it seems probable that only a Christian society could create a milieu propitious to virginity and eliminate its grave disadvantages. If Christian asceticism extols virginity, it also wars unceasingly against these perils, the chief of which is repression; it constrains its converts in the world to a life of devotion and, in the cloister, to over-activity by the parcelling out of time and the variation of tasks. For the virgin who dreams has already fallen.

Before pursuing our enquiry, it must be emphasised that the problem of virginity is not the same thing for woman as for man: with woman the crux of this condition is not in its beginnings. The undertaking is facilitated by a modesty natural to the sex, because in certain social situations, the young virgin enjoys a respect which marriage often causes her to lose, because, in fine, in our Western societies, the virgin is still popular and remains a queen. But as woman ages, as her natural gifts disappear and the brilliance of youth diminishes, so barrenness of body and the drawbacks of solitude become apparent. This is the reason why virginity almost inevitably breeds its parasites: bitterness, secret jealousy, a managing and repressive spirit, a masculinity more harsh in woman than in man, austere forms of devotion, perhaps also regrets at not having loved. It is at the menopause that the virgin needs to make a real effort to avoid the inhibitions of the elderly spinster; that is why, with woman, sanctity is usually a phenomenon of youth.

It is quite otherwise with man. The crux comes at the beginning, for it is then that the call of the senses is most strong. When man comes to middle age continence is less and less exacting for him, and it is then that he develops to the maximum his propensity for wisdom and that, after passing the meridian point, he realises his own personality. The word 'priest' suggests an old man; with men sanctity is rather a phenomenon of age.

We should, perhaps, distinguish at this point between two neighbouring concepts: that of *continence* and that of *virginity*. Common usage, moreover, suggests a similar distinction in that continence seems to be reserved for the male species (one can hardly speak of a continent woman) while virginity seems to be the perquisite of women: it would never occur to us to speak of a *male* virgin, except in ridicule. Continence suggests an *effort* whereas virginity implies a *state*. *Continence* might therefore be termed the effort of a being who *contains* the immoderate stirrings of the life-force within himself. On the other hand, virginity might be termed the state of a being who, without having, strictly speaking, to make an effort, at all events in any deliberate fashion, refines, purifies, ennobles and sublimates the vital impulse by assuming it in the order of *spirit*. From this point of view virginity would be a kind of celestial gift, but continence only a human discipline.

We have hit the mark: the criticisms invoked by all asceticism can always be applied to continence: if the continent person *represses* without *sublimating*, his effort will prove to be a psychological ill, even if, morally, it is laudable. Just as disobedience to the State is praised only if it triumphs, so continence is only virtuous if it is victorious, if it is gracious, if the qualities which we attribute to virginity are latent within it. It will, no doubt, be asked why it is that the virgin should not have to submit to these exhausting conflicts. It is surely because, at root and in essence, in virginity love is already present in its purest form.

It is the unconditional gift of the self which renders virginity possible, and it is love alone which gives this victory over love.

We thus move towards the conclusion that, to a discerning person, if these two states are thus both inspired by oblation, there should be no radical difference between virginity and fertile love. It is true that we are quite unable to combine them in experience. Parthenogenesis could only come to pass in the human species by an exceptional submission of nature to pure spirit: that is, by a miracle. Whether myth or reality, virgin-birth remains an unattainable mark, but yet one which is pleasing, poetic and congenial to the mind. It is curious that Auguste Comte, from a purely positivist point of view, had noted the intellectual fecundity of this idea of parthenogenesis; he even thought that 'the utopia of the Virgin-Mother' might contribute to the progress of biological science and the economy of society, as the utopia of the transmutation of metals had stimulated the pre-scientific activity of the Middle Ages. An ideal aim, but one which, on the winding way towards it, permits the making of further discoveries by the wayside.

However that may be, the view, traditional in Christian lands, of the outstanding merit of virginity preserves a profound philosophic value. It is true that the best use that can be made of a good is to renounce it for a higher good: not indeed through scorn for that first good, but in order the more to reverence its essence, to purify it, it might almost be said in this connection, to glorify it. It is thus that virginity can but be illuminated by the nuptial reality which it sublimates. If, in fine, it is remembered that nuptial love is itself a process of ineffable renunciation, it will without doubt be perceived that virginity manifests the dialectic immanent in love. By a voluntary choice it takes its point of departure where the other love should reach its culmination. That which in normal love is realised little by little, which matures slowly, is achieved sorrowfully, this donation of the self spread over the years, is imposed upon conjugal love

more by circumstances, by necessary metamorphoses than by
the conscious will of man and wife; whereas virginity realises
all this in a kind of timeless moment repeated through time.
From this aspect, between nuptial love and virginity there would
be the relation which exists between thought and speech, theorem
and demonstration, or, to use a metaphor, between a gold coin
and its copper change: virginity would be given the whole of
love at a stroke while the other way of life parcels it out in
successive instalments.

★

But it may be asked if the life of virginity may not have a
new and even more remarkable result, that of initiation into the
mystical life. By that, in the strict meaning of a term so
ambiguous, are implied those strange experiences of invisible
realities enjoyed by certain privileged souls in Christianity, and
sometimes by those beyond its range. Virginity would thus
have the effect not only of developing charity in the ordinary
sense of the word, that is, of love for others, but would also
awaken in us a life of a new kind for which every man is made,
a life which is not realised because the fleshly matrix op-
presses, obscures and dissipates it. Virginity would develop
potentialities latent in our nature but stupefied by the ordinary
habits of bodily existence. We are confronted here with a very
delicate and knotty point. It was already a difficult matter to
define the precise relation between love and sexuality. The
question is further complicated when the relation between
mysticism and sexuality is concerned.

The hypothesis that mysticism may be allied to sexuality confronts us; it may be that, by some sort of transference, sexuality
transforms itself into a mystical state. It is true that the
relation between virginity and the mystical life is not invariable.
Cases are known in which conjugal relations have been no
obstacle to mystical experience. Mme. Acarie and, more
recently, the blessed Taïghi, are cases in point. Those of Jeanne
de Chantal and Marie of the Incarnation who, before becoming

mystics, were young widows, should also be recalled. It is possible for conjugal life itself to arouse mystical inspirations. But the case of Mme. Acarie, recently studied by Père Bruno, is not conclusive, for the fixation of mysticism coincided, for Mme. Acarie, with an accident which rendered her unfit for conjugal life. These exceptions do not alter the fact that the majority of mystics are celibate and are often women. That would suggest that mystical development is in some way connected with a latent sexuality.

The language of the mystics, moreover, permits of that interpretation. The rôle which the *Song of Songs* has played in the language of the mystics is well known. And if the *Song* is taken in its literal sense, it is impossible not to realise that it is full of amorous expressions. Now the mystics have found in the *Song* the most adequate grammar of the operation of divine love and they are never weary of commenting upon it, as though its pages contained an anticipatory description of their experiences. It will be said that this is a matter of symbolism, but the problem is precisely that of ascertaining why this symbolism seems, for the mystics, superior to other equally plausible symbolisms which they also accept, such as those of the fire, the court, the banquet, paradise.

From this angle there have been mystics who seem to have provided arguments against the specific nature of their experiences. Our contemporaries have gone much further than they; one can only infer that the temptation was too strong for their sagacity to resist. Many have seen in mystic states a transposition of sexual states. The explanation by transfer, disguise or transvaluation of values is one of the most common in the contemporary world. And here I find Nietzsche, Marx and Freud, those three gloomy pillars of the new temple. If it is true that religion originates in mysticism and mysticism in sexuality, then that which is most lofty is reduced to the level of that which is most low, and the idea of God lowered to the level of the glandular system. Religion would then be fundamentally no more than the transmutation of a maladjustment which, for its cure, fabricates hallucinations, false experiences and beliefs, just as a malignant disease causes a rash. And, like disease, religion would be at once an ill and a boon, an ill since it creates belief in its objective reality, and a boon since, stabilising his disquiet, it liberates the subject of it from an inner disequilibrium.

The defect of these explanations is, perhaps, that they prove too much. They are not of a kind which criticism can touch. For a theory to be irrefutable is a bad business. A scientific thesis is one which can be taken on to the level of experience, and can raise precise questions formulated according to the nature of things, of which the conclusions will be incontrovertible for all experts. But here the experimental basis is, in truth, too vague, too subject to the distortion of interpreters. If religion were derived from the cloisters of women, if it originated with a Diotima of Mantinea, one would, perhaps, have the right to suppose that sexuality is at the root of mysticism. But it seems clear that, even in pagan religions, the mystical impulse has preceded the erotic manifestations with which it is sometimes associated. And the only religion which has triumphed over all the others is precisely that which has based its mysticism upon a radical condemnation of eroticism.

The share of mysticism, in its proper sense, in the origin and essence of religion is, however, exaggerated. Prior to mystical experiences (which, moreover, save with minds which clarify them in doctrine, remain extremely confused) there were cult, religious ideas, facts true or suppositious, histories of heroes or saints, perhaps even systems of thought. If the mystics have found a place in Catholic Christianity, it is because their experiences are found (naturally or artificially, for this purpose it is immaterial) to be in conformity with the dogmatic, cultural and historic system of religion. Much more that, mystical experience has illuminated this system in an unusual way. Thus lamps lit on the pediment of a monument on a fête-day do not in any way alter its architecture but rather serve to throw the design of it into relief. To explain mystical states by sexual repression one must, moreover, leave out of reckoning the witness of the mystics themselves. On the other hand, sexual repression is a constant factor in the human race whereas mysticism is quite a rare phenomenon.

But if the relation between sex and mysticism is not what the writers whom we criticise suppose, is it necessary to conclude forthwith that there is no relation at all? We are far from comprehending the relation between the physical and the mental in all its intricacy. To speak more generally, it may be said that the relation of essences, and, in particular, the relation between the higher essence and the lower essence which sustains it, in cases in which they might seem to be indissolubly linked to each other, remains, for the most part, incomprehensible for lack of adequate analysis and appropriate language. When theologians remark that mystical states are often accompanied by sensible phenomena, as, for example, with St. François de Sales in his *Treatise on the Love of God*, they note also that the base part of our nature is not independent of the other and that, if the spirit is stirred by a divine impulse or motion, the body may also experience its own reaction, like an echo or the wake behind a ship.

To translate this idea into more modern terms, it might be said that grace acts fully upon the central nervous system and that it excites reactions remote from those which are strictly necessary. But these vagaries hardly matter since what is really essential is attained in the simplest of ways. But, even though, for the mystic, there might be an analogy between the states of human love and his own personal experiences, when taken onto these higher levels, the soul discerns clearly that there is, in fact, no common standard of values. We may go further and even admit, as we have just suggested, that, in consequence of the frailty inherent in our nature, the mystic impulse is still expressed through the medium of sensory reactions. The spirit of the mystics eliminates or excludes these reactions without even having to sublimate them: their consciousness, serene and pure, ruling the body in all its aspects, knows that it has no part in these things and abides in its own calm.

Finally, it may be asked whether the exaltation which, amongst men, nearly always accompanies the stirrings of sexuality might not have a mystical origin. Can this obscure ecstasy be fully accounted for in a mere fortuitous and banal creature? And if its object were only a limited personality, even though supposed to be immortal, would it have any sufficient and final reason? Can ecstatic love project itself towards any other end than that of infinite being, the beauty of which, although immaterial, is beyond all conceivable expression? Plato held this view when he described Eros reascending to the Highest and there finding rest. His error lay in underestimating the intermediary stages and failing to do justice to the personal created being.

But we are entitled to ask whether this *transport* which is so natural a phenomenon in human love might not be the residue of an obscure and inveterate love for the divine of which this particular attachment is the symbol. From this point of view, as Bergson divined, the problem of the resemblance between the language of human love and that of mysticism must be completely reversed. It cannot be denied that these two languages are similar to the point of coincidence, and that the mystics have taken this fact into account when they interpret certain expressions of passionate love after their own fashion. But the question is whether there are not lovers whose love has been enriched from the first with sentiments which can only be accounted for in the context of religion. In that case the mystics, in speaking the language of human love, do no more than reclaim what was, from the beginning, their own prerogative.

To return, in conclusion, to the theme of this chapter, we shall affirm that the oblative forms of love, far from being an obstacle to the understanding and practice of its normal manifestations, help us to enter into and to live them more profoundly. That which is least is justified by that which is more lofty, the commonplace by the sublime. The saying of Leibnitz may very aptly be cited here: "Low things exist in those more lofty in a manner more noble than their own." In the course of the life we lead now, dependent upon time, flesh and the finite, no solution of the relation of flesh and spirit can be fully satisfactory. As the contemplatives have remarked, the life of marriage and family imposes an irksome servitude upon pure spirit.

But it might equally well be maintained that virginity, apart from the fact that it cannot become a universal vocation without cosmic suicide, diminishes experience; and, since it involves a detachment from the duties of paternity and maternity, is impoverishing and even imperfect. For then man does not restore to life what he has taken from it. This last criticism would be true if there were no other life than that of the body, but, as Plato observed, generation after the spirit is superior to that after the flesh. And it is hardly debatable that the state of virginity, even though without intrinsic virtue, allows more liberty for such spiritual tasks as the education, service and redemption of other men. And humanity as a whole would be the poorer did it not make some of its members experts in the special functions of the life of contemplation, which it alone can achieve, such as reflection, silence, peace, prayer, the submission of the natural faculties, and the sacrifice of that which is only in part and temporal. From this point of view, no lover of the unity of the spirit can deny that virginity offers incomparable conditions for oblation.

To give one final consideration to these two states of virginity and marriage which are the only possible solutions of human love, it must be recognised that they should inspire and emulate each other in spirit. For, if it is true that contemplation is superior to action and that the state which, by its sublime leisure, permits it, may be more in conformity with the ideal life, it should also be noted that, in order to attain to wisdom, virginity should share the generous spirit which animates the founders of families. And, from another angle, in order that marriage may be really worthy of man, it is fitting that its fruition should derive, not from the impulse of instinct, but from a desire to transmit and multiply the spirit, in a veritable love for being.

> And wedded lives, which not belie
> The honourable heart of love
> Are fountains of virginity.[1]

The mirror of human love is as though broken into two fragments each of which can deny fulfilment to the other. Everywhere there must be renunciation. In this world accomplishment depends upon specialisation, and, in consequence, upon accepting deprivation of what might otherwise have given us fulfilment. The meeting of the contraries is at the point of convergence. Each of these two loves ascends towards oblation by different paths. One of these ascents is immediate, very intense, very direct, secure from vicissitudes. And this same oblation is also the goal of the other. But, though it can be effected at a stroke at the threshold and without experience of life, it nevertheless supposes a dim realisation of the benefits it has chosen to eschew; if it were not so it would hardly be sacrifice.

Here we encounter again a difficulty inherent in morality in that it counsels us to detachment. The renunciation demanded by asceticism is difficult: for it is not enough to reject what was evil in the nature which one transcends; it is still more necessary to gather into oneself and to assume what was good.

[1] Coventry Patmore. From *The Vestal*, *Tire*, written for the fourth section of Book II of *The Angel in the House*.

St. Paul understood this when he said that the way of the inner man is not of one stripped bare but of one who is 'clothed upon', in order that what is mortal in him may be subsumed by life. It is true that he spoke of death: but all *surpassing* is like death and prepares for it.

THE SIGNIFICANCE OF SEX

7 *The significance of sex*

IT is appropriate at this stage to recapitulate the steps we have taken before proceeding further.

We have examined love first in its most characteristic manifestations. The second approach to its mystery was by way of analysing it in its lapses, through the negative medium of defect. Then we tried to construct what might be called the *statics* of love by describing the poignant moment of its eruption into the field of consciousness. This study led us to the consideration of love in its development: it had become necessary for us to delineate the *dynamic* of love. The study of this development of love in human existence led us to the consideration of its final phases, and we believed that there we best discerned the essence of love, which consists in a kind of oblation. This induced us to pay attention to those seemingly rare and paradoxical forms in which love appears no longer to have any connection with the flesh: virginity, mystical states. And, just as in the most carnal aspects we found, by deep analysis, an element of pure oblation, so in the most oblative states of love an audible echo of the carnal was also inescapable.

It is one of the marks of this mystery that this ambiguity is constant. The complete separation of body and spirit is impossible. But all the studies which have been made up to this point belong to the order of appearance or at least of description. Those which we now wish to undertake relate to a different and a higher order, that of significance and perhaps also of justification. Hitherto we have mainly posed the question *how*; henceforth we shall also ask *why*. It will be our business to consider the phenomena of love in their total range, extending from physical generation to deifying union, or, even more, from sin to sacrifice (filling in all the middle, the whole properly human domain); we must examine the relation of all these to the destiny of the spirit. It is in fact the supreme duty of mind to seek the *meaning* of a reality, that is to say to ascertain its place in the sum total of beings, to perceive in what respect it is in accord with the harmony of the universe.

We are perfectly aware that in our approach to these final questions we may enter the domain of the unknowable and sometimes of the ineffable. Some will say that we are abandoning appearances in order, at last, to reach realities; others that we are leaving the plane of the verifiable to which human research should be confined.

It is important for the lucidity of these discussions to define our point of view. We start from the postulate that the beings composing the universe are not products of chance but are related to a higher end. Even the partisans of chance who were given the name of evolutionists admit that, of the multitude of combinations produced by chance at each moment of time, only those survive which are adapted to their own needs and circumstances. That is to say in other words that everything that is has its reason, and that the reason of being should be found in conformity with its own equilibrium and that of the universe. No doubt the partisans of chance reckon it an unforgivable sin to seek the purpose of nature, the ends of creation. But since the human intellect cannot comprehend a reality without knowing its function, destination and use, those who deny finality utilise the concept of an end no less than their opponents. The difference is that they do not confess it, or at least only consent to utilise it in a restricted area. They accept enquiry into the function of the eyelid or the liver, but they refuse to put the same question concerning man and life.

We shall not entertain such scruples. At the risk of scandalising our contemporaries, we shall pose questions which seem addressed to the Author of life Himself. Can nature and the ways by which she moves be justified? Is there any ratio between means and ends, cause and effect? Philosophers once tried to justify God concerning the problem posed by evil: such was the attempt of Leibnitz in his *Theodicy*. In our turn, and in a very modest manner, we have recently tried to justify time, that is to say to explain why a free spiritual being is confined to this form of fleeting and disintegrated existence which is called temporal. To justify is to seek the most profound significance, the reason for the reason. To employ the language of the ancient Jews, to justify would mean to penetrate into the secrets of Elohim as Wisdom is said to have done in the first days of the creation: *Cum eo eram, cuncta componens, ludens in orbe terrarum.*[1]

★

It is remarkable that man has kept silence concerning the problem of sex for so many centuries and that he has not found any justification, or at least has never (save perhaps at the dawn of time and in the first pages of the first of books) fully elucidated the question why nature has linked love to sexuality by such subtle bonds, and the most elevated of states of feeling to acts which make man feel his resemblance to the superior mammals. It seems that it would have been easy for the Creator to follow a different procedure and the study of the vegetable realm suggests many other types of reproduction which would appear more suitable for the spirit. Must it be said that He did not really will this and that this strange conjunction of flesh and

---

[1] "I was at his side, a master workman . . . as I made play in this world of dust." (*Prov.* viii, 30, 31, tr. R. Knox.)

spirit, as it exists in humanity to-day, was the chastisement of an initial rebellion? Such, it seems, was the Jewish conception which the Christians have inherited. It seems that, previously, man had full control over the flesh, that it was no more than the sheath and symbol of the spirit, somewhat as Christian hope expects it to be reborn after the final change. The first transgression would thus have been the occasion and the cause of the submergence of spirit in the flesh, whence it follows that the human order, in so far as the balance of being is concerned, is inferior to the animal order where all is nature in tranquillity.

But, even though sin should have changed the manner in which spirit uses the flesh, it does not follow that it has transformed the biological mode of conception, the mechanism of which was, from the first, related to that of the mammifers. For long centuries, this explanation of our basic disequilibrium has been the accepted one for the majority of thinkers. We do not intend to study the question here along theological lines, seeking to discern the respective contributions of revealed teaching, mental environment and language which it suggests. We limit ourselves to remarking that, from the point of view of a philosopher, the second chapter of *Genesis*, for the expert eye, undoubtedly contains an explanation of love in its relation to sexuality which already provides an answer to the problem which, with the aid of science, we wish to study anew.

And this is the course which we must pursue. We shall first consider sexuality in the cosmos and the biosphere; we shall relate it to the problem of reproduction which itself depends upon the problem of life. We shall enquire why, among so many possible modes of reproduction, nature seems to have preferred that of sex, at all events for the higher species. We shall then enquire why nature has not modified the reproduction of the primates for the purpose of the human species; what advantage or disadvantage there was in the creation of a preeminently spiritual being in the dual form of male and female; and how the psyche is affected by the influence of sex-conscious-

ness upon this spiritual being. In other terms we shall put to
ourselves afresh and on a higher level the problem which has
not ceased to challenge us—the relation of flesh and spirit.

I say on a higher level, for this time we shall seek to ascertain
if the spirit has in any way profited by assuming the knowledge
of sex. We shall enquire later if the relation of spirit and flesh
is not fundamentally modified by the quite recent discoveries of
science, the structural changes in society and the new conceptions
of marriage and the family which derive from them. We shall
put to ourselves the question whether we are not witnessing a
mutation in humanity as profound as that to which Christianity
gave rise twenty centuries ago, although with a very different,
if not even a contrary orientation of meaning. Thus we shall
have made every possible effort of the understanding to penetrate
in spirit into this most obscure problem which nevertheless
pierces to the quick of our being.

The principal purpose of this study is to give sexuality its
proper place in anthropology. But, as we have just said, it is
first necessary to study the place of sexuality in nature. On the
planet we know, which forms the universe of our experience,
life presents itself in a form at once invariable and precarious.
Invariable, since the same species seem to persist without change;
precarious, since each individual is the bearer of a limited vital
force subject to the servitude of beginning and end. Perhaps
in other planets it is otherwise? It is possible to conceive
of living organisms which may be durable after the manner,
for example, of crystals. In this world of ours, the duration of
each individual is limited and the species can only survive by
means of this artifice called reproduction. The principle of
it is clear and can be deduced *a priori*.

In order that any being may reproduce itself it is necessary
and it suffices that, at a certain moment in its development, it
detach some part of itself capable of existing autonomously and
of repeating the pattern in another substance.

All reproduction thus implies a separation, a division, a kind of dichotomy. We give here the simplest, the most abstract form of reproduction. Everything points to the belief that, in nature, so prodigal of invention, this mode is to be found in the most varied and complex of forms. The easiest to understand is, doubtless, that of dichotomy. But it is evident that dichotomy implies forms of being in which individuality remains elementary. When individuality develops, a portion of being specially adapted for reproduction should begin to appear; or, more exactly, in the primitive being a probably very small fraction of its cells should be found possessing the property of reproduction, while the others are without it. That principle of economy would thus be applicable which requires that a function, after being divided in the organism, is found in the end to be located at a particular point. It is that to which the classic distinction between *soma* (body) and *germen* (germ) corresponds; the *germen*, moreover, may be as diminutive as possible.

Thanks to this specialisation of the cells destined to transmit the type and life, reproduction no longer results in the fission of the unity of the reproducer nor even in disturbing its equilibrium. The separation of *germen* and *soma* can, no doubt, occur in conditions so violent that the *soma*, deprived of the *germen*, and now lacking some necessary stimulus, finds itself speedily given over to death; this seems to be the case with those insects which, after fecundation, no longer survive. But, in general, and thanks to the division of *soma* and *germen*, the living creature is not affected by generation; before generation becomes possible it can develop its own personality without being absorbed by the generative function.

As for the *germen*, after having known a first life hidden in the interior of the *soma*, as though in order to become impregnated with that *soma* and so that it can convey the likeness to its parent, one day it escapes from the maternal circle to pursue its own separate life and growth: this is what we call birth. There is, moreover, nothing to prevent the *germen* from preserving a certain independence in relation to the *soma* and a certain dependence in relation to previous *germens*. This permits the individual to escape the influence of space and to receive that of time, or, to speak more clearly, to relax the relation with his own parent and, in compensation, to form a bond with a great-grandparent or even with an ancestor still more remote.

Thus, by means of this distinction between what we call the *soma* and the *germen*, nature is found to resolve a difficult problem in a graceful fashion—that of reconciling the identity necessary for the permanence of the species with the diversity and individuality of beings which will later, in the human species, be the foundation of personality. Again this system, in that it obliges each individual to exist in a micro-organic form, and then to pass, in a continuous progression, through all the degrees which separate the humblest beginnings from fulfilment, is found to be in accord with that requirement of growth and regular development which, in the realm of the living, already typifies a law of spiritual existence.

It is remarkable that, in this system of reproduction which we have first deduced by the argument of conformity to type, the necessity for sex is nowhere apparent: for each *soma* could equip itself with its *germen* without external intervention. Sex would thus be a luxury in the biosphere. I mean here by sex the division between male and female, or, better, the distinction between the male and female organs which can be found, as one knows, in the same hermaphrodite-person, but generally exist in two distinct and separate persons and are only rarely conjoined. It seems as though reproduction by means of sex were a uselessly complicated mode, hardly conforming to that universal principle which wills that nature should always function in the simplest of ways.

This conclusion holds good for both finalist and evolutionist. For the finalist the abnormal complication indicts nature or its author. For those who explain every organ by the struggle for existence and selection, it is difficult to understand how sexed species have any advantage over those which are not, or at least why chance did not cause other more perfect and more simple forms of reproduction to prevail over that of sex, which is an awkward contrivance. It seems, indeed, that the most normal mode of reproduction would be that which we call parthenogenesis: it would, in fact, be sufficient if a female organ could reproduce another being in its likeness. It is credible, on the other hand, that nature has divided the parental task into two equal shares. The two generating cells seem, in fact, to contain the same quota of hereditary elements: the enumeration of the chromosomes has verified this fact for us.

But if the influence of the two parents is thus equal, their labour is not. In all sexed creatures the ovule, which is stored with reserves of nutriment, is of considerable bulk in comparison with the spermatozoa, which are limited to a simple nucleus without protoplasm and have a function which is purely momentary since it seems sometimes to disappear upon emission. This rôle of emission is, moreover, so slight that, in certain cases (perhaps in all cases) it can be replaced by physical or chemical agents. There is more than this: the aptitude for parthenogenesis seems no longer to be the specific property of certain eggs but a generic property of the animal egg. Everything happens as though nature has kept the possibility of parthenogenesis in reserve, not only because the male functions only by a stimulus which can be supplied, but also because the female can find in herself the means of assuring her complete hereditary equipment.

Is that tantamount to the assertion that sexuality is altogether useless and that parthenogenesis would produce the same results? Upon this point the case of the most elementary creatures might, perhaps, give an indication. Amœbæ and infusoria are reproduced by division. Nevertheless a process analogous to what we call sexuality is already apparent in the development of these protozoa, at least in so far as the infusoria are concerned. In fact, at a certain moment, two individuals are seen to blend partially or completely, to be conjoined in a temporary rapprochement which results in interchanges. Emmanuel Maupas, who was the first to experiment with these facts, thought that this conjunction was necessary for the rejuvenescence of the nuclei and had to occur periodically. We should be much less positive to-day, for, in favourable cases, multiplication without conjunction can be indefinitely repeated. According to M. Caullery, it amounts to the probability that, when sexuality appears, it has the function of reconstituting the nuclear apparatus by a fusion of the nuclei of the two gametes and, in consequence, of the properties of the breed.

Thus, in the order of the protozoa, as a simplified and privileged example, we see that sexuality, although not strictly necessary, produces an activation, a rejuvenescence which may be indispensable.

It is evident that sexuality favours the variability of the species. If the parent belonged to only one type of being, the product would be identical with that which begot it; daughters who were daughters of their mother alone would resemble her in every respect. Moreover, all the variations which could be produced in the maternal chromosomes would reappear in the second generation and so on indefinitely. It is probable that, under these conditions, the species would disappear through impoverishment and perhaps also through degradation; for, in hereditary transmission, the bad generally prevails over the good. The aberrant and monstrous forms which appear so frequently in the existing world would occur more frequently still and that without any mechanism which could neutralise them.

Suppose, on the contrary, that an individual derive from two parents, the one male, the other female, that he possess two different heredities and that this be repeated in each generation: the potentialities which are in the species and, in some manner, materialised in the chromosomes, will then group themselves in every possible combination and at the same time be capable of mutual compensation. The two fundamental needs of life, the permanence of the type and the variability of individuals, will thus be better assured; above all new, original and creative combinations, like the highest prizes in a lottery, have the chance of being drawn.

Sex-differentiation thus corresponds to that of the two functions necessary for development: the female represents heredity and identity: she is the race, permanence; the male, on the other hand, guarantees the variations. And the combination of the two factors makes progress possible, above all if the permanence is sufficiently strong to prevent the variations from changing the type. It will be said that monstrosities could still make their appearance; but the monstrosity is eliminated by life, whereas genius is favoured by the better adaptation which it enjoys.

When certain animal species are considered, it seems as though sexuality may have been the method chosen by nature in order to get round difficult corners: were she once more a free agent she might perhaps prefer parthenogenesis. With the bees, among which the queen, after the nuptial flight, fecundates herself for many years, sexuality is limited. With the aphis several generations of self-reproduction by parthenogenesis are to be seen: it is only in a bad season that we find the male and female elements once more. In the same way, with certain crustaceans, sex appears only when fresh water fails. Thus reproduction of like from like seems the most convenient process, under favourable conditions, for the swift colonisation of a society. But it has the disadvantage of enfeebling the species, and sex manifests itself in order to revive the vital energy. Here, as everywhere, difference acts as succour and stimulus.

Thus sexuality is conducive both to the variability and to the vitality of the species. Some say that, on the contrary, it hinders reproduction in that it makes it contingent upon an encounter which is itself an affair of chance, that it is a lottery in which any hereditary stock is associated with any other. The objection would have weight if nature had not provided a kind of selection which brings it to pass that the better stocks are matched with their peers. The behaviour of animals, particularly of the female, is characteristic in this respect. If animal behaviour is compared with human habits it will be remarked, moreover, that sexuality plays a much more restricted part among animals. It functions, at least in the higher species, in phases and restricted periods. If the case of the great apes, which are undoubtedly degenerate, is excepted, the female admits the male only in strict accord with the duties which she has to fulfil towards the species. One knows that there are even cases in which a single coition renders the female capable of a great number of births, as is the case with bees and aphides. Besides, animal sexuality is confined to its strict rôle and is not concerned with the creation of a shared existence between individuals. Symbiosis in mating is indeed known, as, for example, among frogs and tortoises; but mating is not society.

All the observations and reflections which we have just made concerning animals have been made with the purpose of clarifying the difference between them and man. In our species the physiological mechanism is the same as that of the higher mammifers. There is, indeed, no reason for supposing that the processes of artificial insemination, ectogenesis and parthenogenesis could not, one day, be applied to the human species. But, with man, the mechanism appears in a context and with a significance which completely change its meaning. And the chief problem is not that of knowing how the sex organs are adapted or how conception takes place; it is that of knowing how the instinct of reproduction possessed by the animal changes in form when encountered in the human consciousness. In other terms, that which interests the philosopher is the development of one order of being in another, or at least the envelopment of one order in another: the way in which the transition from the biosphere to the psychosphere comes to pass must be described, the way in which the biosphere is transfigured when found within the psychosphere.

It is easy to observe how often, with man, the sexual instinct is but little adapted for the rôle which it ought to fulfil. Endow the animal with consciousness, and try to imagine how the instinct of generation would appear to it! In the ordinary course of events it would give no sign of being present. Suddenly, at stated periods, it would invade the field of consciousness. It would then, no doubt, be the sense of an irresistible inward constraint, as is our need for micturition. Once satisfied, the instinct would again become atonic. This instinct of reproduction, limited in time, would, above all, be independent of the other instincts and behaviour of the animal, or, if it affected other organs such as those of sight or smell, it would be only during the instant of its efficacy.

If the animal which we imagine were endowed not only with consciousness but also with reflection, it would be able to explain itself to itself by relating all the manifestations of this instinctive mechanism to their purpose. This intelligent animal would be able to apply to itself the maxim which Taine ascribes to Thomas Graindorge: "I have reduced love to a function and that function to a minimum." And perhaps, comparing itself to man, it would rejoice to see how nature, by not complicating its sexuality and confining it within its limits, has effected a precious economy of love.

It is to suppositions like these that the Encratites of old, like the first Russian Communists, had come, seeing in the rôle of worldly love, even when not vicious, a superstructure, a quite useless psychical derangement. In view of the deviations of love they cannot always be refuted; but their error lay in the belief that this superstructure depends upon political or social conditions and that a revolution or a legislator would suffice to transform the mode of love among men. In reality, this mode is incarnate in our nature. It is true that, in one respect, the sexual instinct allows man more liberty than the animal, and that it is thus distinguished from the instinct of nutrition and of respiration which cannot be flouted without suffering and eventually dying.

There is certainly a whole literature that would have us believe

in the necessity for satisfying the sexual instinct. But neither
the reasoning of the physiologists nor the lyricism of the poets
would ever, as has been remarked, prevail against the fact of
continence, which neither harms physical or psychical health nor
impairs the organs of generation. It is in this way that the
sexual instinct, which in man, and in man alone, can be detached
from the equilibrium of life, permits him to free himself
from it.

But, from another aspect, the sexual instinct leaves much less
liberty to man than to the animal. It is bound up with other
instincts; as a stimulus it enters the realm of the human psyche,
its roots ramify throughout the whole man. This capacity for
liaison is peculiar to it. The instinct of respiration may be
associated with the desire to enjoy beautiful landscapes, with the
love of mountains, with the quest for all that is fresh, pure and
perennial. Pleasure in food may awaken the love of fine linen,
of gold and silver, of precious stones, of friendly conversation;
it has its echoes in social life and even in the life of the spirit
where the breaking of bread draws together the disciples. But
these influences have a limited field.

The notion of trying to trace the connection of hunger and
thirst with art and mysticism would occur to no one, save as a
study in the play of metaphor. The case is otherwise with the
sexual instinct. There is no psychical function, there is neither
sensation nor image with which this instinct cannot be associated,
without the subject of it always being cognizant of the fact, and
the more so perhaps in that the subject is not fully conscious
of it. It can mislead the noblest of sentiments, make dubious
the purest of spectacles. It can also feed with its fire the
loftiest of activities, stimulate self-donation, promote artistic
creation. And it can be said of it that, though contained and
suppressed, it still functions since it is transferred to a similar
object in such a way that there would seem to be no question
of suppression, but only of controlling its trends and causing
them to abet what is good.

On the other hand, while, with the animal, the instinct is regular and subject to the cosmic rhythm, with mankind, and especially with the male, it is subject to an almost continuous excitation. It is released from vital necessities, it makes its appearance in season and out. It might be said that with man instinct disengages itself from the life of nature in order to become engaged in that of the spirit and to disturb the relations of spirit with life; it is infinitely stronger and more persistent than need be. Everything occurs as though, in this instinct more than in any other, nature had detached *desire* from *need* and that counter to the good of the species.

Here, more than anywhere else at all, there is a marked difference between the claims of need and the impulse of desire: between physiological appeal and psychical attraction. Need reduced to mere bare need is rare; it is noticeable that it is never compulsive. Desire, on the contrary, is so intense that not only does it constantly exceed need but also substitutes for it a kind of illusory need which is much more difficult to overcome. For it is based entirely upon imagination; and everyone knows that the fear of a danger is far harder to endure than the danger itself, that we can contend against actual pain and yet with difficulty control the frenzy of imagination. Add to this the fact that social life (even in the most moral societies) encourages desire because it is compelled to regulate the life-instinct and all prohibition stimulates the imagination.

All these observations suggest that, from the sexual point of view, the human realm is disorderly, ambiguous and paradoxical. We are tempted to suppress such unfavourable conditions in our thoughts, to dream of some new Eden where the relations of spirit and life would evolve in a normal fashion. It may be that man would benefit therefrom what the scholastics call the *dominium*, that is to say the absolute power of his instinct; it may be even more likely that, after all, man possesses the faculty of assuming the forces of life in the spirit by a felicitous sublimation.

But, before having recourse to the unverifiable idea of some disorder in being itself, it may be asked if, in creating sexuality in man, nay, even in leaving human sexuality in this ambiguous form which we have just described, nature has not obeyed a final purpose the meaning of which we can perhaps discover. What would a society be like in which sexuality were functional, as with the animal, or reduced to a *debitum* after the formula of the jurists, or even to a *solatium concupiscentiae*, without the psychology of the person being involved? Or what kind of a nature would it be that would not have to engage in conflict with itself at the core? Or again, how should we like a world where love was purely intellectual, as in the universe of Spinoza? What would a parthogenetic cosmos be like? Would the most sublime forms of the life of the spirit be realised in it?

There are, as may be seen, plenty of questions posed by the subject of sex which concern man himself. With every difficult question I believe that the first task of thought is to discover if the problem under consideration does not offer a point of cleavage and, as it were, two definable approaches. Obscurity and confusion generally arise from using the same terms for different aspects of reality which, even though not separable, should be distinguished from each other. The greatest achievements of thought have been attained by this method of disjunction which seems to enable us to probe the very quick of things.

The problem which occupies us at present would doubtless be simplified if, in this confused notion of sexuality, we were prepared to distinguish two elements which are closely associated in man though often confused in practice, but which nevertheless have their separate existence. In all consciousness of a sexual act one can easily separate the knowledge of the other, that is the concept and image of a being physically and psychologically different, from the desire for contact, of whatever kind, with that other. This difference is so evident that incest has always seemed a monstrous thing to humanity; yet it is obvious that a father does not love his daughter, a mother her son, a brother his sister in the same way as they love a relative of the same sex.

These affections between different sexes within the family without any sexual element are one of the secret charms of social life. They give birth to the most sublime sentiments, for they combine unity, purity and variety at the highest possible level. That which, among living creatures, is associated with the dyad might be styled *sexism* and the term *sexuality* be reserved for that which concerns the conjunction of the sexes with a view to the reproduction of the species. Or again, the sexuality of otherness might be distinguished from the sexuality of conjunction.

These two concepts are separable. It is possible to conceive of beings without the need to propagate, a species of angels or *eons*, who would none the less exist in couples, finding profit and joy in thus beholding the duplication of their experience of existence. It is also possible to imagine beings united without any resemblance: it seems that this is what occurs in the microscopic order where the spermatozoa have no relation to the ovule. This all amounts to the statement that the notion of *sex* can be detached from that of *dyad*.

Let us first consider the *dyad* and ask ourselves what advantage this doubling can offer to human psychology and, more generally, to the spiritual life. It is perhaps fortunate that the human type, in all its functions, from the less to the more elevated, appears in two different forms which complete and react upon each other. It may be added that the knowledge of the other is, perhaps, an attribute necessary for self-knowledge. If Adam had been alone, being intelligent and tormented with desire for knowledge, he would have been in love with his own image. If there had been only two Adams there would soon have been more than one Cain and crime would have immediately begun upon the earth. If there had been only an Eve she would not have thought of giving birth. If there had been two Eves they would have torn each other to pieces for the sake of their children. But Adam, being able to reflect and know himself in Eve, sought in her the consciousness of his own vigour, and, no doubt, when he regarded Eve, saw in her the birth of the sense of all that is rare, exquisite, precarious, of all that is contained in the word *grace*, at once the contrary and the consummation of vigour. The like might be said of woman, who becomes aware of herself in the mirror of man. It is in the other that we have life, for it is in the other that we find renewal and fulfilment.

The punishment of Narcissus is not to see himself and to be himself only in appearance. It is true that it may be asked if love does not lead to Narcissism, if Adam really loves Eve or only admires his own image in her. That is indeed the most subtle temptation of love. But it is of the very essence of love to surmount or rather to avoid it from the first. Yet every finite being is limited and, by the same token, incapable, while he remains solitary, of escaping from himself except in appearance. And in that solitude what, save the world and God, is there to be known? But the image of the world enhances the isolation of the man who feels as though lost in himself; for him who feels himself to be alone in His presence the concept of God is formidable. That is why it is not good for man to be alone, even in order to know the world and to know God.

M. Lavelle once remarked profoundly that "duality is the consolation and the temporal remedy of finitude". Moreover, it is evident that the existence of the dyad increases the significance of paternity since the child, instead of being descended from a single progenitor, bears a resemblance to two contrary types. And it is important to observe that it is not born in some third sex which would be, as it were, a synthesis of the other two. The child is itself either man or woman, a fact which implies that, for the fulfilment of the first couple, there should be at least a brother and a sister. The boy will then bear a resemblance to the maternal element, and the girl to that of the father. Thus a multiple unity will be realised capable of increasing the variety of persons without confusion.

If that is agreed, it remains to ascertain why knowledge of the other is often troubled by the sexual instinct, in that the pure representation of the other is mingled with the stimulus of instinct. Here we return to the problem which we have just touched upon, that of knowing whether the impacts of sexuality cannot themselves convey a spiritual value.

If one observes the development of the nervous system in man, one notices that nature tends to furnish mechanisms capable of giving more and more scope to excitations becoming more and more faint and far. The progress of the nervous organism occurs in two ways. At the centres the nervous mass is seen to increase in volume, but it remains undifferentiated and homogeneous. On the other hand, in the organs on the periphery and, in particular, in the sense-organs, the slenderness of the nervous filaments becomes extreme, so that the brain seems like an organ capable of giving a more and more profound significance to excitations more and more detached.

It may be asked whether the erotic impression has not a similar destiny for the psychical being, that is to say, if nature has not intended that the excitations of the generative sense should become more and more delicate and, at the same time, capable, through the medium of the brain, of acting as a stimulus and hormone for a wide variety of other psychical attributes. In that event the case of man would be like that of the animal from which castration removes not only the faculty of reproduction but also the original energy and vigour.

With those in love one can perceive a new zest in the use of the whole body, of all the thoughts. All the other senses are stimulated—sight, hearing and the sudden perception of form and compass. *Sexus intus alit et magno se corpore miscet.*[1] It is a kind of natural magic. The time of life when these excitations begin to be felt in body and mind is called puberty. It is noticeable that this is the time when originality, personality and, too, the sense of the heroic awaken. On the other hand, the

---

[1] An inward power of sex nourishes it and mingles itself with the great mass.

force of habit, tending to transform *spirit* into *nature* in us, lulls the unrest, puts initiative to sleep; and, just as a monotonous melody hypnotises, so the sameness of custom, aided by a sameness in the order of nature, creates a state of inertia and gloomy contentment which is not favourable for the progress of consciousness.

It would therefore be exceedingly useful were there, in our organism and even in our moods and our blood, a kind of slight disturbance sufficient to release the first stirring of spirit. There is no doubt that the sexual instinct has, in part, this secondary function: whether yielded to or resisted from a sense of duty, it leads to an emotion favourable for creation. That is why it is to be found, in a positive or negative form, at the root of many of the works of man and, above all, in the domain of pure invention. And, from the point of view adopted here (which also vindicates the fecundity of continence) many a moral triumph, many an enduring foundation may, again, be attributed to the struggle of the nobler impulses against this urge.

To our view it will be objected that the sexual instinct of mankind is distorted. But, to refrain from trespassing upon the domain of theological history, it may at least be noted at once that every complicated multiple and polyvalent mechanism is so delicate in its nature that it seems, in many cases, as if destined to failure, error and even aberration. In times of decadence the perversion of sexuality is almost an industry with its own technique, experts and propaganda, but this industry has not penetrated life as profoundly as literary accounts might lead us to believe.

When the history of humanity is envisaged in its long duration it may also be asked if the sexual instinct has not been mitigated, if it has not lost its first violence and acquired a very surprising delicacy. It should be sufficient to re-read certain passages of the Old Testament and, in particular, the nineteenth chapter of the Book of *Judges* where an abominable story surpassing the greatest audacities of modern authors is serenely told. This progressive refinement of instinct is to be seen in all civilisations. Everywhere, in Egypt, in China, in Rome, woman is seen to be honoured. In non-Christian civilisations, indeed, this progress consists in doubling the function of woman by distinguishing woman for abuse from woman for love. But in Jewish and Christian civilisation this duplication of function has always been proscribed and the sexual instinct has become refined.

There is therefore ground for enquiry as to whether Christianity does not foster a tendency inherent in rational beings. The whole progress of Christianity is generally represented as contrary to nature. But, without wishing to minimise the rôle of grace, it is clear that Christianity would not have been able to elevate humanity to a higher level if human nature had not already desired that elevation. And, in the matter of sex, it may be asked whether, in spite of corruptions and monstrous perversions now culminating in man's loss of mastery of his own being, we shall not see the sexuality of mankind as a whole diminish in violence, if, indeed, it does not once again become what, in principle, it ought to be: the collaborator of love. Minds as diverse as those of Comte and Bergson agree in hoping for this, and it is also one of the points where Catholicism and Communism meet in their condemnation of the sensual and licentious spirit to which the bourgeoisie of the last century had accustomed us.

We come to the conclusion that, in the conscious being, sexual stimulation, provided always that it does not become violent, could have beneficial results. But this proviso seems to have been fulfilled by the very progress of the human race in which, as we have said, sexuality is found to lose the ferocious form which characterised it at first in order to assume modes of expression more subtle and gentle. Having examined the share of sexuality in the development of the psychical, we will now proceed to consider its rôle in that of the moral consciousness.

If it is true that the sexual instinct is maladjusted and ill-regulated, it must be recognised that it shares this defect with many other instincts. M. Pradines made some very penetrating observations concerning the irresponsibility of instinct. Like so many others he remarks how pleasurable suggestions deceive us as to our true good, and suggestions of suffering as to our true ills, so that, were man to be guided solely by the appeal of pleasure or the fear of suffering, he would eventually impoverish, perhaps even destroy himself; this may be seen in the case of drug-addicts. Thus man, guided only by animal instinct *plus* consciousness (if we suppose this consciousness to be inspired by the will-to-live alone), would encompass his own destruction just as surely as children who did whatever they liked would, in consequence, be spoiled.

But to consciousness nature has added a faculty called reason which is, in part, detached from the will-to-live. And it is reason, correcting immediate and often erroneous impressions by the calculation of future consequences, which halts man on the slope whither he is led by instinct. Thus the idea of duty, which very frequently prompts the refusal of a passing satisfaction, is *biologically* necessary for the adaptation of man to the task of living. The psychological consciousness alone would derange the mechanism of instinct; while deeming that he was fulfilling, man would in fact destroy himself. It is necessary that the psychological should join forces with the moral consciousness and that this process should take the form of an obligation. Calculation of self-interest might, indeed, suffice, but the preference for an intense present rather than an uncertain future will always be too strong unless duty speaks unconditionally; and that is obligation.

Such considerations help us to understand the profound relation of sexuality to the moral life. For the most part the conflict is represented as that between two tendencies and two laws perpetually opposed within us, the one of the flesh, the other of the spirit. It would seem that, in the domain of sex, duty obtrudes itself as an external command, an incomprehensible imperative, a brake upon life, a futile sacrifice. The more searching study which we are about to make compels us to reject these opinions. The evolution of life in the human species is incomprehensible apart from the existence of a certain sexual duty. However immoral in its habits a society may appear, fundamentally it comprises far less immorality than seems to be the case; if it were not so it would have already perished. And, from this point of view, from which duty is found to be related to its biological function, the concern of a living and moral being with this conflict between spirit and flesh becomes comprehensible.

No doubt a being in whom such a struggle did not exist is conceivable, but he would have to be capable of anticipating by intuition the painful sensations which may result from a feeling which, at the moment, is pleasant and powerful. And that is an impossibility since instinct lives in the present and for the sake of the present. Moreover, in a being such as we describe, could freedom exist? Freedom (and, consequently, merit and moral value) find a fitting arena in what we call the struggle against the flesh, since it must be incessantly correcting appearances and even present realities by real *creations in appearance*: it is continually making a kind of new man who does not yet exist whom it sets over against the existing man. It is a curious fact that it is thanks to this continuous creation that man escapes from the disequilibrium of instinct and adapts himself to his rôle in the world.

The perspectives thus attained are found to coincide with the most familiar affirmations of tradition. Truth to tell they meet with rather than proceed from them and this is our authority for introducing them. For, in this study, we have never made the moral and religious point of view our point of departure, but rather that of existence and profound experience. We are all the more justified in claiming that, without definitely intending to do so, we have, in this way, rediscovered the verdicts of the moral sense. It is the proper function of philosophy to reach by its own proper procedure, by the most exacting methods, what morality and good sense have long since affirmed.

★

In the course of our enquiry we have frequently encountered the function of sublimation by means of which sensuous experience acquired a spiritual significance and use. We believe it to be the peculiar characteristic of human nature and incarnate existence to be able, by an art most ordinary yet most rare, to transmute *vitality* into *spirituality*. It is incontestable that there are two poles and forces within us, one of which is called *life* and the other *spirit*. Between these two faculties there is a secret intercommunication. Both of them are, in truth, imperialistic; each secretly tries, as though that were possible, to substitute itself for the other and monopolise the scene. But neither of them can, in fact, disappear and they even sustain each other. For, if spirit were not sustained by a vital energy, it would lack both fire and support, and if life were not animated by spirit it would lack all humanity.

Thus the hypothesis that there are two very different attitudes to which the term 'sublimation' can be applied will be our guiding clue. The first is a *normal* function enabling us to cross the *limen* (the frontier of flesh and spirit) in an upward direction and, that frontier once crossed, to attain to a more fully perfected state. But there is also an abnormal form of sublimation which is much more evident, tempting us to contaminate the higher life with carnal elements and so with the possibility of causing a disturbance which is often equivocal and sometimes perverse. To be precise we should speak of *sub*limation in the first and of *subter*limation in the second case. But since we cannot reform the language, we shall speak of infra-sublimation in the second and of supra-sublimation in the first case.

Abnormal sublimation is thus a movement from above in our nature; it descends towards its roots and through *life* contaminates *spirit*. Its effects and modes should be described in detail. Moralists have not been wanting in this respect when they have elaborated the history of divine love and even of all love, for those who love cannot fail to encounter this angel of darkness, and most of all in love's beginnings and in all its moods of fervour and zeal. For all lofty passions, as for the *sublime* vocations, there is a dubious sublimation which brings it to pass that the greater the elevation, the greater is the risk of confusing spirit with its opposite implanted within it. Since all that is of the spirit has an immediate echo in life, which wants to transpose it into its own key, the progress of spirit, especially when occasioned by love or some zealous passion, has the effect of arousing bodily and specifically amorous reactions; the activity of the neophyte is suspect. Immediately he is converted the young Pascal falls to censure and denunciation: in him grace arouses this desire to excel which it afterwards mitigates and annihilates, but, at first, it stimulates all that is most contrary and yet most similar to it in human nature. The love of God impels towards sacrifice; when it appears in a soul it is for the purpose of detachment. But the joy which this new freedom wins is imparted to the nature. The spiritual pole seeks in the vital pole a living image, an echo, a resonance, such as fervour, poise of power, buoyancy of being, a gentle grace in love and in action, and even a real and poignant joy in self-sacrifice, silence and suffering. But this fire kindled by life, like all that is tainted by natural energies which become corrupted in use, remains a temporal phenomenon. Beginners, suddenly deprived of that aid, become distracted as though all were lost.

The sublimation which we describe is to be found at other moments in the life of the spirit, and it is particularly to be feared among those more akin to nature than to spirit; it is thus, it will be recalled, that we have defined the feminine character. And that is doubtless why women mystics have both so much assurance and so much disquiet; they feel the need of re-assurance, for they are more conscious than men of the kinship of spirit and life. The friendships peculiar to adolescents of both sexes provide a further example of these imperfect sublimations even when they are veiled in innocence. For friendship, though unwilling to realise it, is readily transposed into instinct; thence derive both its agitation and its exaltation. The services, the rites, the chants, even the purifications of religion, when continually transposed into the key of instinct by this sublimation of descent, serve to foment rather than to heal this stirring of the senses.

We are in an equivocal zone where, being dependent upon the nature of souls, the cure may become a poison. Who is to say whether the author of the *Génie du Christianisme* was not the victim of this false sublimation when he demonstrated in the religion of Jesus the fulfilment of the religion of nature? For him, did not Christianity serve as a means to endow passion with the character of holiness instead of teaching him to sacrifice it? The same questions could be asked concerning the *Jardin sur l'Oronte*.

But, to return to the characteristics of the love-fervour, it is very remarkable that, in its beginnings, love can hardly avoid the sublimation of descent and illusion. As we have said, love is a gift: it is a projection of the self upon another, it is a reception in oneself of the projection of another self. And these two ideal and perhaps unreal images, being projected, create conditions of possibility, development and efficacy in such a way that love, were it pure, might be a means of perfection. But no human sentiment is more rooted in the bodily powers, none more strongly stirs the very entrails, so that it might well be asked if love is not unleashed by a lure derived from the senses, those blind carriers of the message of the spirit. It is a fatality that there should be this repercussion of love in these depths, that the lilt of spirit and the lust of nature should be confused. That is why love is often so ambiguous, so deceptive for others and itself, in its first avowals, its unlimited promises, its sincere declarations of sacrifice, above all with man who is perhaps more easily deluded, being less capable of ungrudging and natural sacrifice.

Love is also apt to intensify faults, especially those of bombast and those bred by the will to dominate. In those who desire, nature speaks the language of egoism: she wants to increase and propagate the species; yet with their lips lovers speak a language opposite to that of egoism, that of radical self-donation, that of death on the other's behalf. These two conflicting voices compose a perplexing unity. How hard it is to discern what is pure, to dissociate it from what is impure, to seize its distinct reality! Love, for the most part, reveals to the spirit a life which it ought to sublimate; but, being incapable of it, it is the spirit which, through pretence or through sin, becomes carnal.

He who comprehended this mechanism would have gone far in the knowledge of eternal man and still more in the understanding of existing man. For he, more truly *spirit* than anything else in history, is nevertheless incapable of living this life of the spirit which is offered to him: we see him incarnating the spirit in appetite, in instinct, in aggressiveness or exaggeration, in voluptuousness, in blood. And we come to accept these merely transformed instinctual urges as spiritual values.

The modern myths stem from transpositions of this kind. For example, in what does the magnificent lust for liberty differ from the instinct to envy and power? Are the sacrifice of masses of men and that kind of frenzy which still drives so many young men so readily towards death genuine sacrifice? Is there not a death-wish to be found there which is very different from true sacrifice, the desire for life beyond death itself? In all such conditions the enumeration of which is not our task, travesty is to be seen: the inferior pole becomes central or at all events brings into being a bastard blend.

But there is no need to insist too much upon these aberrations of infra-sublimation; that might lead us to overlook the lasting, superior and necessary forms of it with which the economy of our nature is bound up. These forms are related to the very rôle which we play in the cosmos and in history: for, since we are both sensuous and spiritual beings, it is our duty to act as a channel and filter for all that is of the flesh for its assumption into a more lofty and sublime existence. That, without doubt, is the meaning of our destiny. These forms of normal sublimation are manifold and to see them only in the domain of love and the sexes would be a great error. The sublimation to which we refer here goes much further than that; it extends to the whole physical and moral life, both kinaesthetic and pneumatic. But since its primary and most misunderstood extension is in the sexual sphere, it is with this that we must deal first.

It is well to note how handicapped we are by the poverty of our language. The word sexuality, apart from the fact that it has become corrupt in common usage and is unseemly, concentrates attention upon a single point. But, in addition to this localised and fixated sexuality, there is also a diffused sensibility, no doubt allied to still obscure urges of the hormones which influence the use of the other senses. It gives them a vibration, a radiance, an effervescence of a peculiar kind. We have already noted how at puberty or at the moment when love awakens, colours and sounds, the sweet influences of nature, the impressions of art, are transformed and find an added felicity and fervour. The poets have told often enough how the absence of the beloved dissipates joy, quenches the light of day, robs all things of their depth and stability. That suggests that an ethereal and more subtle breath stirs in the depths of the other senses, some ineffable vital sense which cannot be described as sexual but which, none the less, depends upon the sexual life.

Where are the first stirrings of this sense to be sought? It is, no doubt, associated with the moisture and warmth of the maternal womb, with the fecundity of fire and hearth, with the sweetness of water, air and everything that encompasses and breathes upon man, with all those primitive elements in our life which the romantics have sung. Dawning love certainly awakens these prehistoric emotions, these quests for the lair, the nest, the intimacy, and the cradle where amid the breath of beasts, the child is born. And that is why love alleviates the anguish of solitude in the midst of the world; *bonum est nos hic esse.*[1]

Here, then, there is indeed a first and seldom realised sublimation: that of vital warmth, penetrating while stimulating the other senses and even the spirit, which, in its own turn, will be assumed and transformed into thought. The child reposing in its mother's lap and feeling the warmth of her arms is at peace and revitalised. It is the same kind of delight as that bestowed by the caress of the sun: here is sweetness without fever, the very contrary of that giddy torment of which sex partakes. A body considered as an object for the excitation of the senses is a concept far removed from that of this same body regarded as the integument of the soul, as a form of nature replete with symbols which our minds can make their own by an act similar to that of knowledge.

There are many other regions where the soul thus sublimates the harvest of the senses, making it fit for its own food. I doubt whether the sublimation of sorrows and vexations has been adequately considered. It is not only enjoyment which is liable to corruption unless assumed by the spirit. Sufferings, moreover, have this privilege also, which is, I fear, what causes their chief bitterness: the impossibility which we sometimes experience of utilising them as trials for the development of the inner life, the compulsion to hide our troubles in the secrecy of our self-respect, like wild animals roaring and untamed. We repress our sufferings; that is why they torment us. The real art is that of bringing our troubles into the orbit of the soul, so that it may extract from them a mysterious increase, may acquire new perceptions, may become sensitive to new ways of understanding and compassion: for each trial which is sublimated is an apprenticeship to a new language.

It is an art that discovers a universe of perceptions which,

[1] It is good for us to be here.

until then, had been hidden from us; it enables us to hear and to communicate. That is so even in the case of irremediable sufferings piercing to the very sundering of body and spirit: thus Nietzsche and Dostoievski fashioned means of vision from their strange sufferings. Charles du Bos, in his *Journal*, describes almost daily these new dimensions which the dissociation of nervous suffering lays open for the spirit, so much so as to pose the question whether creation, of whatever kind, may not be the fruit of some tribulation overcome. Sublimation also explains the operation of memory with its incessant transformation of fragments of the past into beauty, making of them those works of art which we call souvenirs. It is by grace of this sublimation at work in all memory that even now time becomes non-temporal for us.[1]

Up to now our focus has been upon man. We have treated the subject as though the only objectives of man were his own inner equilibrium and perfect adaptation to nature. Henceforward we shall rise above these aspects. Human thought, like the scientific method itself, proceeds from cause to effect, from the antecedent to the consequent: it follows the order of succession given in history: it supposes that each phase of an historic series is produced by preceding phases and that it is unnecessary to look for any other cause. We shall suggest, however, that it is the idea of effect and not of cause which is given first. Thus, according to this hypothesis, we affirm that, in order that there may be civilisation there must be humanity: that there may be humanity there must, in a world animated by life, be organic bodies; that life may be able to appear there must previously have been matter. . . . Otherwise stated, we suppose with Aristotle and perhaps with all thinkers of every kind, that the historic order which sheds its seeds in time, seeming to pass from one form to another under the influence of mechanism or

---

[1] These pages are only an outline of a *Traité de la sublimation* written in captivity. This treatise was entrusted to a young officer in July 1945, in the Magdeburg camp, who had promised to see to its delivery. May these lines come to his notice!

impulse, is in reality the *reverse* of the real order. This real order we picture as a non-temporal progress proceeding from an end posited from the first to the most appropriate means for realising such an end.

We assume, therefore, that the final term existent in the eternal mind dominates the whole development. God seeks saints that they may rejoice in His glory: to obtain saints there must be men in society; that there may be men there must be living bodies and a biosphere; that there may be life there must first be the abundance of galaxies. Let us begin therefore, says God, with the galaxy.

This regressive analysis, moving from end to means, seems illusory and arbitrary to the modern mind for which the sense of essence and end has become enfeebled. It cannot be denied that, when employed ineptly and prematurely, it leads to devastating results. Perhaps it should only be employed in an instant and as though in a lightning-flash, as Bergson exemplified for us in that work where, after a long train of thought, he suddenly styled the universe 'a machine for the making of gods'. Nevertheless, the stone upon which the vault rests, although only an undermost part of the mass, is that upon which the building depends.

Up to this point, reasoning like the mob or, rather, like scientific thinking, we assumed that it was the sexuality of the sort apparent in animal nature which was really fundamental, that is, the momentary coition of two individuals with a view to generation, with all its train of instinctive urges and sensuous satisfactions. Upon this sexuality, as though by chance, love was grafted. In other words, a purely material process little by little subtilised, transformed, intellectualised itself, through a series of hazards, through the gradual action of society and civilisation, up to the point at which that product of sexuality which is love could detach itself from its peduncle. Thus the final term of the series *animal sexuality*, *human sexuality*, *love* would be produced by refinement of the preceding terms.

If we accept these ideas we are forced to admit that, through a combination of favourable chances, the higher term is derived from the lower. But is it not asking too much of chance to suppose that it has multiplied and serialised these felicitous variations for the benefit of our species, unless we imagine some genius of the species manipulating the lottery? And, in that case, however inadequate such a formula may be, would it not be better to affirm that nature travails in some way to realise love?

Now for that purpose, there must be beings capable of self-consciousness and self-examination, distinct yet similar beings who, though remaining separate and incommunicable in essence, could always conjoin in such a manner as to become a single entity. If this is so then sexuality is seen as a means for the realisation of love. The change of perspective is radical. It is now no longer love which is conceived as an artificial and accidental consequence of sexuality: on the contrary it is sexuality which is seen as the best means for arousing and sustaining love in a society composed of manifold beings more or less involved in matter and corporeity.

This difference in point of view presents us with a different set of problems. In the former doctrine it was human sexuality which was hard to justify, for it seemed to be a mere chance offshoot, a curious sport of nature. Upon that assumption it is animal sexuality which is the most inexplicable phenomenon, for then it seems no more than a useless luxury. If the animal is denied inwardness, what meaning have these parodies of union guaranteeing no symbiosis of being, no communion of consciousness? Such is indeed the impression which we are apt to get when we watch the coupling of beasts. Such too is the feeling of many contemporary biologists concerning animal sexuality; they see in it only a troublesome complication which, from the orthodox Darwinian point of view, is not easy to explain.

But if we assume that the supreme intention of nature is, as

Elohim pronounced on the sixth day, 'to make man', then the antecedent orders, no longer containing their ultimate purpose in themselves since they were merely preparatory stages, would present characteristics which, if unrelated to the definitive end which alone explains them, could but strike the mind as absurd. Apart from that postulate they cannot avoid seeming irrational, aberrant, futile or superlative. Such is, indeed, to our thinking, the case with animal sexuality, above all when considered in the higher species and notably with the anthropoid apes. This chimpanzee-sexuality which Dr. Zuckermann has so well described for us, conveys its full significance only when looked at as a foreshadowing of what was to come—the often monstrous picture presented by human sexuality which is so easily perverted, moreover, that the aberrant behaviour of the great apes seems—alas!—pre-human. In other words, there would not be sexuality in the animal (at all events in the form in which we see it) were there not sex in man. And the history of animal sexuality, from the infusoria to the anthropomorphous creatures, enables us to perceive the preparations, at first remote, then more near and immediate, for that human sexuality in which alone their reality consists.

In order to comprehend sexuality, it is desirable to relate it to the general structure of nature. Without wishing to burden this essay with metaphysical considerations, it is always well to remember that, in nature, every degree of being is animated, possessed, enveloped and as if transformed by the order immediately superior to it. Just as space must be sublimated by energy in order to become what we call matter, as the physico-chemical body is, in its turn, sublimated by a principle of internal organisation in order to receive life, so animality must be sublimated by reason to become humanity, so too, doubtless, humanity is summoned to receive a sublimation in order to become that new type of being which we have no word to designate.

The idea that actual humanity is a humanity only in its infancy is to be found in the religions, and also in those substitute-religions which, in our day, are theories of progress. The difference between them is that while religion refers super-humanity to eternity, the doctrinaires of progress look for it in the future. Thus the sublimation in which we have hitherto seen only a psychical function, can now be perceived in a wider context. Instead of perceiving in it only a process restricted to man, we should try henceforward to recognise in it a fundamental movement of nature. Much more than that, this raising up of the person above himself which the mind discerns and considers from without (when, for example, he envisages the relation of matter to life, of life to humanity), the experience of sublimation would perhaps enable him to apprehend from within. In some such fashion the formation of habit and the degradation of *act* in *effect* which we experience in ourselves every time we act freely, enables us, by a true analogy, to comprehend the act by which a pure spirit is self-naughted and freedom flowers in nature, and indeed, by a détour, to penetrate into the mystery of creation. It is thus that man is the mirror of being.

Sublimation, which is, in essence, allied to sexuality, would, from this point of view, be a kind of fault or fissure through which we would be able to perceive the movement, from degree to degree, from form to form or rather from assumption to assumption, which draws matter to the threshold of spirit. The purpose of sexuality would then be that of affording a form of transition: it should be surpassed, like a springboard. Yet the springboard comparison is not really exact, for the athlete who takes his stand on a springboard in order to jump higher retains nothing of the springboard in his leap: he uses it as a thing which participates neither in his action nor in his flight, which serves his purpose for an instant only. Sexuality, on the other hand, in spite of being a means to attain to love and to supersexual love, is not entirely abolished and renounced in the act which surpasses it and which it has made possible; on the contrary, it is found to be assumed within it.

Some will say that, in ascribing this function to sexuality, we yield to an angelic illusion, and that if our hypothesis is correct it can only be realised by an extremely small minority of human beings. It would indeed, from this angle, be quite incredible that nature or its Author should have taken this spiritualisation of sex for His goal. We observe, on the contrary, that an incarnation of spirit in sexed nature leads either to the degradation of love in sensual excess or to its inertia in the exactions of daily life. It is, however, quite impossible to sunder love from its physiological context, at least without committing the angelic error. The physical and the social exhaust all the aspects of the phenomenon: the rest is fantasy.

The objection has its weight and must be reckoned with. It cannot be denied that in love there are two aspects and, as it were, two poles. The whole problem is that of defining precisely how far these two foci converge and which should be eliminated. We should respect the peculiarly profound structure of this matter, which is perhaps unique of its kind. It is here that the distinction recently suggested by certain German theologians might be of help to us. Doms suggests distinguishing between what he calls the meaning (*Sinn*) and the end (*Zweck*) of marriage, between its significance and its destination. In the animal world sexuality would be unconscious of any significance other than its destination: among the animals, whose only function is that of living, there is no place for love. But this power of giving meaning to things is characteristic of humanity. An act which has, according to nature, a limited end can thus, according to spirit, acquire an indefinite importance. In the utterance of a cry thought produces a word; in animal behaviour it produces demeanour, movement, act. In the same way, when spirit assumes sex, it ennobles it with a mysterious meaning which is no other than love.

These observations are of weight, for they are able to transform the concept of marriage formed by the theoreticians. In reality, if the moral value of an act is defined by its relation to the end, then, because marriage has no other perceptible end, socially and psychically, than the begetting of children, we shall be inclined to regard the use of the flesh, when not directed to that end, as of no significance or even as an abuse: at the most it could be regarded as a concession to frailty, as an alleviation of the fires of sense.

Although the martinets of orthodoxy often tend towards this construction, popular opinion has not followed their lead in this matter. The Church is bound to condemn every artificial means of diverting the sexual act from its purpose; yet it does not forbid the choice of periods for sexual intercourse when conception seems improbable. But now at last we know the mechanism of these first beginnings of our being which, for so many centuries, has defied enquiry.

Now the knowledge of this so complex, lavish and opulent economy suggests that nature has wanted much more from the meeting of the sexes than was needed to ensure conception—whether she has acted with her habitual super-abundance, or rather, with the human race, has pursued some other purpose than that of ensuring the mere propagation of the species. And what could that purpose be if not a humane one and one which ought, therefore, to be related to the spirit? It might be supposed that this purpose is that of providing an opportunity for or a symbol of the union of incarnate persons, of permitting the foundation of a community in which every man may participate. But, if it is so, this relation between two persons which does not essentially aim at generation or could no longer hope for it has none the less a humane and spiritual significance. The idea that conjugal love has two aspects and two ends which man cannot dissociate has, moreover, always been implied in the Christian tradition, although the civil authority, careful of its duty towards the human race and its propagation, has wisely subordinated love to paternity.

The idea which seems to have guided this perennial discipline seems to us to be metaphysically a very profound one. We shall summarise it best by saying that the distinctions between essences discerned by the spirit should not be interpreted in existence by the will or labour of man, but that he should leave them to the divine will and ways, which are themselves events, and their essential causes. Thus the bridging of the gap between time and eternity, so desired by soul and spirit, can be caused neither by ecstasy nor suicide, nor by any mode of self-expansion or mysticism, but by destiny alone and in that moment of our death which is not in our power. In the same way the distinction between love's delight and generation, although not fictitious, should not be effected through our own initiative. Nature, necessity, accident alone have, so to speak, the right to release what has been joined together in the substance of things. If man wittingly intervenes here, he betrays an order which it is not for us to dissociate even though at any moment circumstance may cause it to fall apart.

Whatever there may be in these views, the full explanation of the significance of love is not at all simple. But that need not surprise us. It is a fairly constant characteristic of the works of nature that they manifest themselves in senses which, though dual, are closely united and, for an outside observer, easily give an impression of ambiguity. Without wishing to encroach upon what an ontological study alone could give us, we will say that being often presents two aspects, two axes firmly interlocked which would nevertheless, if separated and allowed full freedom, move in contrary directions.

The more spiritual a being is the more this inward duality of the elements which constitute it becomes a source of difficulty for the spirit. Those who reflect for long upon love always discover this duality of meaning. Love is at once propagation and exaltation; it has both a social and a quasi-mystical function. All who have concentrated on the subject have been forced to distinguish these two factors in love.

It is a curious fact that when the Greeks analyse love they always fasten chiefly upon the second of these senses: we have noted it concerning the *Symposium*. Eros elevates us step by step to the threshold of the supreme good. Among the Jews, on the contrary, love was considered in its social aspect as the source of the propagation of life: 'Increase and multiply'. The Greeks certainly could not forget the generative function of love and Plato did not despise it, but for him it seemed secondary. The Jews, on the other hand, could not disregard the mediating and elevating function of love: it was without doubt present in a veiled form in the ancient tale in which Eve is seen to be drawn from Adam during a mysterious and prophetic slumber (Tharléma) in a kind of mystic ecstasy, as though woman emerged at once from the bone of man and from his prayer. And we know the rôle it played in the *Song of Songs* where there is not, so to speak, any question of progeny, except when the young husband speaks of mandragora, a plant which, in the East, is said to bestow fecundity. Moreover, in the Gospel also there is never any question of the duty of propagation: the 'increase and multiply' is there transposed into a spiritual key as the duty of evangelisation, a duty which also presupposes the other but does not elucidate it.

There are, indeed, two distinct poles in love which unite with each other, and emphasis is laid upon one or the other according to period and temperament. It is clear that, from the point of view of the higher interests of the human species (whether in the period when that species is still in its first beginnings on earth, or again in those periods of lassitude when that species, owing to egoism, runs the risk of no longer propagating), the predominating aspect of the union of man and woman is that of progeny. St. Thomas even asks if marriage should not be a duty for virgins lest they should remain solitary upon a depopulated earth where the number of the elect must be completed. At all events the duty of generation should be taught, recalled and preached to the representatives of the human species. This duty would only threaten to become a danger if nature took no precautions by means of catastrophes to diminish the number of people or to make the resources of the planet sufficient for the increasing population and humanity, multiplied in each generation, found itself unable to exist. The day may, no doubt, come when this hypothesis will be realised and, for certain self-contained countries, it is near. But, given the immense resources which the planet still affords for exploitation and the appalling bloodshed which war causes our rational species to undergo, it still remains only a remote possibility for the human species as a whole. But if generation is, biologically and sociologically, the end of human love, it certainly does not, in this, exhaust all its meaning. One can clearly imagine propagation without the least spark of real love.

In all civilisations, moreover, families are to be found in which man and woman combine for the purpose of having descendants, to supply soldiers for their country and people to take care of them and, after their death, faithfully to carry out the duty of maintaining the fire on their tombs. Bourgeois marriages in our contemporary societies are sometimes reminiscent of those antique unions of ancient Rome or China where the generation of children takes so large a place that it eclipses the consideration of love. It is, moreover, the greatness of Jewish and Christian marriage that it never wanted these two aspects to be separated, these two poles dissociated. In that respect it corresponds to the way of nature, for, in ancient Rome and Egypt, as formerly in Homeric Greece, a sentiment of love between man and wife already makes its appearance within the family institution. At most it might be said that, before Christianity, when love appeared at all it was as the tardy fruition of a common life conceived under quite other auspices. Judaeo-Christianity, however, tends to make the love of two individuals who choose each other, contrary, sometimes, to the advice of their parents ("the man shall leave his father and mother"), the origin and source of their companionship.

Thus, side by side with the pole of generation, becoming more and more apparent, stands the pole which we have called that of exaltation but which it would be more convenient to call quite simply the pole of love. If, socially, it is secondary and even useless, if, in ancient societies, it has always, according to the stage of development of humanity, been veiled, we have nevertheless seen it magnified to such a degree that, in our day, it fills the whole horizon and even runs the risk of impeding generation. That is because, for the person, it has a more vital reality: we marry, not so much in order to have children or to make a woman fruitful, as because we love and for no other reason.

It seems then that, from this point of view, nature has willed that love should exist for its own sake; that is to say, from the first it has had, not the species, but the individual in view. It seems that it has fashioned human love not so much for the purpose of propagating the species as for the education, fortifying and expansion of human persons, knowing well that, if the basic needs of the person were duly satisfied, those of the species would be so too. When reality joins together two distinct yet inseparable terms one of the most subtle temptations of intellect is that of dissociating them. Such, from our point of view, is the essential error and fault.

Without wishing to anticipate the conclusions of the following chapter, we will note that our own age is familiar with this dissociation in an acute form. In societies of the totalitarian type the exalted power of Eros seems torn from the family to be captivated by the State. On the other hand, family problems are resolved in an almost technical manner in which love is not consulted. It is evident that a nation which finds satisfaction for Eros in the exaltation of the social life and of war and, on the other hand, sees its children multiplying under the tutelary direction of the State, acquires a degree of cohesion, a sense of sacrifice, a savage joy which nothing seems able to resist. And perhaps a nation of this kind would triumph over all others were it not confronted with a like enemy. Thence comes an implacable conflict. For between two totalities which have thus dismembered love no compromise is possible.

If the preceding observation is correct, it makes the resemblance between the problems which concern the individual man and those posed for communities a salient one. Everywhere the two elements of which love is composed are seen to tend towards dissociation in the individual as in the State. Their equilibrium is both a most normal and most rare phenomenon—unless some higher power comes to our aid and, in some extraordinary fashion, lends us a hand.

★

May there not be some kind of third essence which would help these two tendencies to combine on a higher level? If so, how should we picture it?

Many contemporary thinkers, and, in particular, M. A. Nygren, distinguish two types of love, one the soul of Greek thought, the other at the heart of Christianity. The first is called Eros and the second Agape. According to M. Nygren, these two types of love are opposed point by point. Eros is desire, aspiration: Agape tends towards sacrifice. Eros wants to lift itself to the sublime: Agape tends to descend in order to lift up the lowly to itself. Eros wants to conquer the divine life: Agape possesses it and, to possess it the more, can but bestow and lose it. Eros is seduced and conditioned by beauty; it needs to have beauty before its eyes, it turns towards beauty as a plant towards the sun: Agape is independent of its object, it does not need its object to be either beautiful or good; it shines upon the just and on the unjust; it needs no value in the object prior to its outpouring of love, it creates that value itself.

Eros is, in the main, an ascending movement: by means of it the egoist approaches and finds God without having to renounce himself. The way of Agape is descending; it is the way by which God approaches and communicates Himself to man. Much more than that, Agape is God's command to man to love his neighbour as himself, that is, by the way of Agape not of Eros. The parallel which M. Nygren draws is full of meaning; it well elucidates the eternal ambiguity of love. It also confronts us with the question whether human love is entirely self-sufficient; whether, to attain its plenitude, it does not need some kind of higher help, related indeed to the depths of its being, but of which it is not itself capable. In other words, we are led to ask ourselves if the erotic and generative impulses, the forms in which we become aware of sexuality, do not in their turn need to be animated by Agape in order to become united. Agape would thus be their bond of union.

Potentially at least these two poles exist in animality. For in certain animal species, like monkeys and rats, we see the generative impulse, in a purely erotic frenzy, conflicting with its own purpose. But, with the animal, the two poles are naturally united by the prevailing impulse of instinct. In animality instinct is thus a regulative power which, even if the dissociation of the erotic and the generative could occur, would prevent it from maturing or at least from having its full effect. With man, as we have said, instinct is regulated by reason. And the disturbing energy of *spirit* is seen to be substituted for the regulative power of instinct and to act like an instinct of death dissociating flesh and soul, even to the point of utilising the vital instinct, present in man, in a sense often totally opposed to that which the normal ends of nature and society would require. Is man then to be abandoned to this fatal schism? Is there not some higher power able to re-establish this lost equilibrium? Cannot some knowledge or power be found to fulfil, for this cleavage of our impulses, the office which animal instinct fulfils with regard to a similar disequilibrium? We believe that this higher power exists and that it is to be sought along the lines of Agape, that is to say, of disinterested love.

Let us now consider the relation existing between these three terms: erotic love—generative love—the love of Agape. This last alone has, in essence, pure being, for, in its most exalted form, it is the character of God. God is Agape: that which is in no way changed by an object or an external interest, but is essentially a gift. Has Eros any relation to Agape? The method of dichotomy employed by M. Nygren, like all dialectic of opposition, leads to a ranging of these two terms the one against the other. We are ourselves confident that the direction of these two currents is different. But we believe also that Eros contains a kind of potential Agape.

There is, no doubt, a deep difference between the love of lovers and the love of charity. In the first, in spite of all appearances, impressions and declarations, egoism is always present like a perfidious fire. As Plato had foreseen, Eros is essentially ambiguous; at each stage of our enquiry we have perceived this disturbing ambivalence. From certain angles love has the character of illusion; its mechanism, like that of illusion, is centrifugal. When we want to describe it we are led to employ words which would equally well describe illusion. But it is difficult to avoid the idea that this illusion also contains the experience of a higher reality.

It may be asked with Plato whether, in the experience of love, however humble its object, however clandestine its manner, however vulgar and base its aim, however vile its instrument, man is not gripped by something which is not comparable with anything which nature offers him. This supposition would explain how Proust could have experienced at one and the same time the most equivocal of sensations and the most exalted and almost mystical of aesthetic states. Similarly, the Parisian street-Arab who meets a shop-girl, in the most conventional style, with gestures inspired by the local cinema, with words derived from street-songs, may have an experience which, however confused, will remain like a gleam from another world.

Love is indeed illusory, but does it not enable us to enter into a super-reality which, by reason of its concreteness, its simplicity, its sublimity, makes our former idea of reality seem like some lower type of existence, or even like a dream from which we have awoken. Between him who loves and him who does not love there is no communication; each can accuse the other of dreaming. Who is to judge? Certainly, in the majority of cases, the lover acts his love to himself like a comedian. But he would not be caught by his comedy were there not some infinitesimal spark of love in him. Just as we can say without hypocrisy that we love poetry when we have felt a faint stirring of poetic feeling, so he who loves, although imperfectly, is able to understand how this palpable world which, for the senses and the mind, seems the sole reality, can be struck by a word into non-existence, become a sombre and stupid apparition, simply because one has lived for a few moments without contact with the beloved.

That is why those who have experienced love of the most physical sort, when they have expelled the egoism of the flesh, are often fitted to comprehend divine love. Eros makes us live in a universe whose arid places and deserts are more real to us than the satisfactions of the world of sense. It gives us the presentiment of a super-consciousness, for it helps us to understand how consciousness can exist upon different levels. If one experiences how, in moments that are almost stationary, duration can become crystallised, then it is possible to conceive how our consciousness, after its mortal existence, will become capable of experiencing entirely new states, but of a kind, nevertheless, not wholly foreign to its nature. And this explains why the Greek mystery cults were oriented both towards immortality and towards Eros, and why, when Christians have wished to represent the life of the beyond, they have imagined it in the form of a love-life purified, exalted and maintained beyond all risk of diminution.

The vistas which thus begin to open out are, no doubt, over-optimistic. In reality, love resists sublimation with very great vigour; and, in order to pass from Eros to Agape, one needs either a predisposition granted only to the élite, or a radical conversion. And when the problem of love is plumbed to its depths the same ambiguity is discovered there. It would be desirable that Agape should acquire the intensity of Eros and

Eros adopt the zeal of charity. But man has the choice between two types of experience, of which one is ardent but egoistical and often blameworthy, and the other, that of charity, altruistic but arduous, arid and devoid of imagination. Our spirits have, no doubt, dreamed of an experience in which the ardour of the senses and mystical renunciation might be merged: it is the illusion of false mystics deeming that they could attain to God through sensuous experience. And it is the privilege of true mystics to know at times, and without artifice, some of those states in which absolute self-sacrifice is combined with extra-ordinary bliss. But, in normal and ordinary cases, Agape and Eros are divergent; charity is born of renunciation whereas the delight of the senses almost always implies a lessening of love.

We touch here upon one of the insoluble problems with which the observation of human nature confronts us. In spite of all the efforts which we have made in the hope of attaining unity, we are here once again in the presence of duality and conflict. Sexuality prepares the way for human love, but, in order to pass from sexuality to love, an act of inversion and of dying to the self is necessary. Although love buries its first roots in a sexuality which alone can give it its full meaning, there is an infinite difference between sexuality and love. In the same way and on a higher level, in order to pass from love, in the human sense of the word, to the divine love or its image which is Agape, a new birth is needed.

There is certainly a continuity between the fire of human Eros and the flame of the divine Agape, and the intuition of the author of the *Song of Songs* is in no way false when he affirms that the flames of love are the very flames of God. But, that this unity may be realised, it is necessary that a higher love should descend to the lower love and become its guide. The lower love might, perhaps, be able to give the taste, the flavour and the first image of the celestial love: it is within the love of the senses like a luminous darkness; but this darkness cannot, of itself, give the light. Nature cannot lift herself up to that which surpasses her, unless that which surpasses comes down, in the form of grace, and abides within her.

★

At the close of this chapter concerning the significance of love we find ourselves once again confronted with a problem which touches the very nature of man. That was only to be expected since man is a privileged intermediary in the creation, and since, at root, he is immersed in nature in its most material form while, in aspiration, raising himself to the level of the divine. He is truly an epitome and mirror of all being since all zones of being meet in him. By his consciousness he ensures their coinherence and, at the same time, by his spiritual life, he sublimates the lower forms of being in order to enable them to live in a higher type of community.

Since love is that which, most of all, dwells in the very bowels of mankind (for sexuality epitomises the whole of the flesh) and since it is also that which is most sublime (for charity is the goal of all spirit), it was to be expected that the theme of love would take us to the heart of man, just as the theme of man takes us to the heart of being. From this point of view we return to the intuition of Plato that love offers a mediatorial force able to set the spirit free from all bounds. What Christianity adds to Plato is the knowledge that this mediator, however powerful he may be, cannot fulfil his desire and is subject to aberrations.

From two points of view love is seen to be impotent to unite the whole with the Whole. On the one hand there is an abyss between the love of man for God and the love of God for man, which, since it alone is disinterested and prevenient, is the only true love. On the other hand the inner unity of the human being is divided; the flesh, instead of succouring, betrays the spirit. Plato did not wish to perceive this conflict of flesh and spirit, this inner dissociation: his work therefore lacked reality. Since the *Symposium* something else has happened—the Cross, and the *Supper* which preceded it, in which the Cross was already present in its entirety as if to show that love, suffering and absence are indissolubly associated. The *Supper,* already a sacrifice before being a feast of union, has superseded the *Symposium* of a preparatory age in which the essential factor was omitted. For only blood can unite and Plato, being too young in this world, did not know it.

8 Conclusions and perspectives

THE last point of view which we shall choose for our consideration of love will be that of the perspectives which our epoch
opens up upon the future. It is almost impossible to reflect
upon any subject which concerns historic man, engaged in time,
without an attempt to divine wither man makes his way,
and the more so since, the future being, in some measure,
the fruit of our thinking, such reflection may itself weigh the
scales.

In the course of its development humanity passes through
periods which colour and modify even the inmost of its faculties.
It passes, from period to period, through climates and spheres
which renew its powers and thrust prior states wholly into the
past. Just as reason, that universal blessing, develops, although
unchangeable in essence, so there is also a development of love,
at all events in its psychical and social forms. Love is more
malleable even than reason. That is to be seen even within the
limits of a single human life. The mode of love of our grand-
parents is not in the least like ours. It is true that we are at a
period of mutation when all difference declares itself. If we
believe in a radical change such as that which characterises a
new era we shall divide the history of love into three periods.

The first would take us to the Christian era, the second to the present time. As for the third, since, for those who live in the midst of them, origins are always obscure, it is difficult to define.

It should be remembered at this point that the succession of phases in a development, whatever its scale, does not imply the entire substitution of a new for a superseded state. All the antecedents pass into the new phase. But they are assumed in a different form of existence. And, even when that development is wrong and shows signs of corruption, within those corrupt forms there is a remnant of good capable of correcting some of the effects of the new evil. That phase of love which, for twenty centuries, has been dependent upon Christian influence, is not necessarily bound to disappear, even though a different and even contrary climate may encompass the modes of love which are to come. There is, therefore, no *a priori* justification for saying that the new phase will be deprived of the Christian yeast. That is precisely the question. For if, with many thinkers, we could suppose that the modern age will put an end to the Christian age in a new antiquity, we could also imagine that the period into which we move will bring new modes of expression to Christianity without changing its original essence and may even serve to realise its intrinsic possibilities.

Let us therefore estimate what modification Christianity has made in the sphere of inter-sexual love. We have already alluded to this at the opening of our enquiry; but, since we were studying love in conception rather than in being, we did so then from a point of view which was still external. The analyses which we have made since then enable us to reconsider these views in a fuller light.

We have seen that Christianity has carried to its furthest possible degree the natural trend of spirit to pass beyond appearance, to renounce all its attainments and to find rest in the absolute alone. This trend was akin to the movement of love, for that sentiment inspires an exaltation of spirit. And in the Greek and Oriental schools of mysticism, this kinship of Eros and ecstasy was turned to the profit of religious experience. But antiquity failed to develop the capacity of Eros for the experience of infinity, or at all events did not know how to purge it of its errors. That is the cause of the crudity of the ancient cults and Oriental religions in the midst of which Israel matured.

Moreover, the conception of the dignity of the human person was not sufficiently defined to allow for those relations of equality and mutual respect which are essential if love is to be lasting. Christianity revealed and, as it were, mapped out infinity for us, gave us precise expressions, epithets and definitions, and made incarnate for us in one historic and palpable Person all those ideas which, up till then, had been jumbled together under the general term *divine*. Since, therefore, it combines these two, hitherto distinct, notions of the *infinite* and the *person*, it must travail to the utmost to give birth to a new kind of love.

A personality which contains, which incarnates the infinite cannot fail to kindle love in man. And if humanity were single-minded and aware instead of being so confused and so distracted, it might have been feared that this infinite Person, existent in the flesh, would so absorb the capacity for love of the human heart that none would remain for the ordinary tasks of life and family. Christ might captivate love and leave for men nothing but sparks or cinders. But, if the love of Christ tended to diminish in Christian society while the impulse to seize the incarnate infinite remained, what could prevent the lure of sex from exploiting those forces aroused by Christianity which thenceforth, owing to the enfeeblement of faith, took the form of fantasies?

Between the love which looked to God through the humanity of Christ and that of the human being for his chosen, there was, no doubt, no radical contradiction: experience teaches, however, that it is not easy for the two to exist side by side, at all events in the same degree. We have seen how, in the old dispensation, the author of the *Song* had tried to diminish this difficulty by restoring human and divine love to the same essence by means of the analogy of exaltation. Later, St. Paul, with a similar analogy, was to identify the love of Christ with conjugal love through the medium of the mystical concept of the Church.

But these are thoughts which could only have been comprehensible for a few spirits already imbued with faith and grace and they had little likelihood of influencing the mass of mankind. Many corruptions followed, due to the fact that this Christian influence was neither rejected nor wholly accepted, but incompletely absorbed. It is the paradox of Christianity that it can only save those who give themselves to it and that, when the gift is adulterated, it risks becoming corrupt. The *amorous* mood verging upon the *dolorous* (for extreme love is related to grief) is one of those cross-currents which Christianity causes in its passage through time and are so frequent in Western history.

To this obscurity cast by Christianity upon the problem of love must be added that of hypocrisy. For Christianity civilises society more easily than it moralises the individual. As soon as it establishes itself members of society are seen to imitate that which is more admirable in each other: it is only virtuous behaviour which can be shown to the world, only noble sentiments are approved. Add to this the fact that institutions canalise the instincts and impose new customs upon them, so that openly evil conduct, in a society of this kind, must confront the whole intricate mass of habits which prohibit ill-doing.

It may be said that a society is well constituted when good conduct is caused by motives which usually produce bad, that is to say by submission to public opinion, by lethargy, by the wish to do as all the world does, in fine, when little less exertion is needed to achieve goodness than to do ill. Now, when to the former *bonae mores* which already ensure a measure of conformity, religion adds its edicts as well as its own methods of controlling individuals and the course of society, then the social order becomes more and more moral. That does not mean that the inner man improves in the same degree, for man ever remains a prey to his initial frailty. Apart from an élite which is often numerous enough, the mass of mankind remains subject to primitive temptations, above all in the domain of the flesh where Christian morality is so exacting that there is no chance of its being put into practice by all men.

The Church has, indeed, confronted this problem set by the perpetual breach between the commands of conscience and the frailty of nature; she has sought to close it with her penitential discipline. But the gap remains and is perhaps no greater in Protestant countries where this discipline is absent and theology tends to construe sin rather as an inherited condition than as a personal act. It is true that the Nordic peoples, where the social bond is more potent and respect for opinion more strong, at one time more easily achieved a public behaviour regulated by decency.

But if Christianity can beget a new Pharisaism and, like every revolution, again discover among its own people the very abuses which it opposed, it must be remembered that this is an accident in its history. To accept the same name for the bond which links man to God as for that which attracts beings provisionally engaged in sex, is to achieve the adverse result of humanising divine and deifying human love. And, since the divine prevails over the human, the latter is found to be lifted to a high degree of excellence. We have, on the other hand, often recollected that love has two functions: one of social generation, the other of inward regeneration. Christianity, in that it causes Eros to contribute towards the foundation of families, identifies them. But we know well enough how, failing a higher unity which ensures their concurrence, these two elements tend to become dissociated.

It may be asked, however, if this function of unification is likely to operate in the world of to-morrow, if it has not been merely a transitory phenomenon. If we were to try to prophesy the character of the age into which we are about to enter, we should certainly say that it will see the invasion of love by two forces hitherto dormant, which have, at all events, not yet come to full consciousness: knowledge and freedom. To follow the ancient Story, and hardly to expand it, one could say that these are precisely the two faculties for which Adam was punished and expelled from Eden, no doubt because, according to Jewish theology, man had wished to know prematurely and to be free before his time. Thereafter, knowledge and freedom strive to re-enter the sacred garden. But the sword of the seraphim which Jahvé had placed at the gates no longer halts the modern Adam and Eve. They have long been climbing the hill of knowledge and will soon proceed to taste the fruits of the tree of life without God being able to prevent them; they may even want to take their revenge upon God and, in His turn, expel Him from this garden from which He once expelled man. If in these symbols the story of *Genesis* summarised a very long history and a bent inherent in many branches of the human family since its origin, it is only necessary to reverse it to describe in a myth the present trend of the times. A new Goethe would not have very far to seek for the theme of the modern drama: it is that of the return of Adam and Eve towards the tree of life and knowledge, of a quite sane Eve drawn, not from man's sleep, but from his pure intelligence.

We may foresee that knowledge and freedom will, at last, be reintegrated in love. Is that to say that they have not had part in it? Had not Christianity aroused and fortified the one against the other, what fruit would it have had? It cannot, in fact, be contested that, in the societies which have embraced it, the Gospel has been a ferment of freedom. If the Chinese or even the Mohammedan civilisations are compared with the Christian and the development of customs and institutions in the West is considered, it is undeniable that, at least until the sixteenth century, the progress of freedom coincides with the track of Christian influence. In the West love has long since been free, in the sense that persons choose each other or at least think that they do, for there are unconscious inner constraints which take the place of social inhibitions. Love, moreover, is aware of its ends, its modes and its mechanism, for literature has made of it its leading theme, as though it were the sole subject of the human drama worthy of receiving the investiture of beauty.

Until now, however, though this dim knowledge may be granted and this mutual choice admitted, love has evolved as though, to some extent, it were an instinct. It was, no doubt, a higher instinct wholly permeated with spirit and promoted by society to the category of the sacred. It was also an instinct which the will could inhibit if it deemed it to be desirable or obligatory to do so. Nevertheless, from the origins of humanity to the present time, man has trusted to nature without overmuch knowledge, calculation or foresight. And that was felicitous. Nature does not depend upon the mind for the regulation of the functions which preserve it: they fulfil themselves mysteriously and as though under the dominion of dreams. If the first impulse of love is to choose and to know, its second movement is that of self-abandonment. Its poise demands that price. It is the same with all those acts necessary for life or formed by habit which our decisions can release or suspend but awareness disturbs.

In this respect, how different are the earlier periods of civilisation from that into which we have now entered! Now the notion of dominating the phenomenon of love by mind emerges, of dislocating its mechanism, of activity with a view to generation according to a new technique, of making man at last the lord and master of life. Had the mind formerly entertained such a conception it would have been dubbed an aberration or a dream. It was not only because science had not yet revealed the secrets of life, but also because any intention of regulating life by knowledge of sex, had it been mooted, would have seemed a fatal impiety for those mixed motives in which religion had a considerable share, but in which there could be found no less the dread of disturbing the destiny of the species and even of injury to nature.

From prehistoric times man had daily used his knowledge of sex to dominate the animal world by the castration of the males. The idea of manipulating sex in order to alter the balance of life was, in origin, a discovery as pregnant perhaps as that of fire: for, prior to the domestication of the animal, man had no other source of power than his own body. Unless there were some inward prohibition keeping man from so simple a discovery, how was it that the notion of applying this same knowledge to the human species did not occur to him or make its appearance till the twentieth century? That the exploration of life might be possible, the advent of an epoch in which nature was completely secularised was necessary, of an epoch sundered from all communion with deity, in which respect for instinct was enfeebled, and the spirit of religion, even of pagan religion, had lost its power. The decadence of Christianity would not have sufficed for that had there not also been a corruption of even that sense of nature which was man's most ancient heritage and perhaps his first thought at his first awakening.

But, in our day, when the influence of Christianity fails, man does not descend once more to nature and reason but to far lower depths. It is in keeping, too, that, at the period of this retrogression, biology should be sufficiently advanced to provide the hope of a technique making it possible to manipulate procreation. We know well enough, and we shall one day demonstrate it at length, that the temptation of *mind*, when it gives rein to its impatience, is to dissect *nature* in order to exploit its elements separately. And our age is characterised precisely by this fact, that, for the first time, *homo faber* has attained to that region where the germs of life are engendered. It can be foreseen that the technician will soon know the mechanism of that encounter or that fusion which gives birth to the new cell and from that knowledge will be able to obtain the desired sex, and that even parthenogenesis will be in his power. In that day intellect, if it so desires, will take the place of instinct. The discoveries of atomic energy, about which we make such an uproar, will be a small matter compared with these. For not only the physical universe but humanity itself is here at stake.

Again, our age is signalised by a fuller and deeper knowledge of love, at least in so far as its lower forms are concerned. It is not that the unconscious movements of feeling were formerly unknown. The periods of sophistication which inevitably follow epochs lacking in culture permit the rediscovery of the subtle difficulties to which love is subject. But formerly descriptions of love were concerned only with its languors, its crises, its origins or its travesties. Romanticism gave its own colouring but did not change the mode of it at all: rather, for all its apparent opulence, it impoverished the grammar of love: for love needs to be defined with an almost abstract precision, as Racine knew. The Romantic Revolution did not deal with its essence as does the as yet nameless revolution taking place under our eyes. If Racine is compared with Proust, Rousseau with Freud, we find a difference which is almost complete, and such a difference is brought out even more strongly in the sciences. But the practice of microphysics, even when it disturbs the universe of the infinitely small, which is its subject, does not affect our faculty of knowledge. On the other hand, analysis of the essence of loving, as practised by the moderns, immediately transforms the very manner of loving in such a way that, passing from intellectual analysis to actual dissociation, we run the risk of annihilating not only love but also the very faculty of knowing love. When a dissociating analysis is brought to bear upon a human essence, it risks begetting a false, though not unreal, nature the separated elements of which, though impotent to re-unite, may destroy each other. The dissolution of essences is, indeed, often an occasion for the appearance of beauty such as that of the rainbow, but, where our essence is concerned, it is a perversion.

We have seen that the unique feature of the present situation is the coincidence of two rhythms which, in another age, might have developed independently. Mental analysis (whether in the form of the novel, the theatre or the poetic treatise) has already split up the inner unity of the essence. But, since no one would think of applying to social life what the mind had dreamt in solitude, that was not over-harmful. The discoveries of biologists and the power of States now give to man the political means and technique to shatter the structures. And what some conceive to be ideally possible others propose to make real. In consequence there is no doubt that, never in the history of the planet, has mind been so efficacious. This trait, noticeable in many spheres, is still more apparent in that which concerns us.

There are several observations which might be made concerning the consequences of the total license which has now been introduced in the use of love. Love and liberty have, no doubt, a real relationship; but our age tends to confuse *liberty* with *liberation* which is only one of the conditions of liberty, doubtless the most important but also that most congenial to instinct. This has been seen again quite recently in the history of this country. If the act of liberty consists solely in rejecting abuse and tyranny without an agreed standard of values, it is distorted and is itself bound in chains which are all the stronger for being invisible. It is the same with the liberty of love. The reader is well aware that we have traced the discovery of this liberty to the Judaic tradition, that we saw its first expression in the *Song of Songs*. But, until the contemporary age, all the premisses which these thoughts contained have not perhaps been developed.

In all societies and even in the Christian, the woman was

chosen by the man without the reverse being possible. When society became civilised man confined himself to asking the girl for her consent. Her liberty, as we have said, was a liberty of veto alone. And our contemporaries should not be reproached for having at last made it possible, thanks to the progress of civilisation, institutions and manners, to develop the axioms of Judaeo-Christianity and give to woman the means to live and act as a person. It may also be asked if many of the feminine traits which we have noted, as, for example, woman's passive attitude towards authority, do not derive from the long centuries when she was unappreciated, oppressed and silent. At all events it may be supposed that the pressure of a society under purely masculine domination accentuated this plasticity inherent in her original nature. When that is said, it seems more dubious whether the still recent liberation of the feminine personality by our Western societies may not be a doubtful boon. Like all that liberty promotes, it is wrapped in a profound ambiguity. It may end in ruining the essence, or, on the contrary, in developing it.

If the principle of autonomy, so right in itself, is to be put into practice without abuse, the person thus emancipated must be capable of self-control. He must possess realism and have become aware of his potentialities and real vocation. For what is power unless rooted in reality? But women, in our levelling age, tend to become more and more like men, and the day seems near when they will be almost wholly so, for political strife and war itself will not for long be forbidden to them. The costume of our time marks the distinction between the sexes less than it did. Femininity tends to disappear. At the same time social evolution multiplies the number of unmarried women, and still more, of women who do not feel the need of marriage. Modern civilisation, in which mystics, both true and false, abound, gives women opportunities, by devoting themselves to the *causes* which are so prevalent, of satisfying their devotion outside the orbits of love and maternity. Formerly woman could only blossom in marriage or religion; she had the choice of either the home or the cloister. Often enough, indeed, she chose one of these solutions, not because of a liking for it, but from dislike of the other.

In our times, and in all Western societies, a third solution is becoming normal; that of an independent life, based upon a profession of her own. This too gives scope for benevolence, but outside the nest and the family home. In Anglo-Saxon societies this evolution seems almost complete; woman can travel, work, choose solitude or society, and repels those courteous attentions which seem to recall her weakness. The present times will certainly accentuate this independence of character since, in the absence of man, woman will have borne the burden of domestic power for long periods; she will have proved to herself that, in almost everything, she can excel man.

This promotion of woman which we shall soon see coming to pass everywhere (even in the civilisations of the Far East where, as the novels of Pearl Buck attest, it is already beginning) is one of the most remarkable revolutions of our age, for it will double the numbers of autonomous humanity. It sometimes seems to transform the relations of parents and children and, for the conscience, to diminish their value. They seem inferior to relations of equality. For, since we do not choose our parents, they are the fruit of nature, not of free choice. Nor should it necessarily be supposed that the disappearance of femininity will enhance virility. On the contrary, a kind of androgynous type is to be found in modern society, the defeminised woman, the emasculate man. Our time is ripe for an author able to write *Hamour* so as to make love give place to some savage state of soul.

We are, indeed, confronted with an aspect of the age into which we have entered—the fact that we tend to lose the sense both of *being* and of *nature*: that of *existence*, plucked from our perils, infers but does not replace them. It is, no doubt, very difficult to state in what the sense of being consists: it is a sense so engrafted in the intelligence, in the most intimate feeling, that we are less aware of it than of life, which is subject to change and of which we know, from the fact of death, that it can cease to be. It is one of those elementary notions, impatient of all definition, which can only be apprehended by a form of vision. But the corruption of these primordial notions, their gradual diminution, their extinction, the impossibility of their finding expression save in a propitious setting and language, can be observed indirectly. The discovery of the material condition and substructures of life, at the same time as the demands of a false and abstract purity, an artificial and mechanised existence, the mounting speeds which diminish the experience of time without compensating by that of space, the fictions everywhere substituted for traditional ideas, the anxiety which causes us to live beyond our capacity, the impossibility of imagining a future as satisfying as the savour of the past—all this seems to help to hide from us the essence of being, or to make us forget the nature of things.

It is, moreover, very difficult to indicate in what climate or for what doctrine the sense of being and of nature would have any hope of revival to-day. For we see the contemporary spirit oscillating between two solutions which are hardly adequate to support it: neither the dialectical materialism of the new schools of thought derived from Marx, nor the emphasis placed upon existence and its drama are philosophies suitable for the restoration of being, although they seem to grope after it. In the former, under the name of nature, matter, the lowest form of nature, is really implied; and in the latter, existence is signalised by being abstracted from all nature in a kind of void.

As for the idealism which is still regnant, in principle it seeks spirit and freedom beyond nature altogether. As happens in all protestantism, the doctrines which, in our day, tend to do away with idealism retain more of it than they suppose. For a future observer, this anxious research for a solid site in which the spirit, after having failed to reconstruct the world by sheer power, can take root, will be one of the characteristic features of this moment of history.

It is—alas!—no longer impossible to suppose that this age, having laid its hands on the essence of things, having disturbed the foundations of being through an excess of knowledge and power, may founder in some abyss. But since hope is more than a duty, a hidden verity which we are bound to affirm, we prefer to think that the man of to-morrow will have a new and finer equilibrium. For every reform effected by humanity in the course of its long history has shown itself to be a return to nature. And, even in so far as poetry is concerned, it is to be noted that the romantic, symbolist or surrealist reforms exhibit themselves as returns to a greater purity and towards the source of things. In all attempts at reform the problem is that of purifying institutions from the dross collected during their passage through time in order to re-discover what, in principle, they originally were.

Modern reform, though it may be related to all reform in this respect, is, however, of a different kind. For we live, not only in a time of crisis, but also in an epoch of change. The issues which, until now, have constituted the substance of modern history are likely to seem as insignificant to-morrow as those disputations upon grace with which mediaeval theologians concerned themselves. For it is evident that, between the conflicting parties, there is a common ground which is more substantial than their differences and renders discussion between them possible. Just as boxers can only fight upon a solid footing, so the strife of parties presupposes an area of agreement upon certain principles.

But it is precisely this area, this ground permitting intercourse even between adversaries, which is now in danger. It seems that there is no common standard of values acceptable to both the man of the future and the man of yesterday. Suppose that science, by an ingenuity which is not impossible, permits the manipulation of life itself, whether by means of artificial insemination or by sterilisation of the unfit, or perhaps by substituting for the male agent a stimulus of another order; it may be asked if humanity, already hesitant between the claims of reason and nature, would know how to forego such incredible opportunities. The most vital and cognate of sentiments, filial affection, paternity, fidelity, are menaced. And with them, consequently, that which former philosophers called *nature* and those of our own age *existence*.

The alternatives are thus clear: either expressly to envisage a plunge into a superhuman realm where we have no rule of conduct nor even possibility of foreknowledge, which may result not, as has been said, in return to animality, but in the creation of a fully conscious and monstrous humanity; or, without in any way condemning progress, really to establish the relation between future and present in order that humanity may recover itself and go forward. It is not a question of maintaining the existing state of things and institutions against the whole world, still less of returning to a past condition. It is a question of maintaining human nature, of, in some fashion, rediscovering nature, without returning to the modes in which nature formerly manifested itself. The future is not in the past: it is in the future. The future should not be unearthed like an excavated antique statue; it should be refashioned in each generation. What we are trying to define is the work of that conservative dynamic which is now called tradition and now progress. In truth tradition and progress are the same thing, for tradition can only maintain itself by advancing and progress cannot advance without conserving.

In the domain of love, as in that of religion, the task imposed upon the spirit is clearly defined. It is a work of criticism, at once purgative, restorative and constructive. It consists in cleansing the fundamental attitudes from all that, in the course of history, has concealed, enfeebled or corrupted them. It consists in rediscovering the very essence of the institution or the sentiment. It consists, finally, in discerning the ways by which this sentiment or this institution can pursue its march through time and adapt itself to new conditions.

★

The Communist manifesto of Marx levelled a condemnation against the bourgeois world conceived in these terms: "Nothing is more laughable than this highly moral dread felt by our bourgeoisie at the community of women, which, by their account, is the order of the day among communists. There is no need for communists to introduce the community of women; it has always existed. As for our bourgeoisie, not content with having wives and daughters of the workers at their disposal and an official prostitution which we do not even mention, they experience their greatest pleasure in the seduction of other men's wives."

Marx then criticised monogamy, conceived as an indissoluble bond, not criticising it as a rule of life but as it is related to a social structure the evolution of which he explained. The domination in marriage which man has arrogated to himself is only the result of the superiority of man as a producer of wealth. The indissolubility of marriage will disappear, for it is the fruit of a religious tradition which ignores the connection between economic conditions and the obligation of monogamy. "If marriage based upon love is the only morality, it can only exist where love endures." And since, according to Marx, the duration of this sentiment is a variable factor, particularly among men, its disappearance with the birth of a new passion makes separation a boon for both parties as well as for society. In the future, the woman of the proletariat, conscious of her worth as militant and worker, will no longer feel the need to seduce man by lies, trickery and deceit. The revolutionary education of youth for labour and combat will defend man against libertinage and onanism by purifying his imagination and directing it towards the great social tasks. And the

time will come, he declares, when all the problems posed
by bourgeois literature and the religious tradition will vanish
before a problem more vast, that of the common life, of
dedication and of the initiation of a society which will at
last be planned.

These views are inherent in all Communist thought. They
have their grandeur, whether as a criticism of Pharisaism
or from the vistas which they open up of a new life in
which humanity will have transcended the problem of sex
in order to accomplish the work of love unhampered by that
limitation which the enclosed family life seems to impose.
And, in these two directions, Communist thought recovers
two of the trends of primitive Christianity which, on the one
hand, attacked the leaven of hypocrisy and, on the other,
envisaged marriage as a kind of *pis aller* in view of the coming
of the Kingdom.

But Communism blends the noblest of conceptions with errors
so profound that they strike at the very substance of being.
And it reinforces this result with that mental process which
consists in disguising (and perhaps disguising to oneself) a denial
of essence under the cloak of the criticism which multiplies the
perversions and caricatures to which that essence is liable among
men and in history. It is thus that, when it is wished to dis-
credit the necessary social order, its corruptions are attacked as
though the latter were inherent in and inseparable from the
former or, if the dissolution of religion is desired, its corrupt
features are emphasised with the suggestion that the corruption
is due to the very essence of it. Should fidelity, engagement,
the institution of the monogamous family, the complex feeling
which binds a man to his wife and is something wholly other
than the comradeship of strife and labour, disappear because a
certain section of the bourgeoisie have abused them, or, quite
simply, even because humanity, being incapable of fulfilling these
precepts to perfection yet desiring to appear to do so, has
often resolved the problem by duplicity? There will always

be a choice between the claims of convention and those of bestiality.

Morality, which in principle conflicts with cynicism, compels man to wear a mask of a finer quality than his inward life. And the majority, by dint of playing at virtue, succeed in surmounting their natural dispositions. But we believe that we have shown in this *Essay* that the love-behaviour which has become the foundation of our Western society, far from being a mere congeries of customs and habits bound up with economic conditions, the influence of religion or the tradition of love, is in fact, true to the very essence of man. In its historic expression, indeed, it depends very closely upon these three conditions. But it is a law of essences that, in their transit in time, they incarnate themselves in some fashion in their conditions of existence and seem to emerge from that which, in fact, only invests them. A person subject to the appearances of history, retaining only the possibility of development, can perceive no reality other than those conditionings, and mistakes the natural mechanism which connects conditions with results for the action of causes. And there is no way of dissuading him from the illusion save by revealing to him this third dimension of being which eludes the social, economic or temporal element as thought eludes language in which nevertheless it is incarcerated. If the illumination is not granted or not accepted, conversation is useless.

A supplementary proof can, however, be suggested. If the engagement implicit in love were bound to convention, it would be only necessary to destroy the convention to be liberated for ever. Russian Communism has, from the first, proscribed the family and tended towards a comradeship of the sexes which would eliminate love: this was the aim of the system. It seems that, little by little, fidelity, and the monogamous family are being re-introduced into the organisation which appeared to proscribe them, or at least being accepted as accessories to it. As Rilke said to Kappus, the social conventions of love are renounced only to be replaced by other much more artificial conventions.

Convention may be defined as the notion of restraining sexual relations in marriage, the care of feminine virginity before marriage, the condemnation of adultery. It is this combination of laws and customs which, for many, *preserves* the essence of love. There are, no doubt, times when these conventions seem false or futile and many have supposed without insincerity that, in recovering their liberty, they would preserve the indefeasible element in their being. We are well enough aware that, in the West, the novel and the theatre are based upon the description of those conflicts in which law and liberty are opposed. But the life of every society demands the sacrifice of some for the good of the whole species. And Western 'conventions' have permitted innumerable men and women to experience true love, when, had they been left to their own resources, they would have exhausted themselves in fantasies.

Love admits of so many illusions, it is so ambiguous, so inconstant, so near to the neurotic, so recalcitrant to all wise counsels, so apt to become inverted or dissociated, so estranged from its normal purpose, so quick to become bestial, absurd or even demonic that society must intervene to protect it against itself. And this is the justification of sexual morality and of the social institution of marriage and of monogamy, as well as of the customs which surround them. Far from being obstacles to love, this collection of tabus, interdictions, fashions, usages, human and divine laws, more or less simulated sentiments, which form the humus in which love germinates—all this makes it possible for a great number of people, in spite of their self-deception and mediocrity, to experience this improbable yet perpetual state.

It would, no doubt, be a blessing if, in this as in all things, that desire of the spirit to fulfil the pure and eternal element in detachment could be satisfied leaving on one side the futilities,

the accidents, the deformities. Let us cut down the under-
growth, we may say, and keep only that which is of value!
Such is the idea of all reform. But no purpose is served by
separating the essences from that which conditions and expresses
them in the course of history; to dissociate the timeless is
vanity and madness. By thus separating the tares before the
fullness of time we risk damaging the good grain. Again, in
the parable the grain and the tares are separable by their diversity,
since they belong to distinct species. But, in the economy of
temporal societies, imperfect conditions are so intermingled
with the substance of the seeds that one cannot see where they
terminate. It is, moreover, the historic characteristic of every
mystery to be thus developed at first in forms which are foreign
to it and seem like ruses of nature. The forms which appear on
the surface are opposed to those which are hidden in the essence
and in the dimension of depth. Hence the hesitation of the
mind in recognising the mystery, its indifference, its perplexity,
even its abhorrence.

This is not the place to enquire why realities of which it is
so essential to know are thus concealed under those aspects
which we can only call similitudes. Isaiah, the Gospels,
Pascal have replied that it was God's method for the gathering of the elect from the midst of the world. Without
wishing to go further into this question it may, however,
be observed that mystery is that order of reality which calls
for freedom of spirit in the highest degree, for it subjects
mystery to a profound study which is, perhaps, the very essence
of intelligence.

As for ourselves, the choice which we have made, assisted by
various types of experience, is clear. The reader is sufficiently
aware that, in sexuality and the love which proceeds from it,
we perceive a kind of mystery. This mystery is twofold: it is
allied to the necessities of temporal existence in a precarious
and transitory universe; it is allied to the preparation for an
eternal existence in which love, detached from sexuality,

will subsist in an ineffable form. *Vita mutatur, non tollitur.*[1]

If love is, in truth, allied to mysteries we can realise with what a sense of humility and surprise, in what a mood of guileless yet wise wonder it should be studied. But when we apply to it the critical intellect with its analytic methods and, above all, the technical intellect with its manufacturing processes, love becomes unintelligible to us. Instead of subordinating himself to this urge of life which love contains and which, as we have seen, draws man far beyond either his capacity or his wish, man subordinates life to intellect and technique. Instead of seeing in it a promise it is shown as a snare.

If it be true that the ground of existence is to be sought in the direction of nothingness it is understandable that the normal and true forms of love may, from that perspective, be neglected or condemned. The consequence of such a spiritual state would be to cause the gradual disappearance of the race in which it manifests itself. This weakening of the sense of love is accompanied by a fear of conscious and solitary death and preference for death in common, and with that desire for unconditional control over the future which impels men to reject hope as servitude to a mere possibility. For love is uncertain, dispossessed and labouring in hope: its very dyad is the combined effort of two solitudes.

From this angle love and what is called civilisation move in different directions. And it should not be too surprising that the civilised countries, in Athens, in Alexandria as in Rome, have beheld, not only their fecundity, but also their power of loving exhausted. Civilisation requires certitude, comfort, the advent of a temporal-eternal or at least the assurance that the moment of perfection will eternalise itself on the morrow: all these states of mind are contrary to the dispossession of love. And that is why countries with an exquisite civilisation run the risk of being once again submerged by peoples whom they call

[1] Life is changed, it is not destroyed.

barbarian but who, though they may merit the name for the most part as regards their actions and behaviour, are not in the least barbarians from the existential point of view, since it is precisely in them that the march of man continues.

If the culture which we have cherished through so many centuries of labour and leisure is to have a chance of survival it is because, in the midst of it (and, in a sense, in spite of it) we shall see the emergence of a type of mind which will accept existence, employing the power of pure mind to rediscover and justify precisely that which mind, when pure, is tempted to dissolve. But a real conversion will be required, a radical reversal of mind, that the dimensions of being may thus be rediscovered. At the same time courage will be required. For the spirit of man, entrusted with the memory of his riches, will doubtless have to live under precarious conditions, maybe in a half-devastated world. Whether he be scholar, artist or even mystic, if he does not wish such blessings to deteriorate, he will have to make them grow again under difficult conditions. It is thus that the man of later times will re-establish relations with the tradition of the first of mankind—a tradition of labour and trust when the universe offered practically nothing but impediments to the frail human species.

It must be emphasised here that this effort to return to elementary existence and its laws will be assisted neither by society nor tradition. Whether we rejoice at or deplore the fact, the reign of instinct is ended. Nothing is done simply and spontaneously any longer. Intellect has arrived and all is changed! We can no longer rely upon the support of the past, for there are ever fewer familiar traditions able, as of old, to reinforce the will. We must, therefore, wait till a new race of men and women arises who will accept existence in all its dimensions of joy and pain, with its harsh but abundant zest, its mysteries impenetrable to science, its burdens which no technique can alleviate.

It is striking to observe that in this situation, a convergence is taking place. The poet, the mystic, the man of faith, the man without belief, in so far as they agree in resistance to the current vogue of frivolity and despair, all seem to be of one mind as to the necessity for this crusade for the sake of existence. Such is indeed the work which the next generation will have to accomplish. ' Its task will be to rediscover the arduous love, the tough and real love which is fit for creation and that in a fashion more worthy of the spirit than past generations have achieved. For it will have to *comprehend* and *will* what man has hitherto confined himself to *doing*.

★

This is perhaps the moment to offer certain remarks concerning the rôle which the woman of to-morrow might be able to play in these developments of love.

It may be said of woman that her 'hour is not yet come' in the history of the world, although many signs suggest the belief that that hour is not far distant. That is not to say that woman has not played a primordial rôle in the human past, a rôle all the more essential for its secrecy. Man rules on the surface of things. He is at home in tempests and at the crest of the waves. Woman, on the contrary, dwells in the depths. It might almost be said that the soul of woman is a stranger in social history, and that is why history rarely mentions her save when she accidentally usurps man's place, like Salammbo, Judith and Deborah, or again when she tempts man as Eve tempted him. But these are but bubbles on the surface of the waters.

The soul of woman is not concerned with history. If it be true that history is interested above all in action, history does not concern woman, for her function is to inspire and sympathise, but not to appear in public. If it be true that history is interested above all in public events, it will not meet woman there either, for she reigns in private. If it be true that history is above all interested in heroism, it will not find woman for, though she transcends herself incessantly, it is in the normal course of things. If it be true that history reaps catastrophes, upheavals, all that is discontinuous in time, it will certainly not come across woman there either, for her vocation is to bind up, to perpetuate, to straighten out. If it be true that history is only interested in initiative woman is a stranger to it; she waits.

Although, in Western literature, the idea of woman has always been associated with pleasure and frivolity, the burden of existence has always, throughout civilisation, been found to rest upon the soul of woman. Woman travails. Every day she begins again those tasks in which rest is inconceivable, for life takes no holidays. She bears children again and again without surcease of labour. We must not be misled by the way of life of the bourgeois woman; it is rare and will become more and more so. Much more typical is that Chinese mother of whom Pearl Buck speaks who scarcely ceases from her labour to bring a man into the world.

Historically, the phenomenon of love has, no doubt, been furtive, sporadic and often even lacking in the human species. The beauty which nature lends to the adolescent for a moment, when not incessantly repaired and preserved by artifice, is so fleeting a gleam. . . . The ordinary countenance of woman in history, as it is still to be seen in our countryside and mountains, is one which is no doubt tender, but it is also work-worn and somewhat hard, like that of mothers. Love, in the literary sense of the term, has very little place in the life of women. For, with them, love is no trifle. Because of her body woman is subject to the drama of existence. When she is not bearing children her organs have their periods related to the rhythm of the cosmos which bring the cadence of the stars and the phases of the moon into her life. Just as the blossoming of spring reminds the inhabitants of the earth that their planet revolves round the sun, so the menstrual periods link woman to the universe. She is thus subject to the respiration of nature and

222

the chain of causality. It is in her womb that the race rises again at each birth and it is often in her arms that it dies. Though she is detached from history, she is attached to life, which is more leisurely and more profound than history; or rather, every day she borrows from history, through the medium of man, that with which she will make life and with which, in his turn, man will nourish himself, somewhat as nature, from the dust of death, makes flowers grow upon graves.

Woman drives man from the house every day so that he can go and take part in the making of history. And while he struggles and endures, man is sustained by the picture of the ever-abiding home. He returns every evening to tell his *tale* in which the history of the world and his own are already becoming legendary. It is there, in front of the serviceable and sacred fire, that he enters into relation with a world which he deems familiar but is, in fact, big with mystery. The objects which the home offers him have no relation with those with which he strives; for example, he finds no weapons there. The sounds which he hears there bear no relation to public talk and there he never makes speeches. The individuals which are to be seen there (those old folk, those children) would tend to make him doubt the reality of history, for they are on the near side of it, like the child, or the far side like the old man, or, like the servants, outside it.

Man thus takes his rest under the gaze of the eternal woman who is careless of time because she is occupied incessantly and bears with her (like an astronomical system or, better still, a living being) the unity of relationships which she needs in order to live. The family is a place where history comes to a halt. Time stops there, or at least time is replaced by something which endures through incessant and unwearying repetition. It is the place of the *timeless*; it is also the place of being. There woman is at home and man is at home with woman.

Such, at all events, has been the state of affairs from the time of the most ancient civilisations to the beginning of the twentieth century. At bottom there is hardly any difference between the Roman family of the time of King Numa, that of Andromache or of Rebecca and those old peasant families which we knew in our childhood. It may be that all that is changing. It may be that we shall soon see the disappearance or at least the transformation of this constant state of human habit, more constant than civilisations, since it is the common bond of all civilisations hitherto known. It may be that what we have called the *timeless* element in woman will to-morrow appear an *anachronism*.

In fact, until now, woman, as such, has never become fully self-conscious; in any case such self-consciousness as she has achieved has remained private; woman keeps her thoughts to herself, 'pondering them in her heart'. The régime of mechanical inventions, political institutions and religious traditions does not permit woman to give any social effect to the self-knowledge to which she has won. And may it not perhaps have been well that it was only very tardily that woman attained to self-consciousness and that, during the fifty centuries in which we have been educated by history, she has existed in a kind of slumber of her powers? I have frequently said that her being is more near to the nature of things. Her rôle, when offered suffering, silence or glory, is to murmur: "Let it be so". Her vocation is to wait, to suggest and to respond, *to be* far more than *to do*.

★

But what are likely to be the consequences of the self-consciousness of woman in a world in which it is becoming possible for her to make her actions effective? That is the question which the promotion of woman poses for the thinker.

It is a matter of exceptional interest to consider carefully the moment (regrettable, perhaps, but sublime) when instinct is changed into intelligence, when consciousness awakes, when, in some fashion, nature becomes spirit. Hitherto woman has found certain regions, such as those of intellectual creation and political power, closed to her. We know, no doubt, of women who have made discoveries, notably in mathematics, but it is remarkable to observe how little aptitude feminine intelligence has for intellectual invention, although the body of woman is perpetually bringing new forms into being for the purpose of life. Artistic creation eludes her; still more philosophic creation, and it seems impossible to cite a single woman who has made her name known for a work of original thought.

As for woman's administrative ability, she is sometimes seen to leave the home and make a dominating appearance in the province of man, in conventual life, in industry, even maybe in a kingdom or an empire. But there is reason for doubt whether the example of dominating women proves that woman is really capable of this power; for wherever history shows us such women in power, we notice also the existence of a quasi-sacral type of society in which woman derives her authority less from herself than from participation in a divine force. The example of Queen Victoria, the last of these imperial women, would not seem to contradict our conclusion, since in England the sovereign power is so symbolic that even a fool has sometimes been able to exercise it harmlessly. As for the story of Joan of Arc, it proves how men will spontaneously obey a young girl who is the prophetic and divine moment of womanhood. When woman rules it is because God speaks in her.

Shall we behold a change in these female characteristics in the future? Shall we behold woman become administrative or creative? It is not thus that we picture the march of human development. When woman is urged on to tasks of creation and power she is denatured. The vocation of woman is not there. And if her as yet unfulfilled nature is married with mind it is all the more necessary that the mind should respect that nature lest we behold the emergence of a hybrid creature, feminine in body but spuriously masculine (the woman-comrade, the woman-soldier, the woman-leader, the woman-professor), who, being in no way the complement but rather the caricature of man, would precipitate the mechanisation of the masculine species.

There, no doubt, lies the danger for modern civilisations, as much in America as in Russia. And perhaps the woman of the East, suddenly awaking from her age-long sleep (if, at all events, this awakening takes place in a world already dehumanised, in a civilisation of the collectivist type) will appear less as woman than as a kind of second man: the spectacle of certain Japanese, Chinese or Indian women, falsely Europeanised, give grounds for this fear. Such are the perils to which the intrusion of mind into nature is exposed when that conjunction is effected in a despiritualised and unhealthy atmosphere.

Luckily we see types more sound and pure appearing in the Nordic countries and above all among the Swedes and Norwegians who have lived, as it were, on the margin of Western civilisation, where climate and race impose a type of society fostering both personality and community. The diffusion of Protestantism has been favourable there to the development of feminine nature. In Latin and mediaeval Catholicism woman has, indeed, been venerated (as chivalry and the preciosity of court life attest) but she has not obtained the conditions of independence essential for her expansion owing to the social situation which Roman Law produced and also to the innate suspicion of the priesthood. The danger of Nordic feminism is that of failing sufficiently to distinguish between law and convention, and in the name of sincerity, integrity and love, authorising divorce, which there appears as a natural right of love.

In Latin and Catholic countries, however, provided that she

appears to be divinely possessed, woman has long enjoyed very great authority, as is shown by the great number of women who have been canonised; but, for this, women must wholly renounce human love and it is very remarkable how the mother and young girl to whom marriage gives importance have until now received little honour. Nevertheless, even there, under the influence of historic progress, new orientations are to be seen. In Latin Catholicism, indeed, movements inspired by the idea of rehabilitating the young girl, the married woman, the mother, the working-woman, the peasant and of giving them a status as respected as that of virgins, widows and dedicated women, are gaining ground. It is an indication of an age when the feminine mystery, being better understood, will be better appreciated, and religion will herself give more recognition to the fruit which she has enabled humanity to bear.

R. M. Rilke, whose genius was so prophetic, wrote in a letter to a friend: "The young girl and the woman will only for a time imitate masculine manners and modes in their own development, only for a time practise masculine professions. Once these fluctuating times of transition are at an end, it will be seen that women, in these often ridiculous masquerades, have only sought to purify their nature from the distorting influences of the other sex. Woman, who lives a more spontaneous, fertile, confident life, is certainly more mature, more near to the human than man, the pretentious and impatient male, blind to the worth of that which he thinks he loves, because he does not plumb the depths as woman does by reason of the burdensome fruit of life. This humanity matured by woman in suffering and humiliation will see the day when woman will discard the conventions which condemn her to be no more than a woman. And the men who do not sense the coming of that day will then be amazed and confounded. One day (to which certain signs in the Nordic countries already point) the maiden, the woman will come to her own. And these words do not imply merely the contrary of the male, but something of worth in itself, not just a complement or a limit but a life, a being engaged in history; woman in her humanity. Such an advance will transform the experience of love, to-day so full of faults, and that in spite of man who will first be outstripped. Love will no longer be the intercourse of man with woman, but that of one humanity with another. (*Von Mensch zu Mensch, nicht mehr von Mann zu Weib*). And this more human love (this love full of respect and silence, sound and sure in all that it binds and looses) is indeed that for which, in strife and pain, we make ready; it consists in this, that two solitudes protect, limit and honour each other."[1]

The truth is that woman is more near to the human than man, so easily estranged from what is human. Through action, through his necessity to take part in history and progress, through the animal or domineering instinct which abides in him, through the abstract and contemplative nature of his intelligence, through the wilful and so often wild nature of his faith, man, had he not at his side a unifying influence, would be easily exposed to a life detached from himself, an eternal unrest, like that Faust in whom Goethe depicted the masculine genius in its essence. One of the missions of woman, after that of generation, is to reconcile man to man and to disappear.

She does not herself perform those deeds which transform history, but she is the hidden foundation for them. It has been observed that great men often have insignificant sons since sons reproduce the thoughts of their mothers: Napoleon, who had not been able to imprint his features upon the face of the Duke of Reichstadt, resuscitated those of Laetitia, the only person who could still give him orders when he was at the height of his glory. "Man," says Gertrude von Le Fort, "is the rock upon which time rests; woman is the stream which makes it move forward." And that is why we behold woman giving

[1] 14 May, 1904.

relief to man whenever the labour of life seems intolerable. By a kind of divine operation she intervenes whenever the situation is really desperate. Then she returns to her place and is lost in it, like Joan of Arc, who, had it not been for the stake at Rouen, would have returned to the shade of her woods.

Our abstract and violent culture, oscillating ceaselessly between the most subtle speculation and the most cruel of conflicts (when it does not combine them), is confronted with this dilemma: either to destroy itself or to return to its sources. This return to simplicity, to nature, to humanity, to being, to a truth commensurate with the heart, to the union of the mystical, the reasonable and the practicable, will undoubtedly come to pass under the pressure of diverse influences: and among them that of woman might well be preponderant. Goethe thought that the masculine monad was often more rich and productive than its contrary; but, he said, since it desires to realise its content while carrying it to full consciousness and by a definite act of will, it is extremely subject to error and disturbance, while the feminine monad is spontaneously oriented towards equilibrium; still more, she draws man towards a celestial realm, she redeems him. Such is the rôle of Marguerite, of Iphigenia, of Nathalie, and Hélène.

Auguste Comte, in the second phase of his life and work, bore similar witness: Clotilde de Vaux revealed the real world of the heart to that intellect, and upon it he was to found the positivist religion and to recover the meaning of virginity, maternity and love. The followers of Saint-Simon, so grotesque and intuitive, looked fatuously for the vision of Woman at the very moment when the Church was painting the picture of the eternal and immaculate Woman, and was enabling a third centre of Christianity to be created, counter-balancing Jerusalem, the male city, with a healing and gentle influence such as only femininity could achieve.

In his *Deux Sources*, Bergson let us understand that, in a civilisation become aphrodisiac, woman can teach man purity again. When Berdiaeff evokes what might be a new Middle Age, he sees woman more honoured in it, the exclusively male culture having been, he says, exhausted by wars. It is true that, in these recent ordeals, women have assumed an exceptional rôle, whether by replacing men, or by assuming tasks of patience, resistance and alertness. They will, Berdiaeff believes, play an important rôle in the religious revival of our age; the day is the time devoted to masculine culture: the night which is coming will be the time when the feminine element recovers its rights. G. Roupnel sounded the same note when he explained that the more humanity returned to a poor, barren, primitive phase, the more it moved towards its reconstitution around the family hearth.

It is, indeed, necessary to recollect that, when we speak of woman here, it is not of the solitary woman nor of the passionate women, nor of woman in the abstract evoked by the imagination, nor of woman reduced to her eternal essence (as Morgan and perhaps Rilke have conceived her) but of that woman who is man's companion, whom she completes and fulfils beside the central hearthstone and the cradle.

We should, therefore, hope for a renewal of conjugal and family life under the influence of a new womanhood to be the salvation of our age, in the quite precise sense that civilisation, in the periods when its rhythm is reduced, can only be reborn and reconstituted around social units made in the image of the original unit whence the human race emerged. Then the problem of Adam and Eve is resolved. Only, while the first Eve proceeded from Adam's sleep, it may be that the new Adam, the man of the age to come, may, not after the flesh but after the spirit, come from the thought of woman who is alone capable of readaptation to nature and of re-establishing the equilibrium of a restless being fashioned for creation, criticism and revolt.

★

But, as Berdiaeff and Gertrude von Le Fort have remarked, when feminine influence increases it is, of necessity, within a religious atmosphere. In this work in which the problem has been that of love, we have often tried to define that most slender link which, if it actually exists, binds human to divine love, in order to discover under the paradox of contrary and opposing appearances, the unity of these two creative forces derived from the same Creator, with, doubtless, a view to the same latent end. It is of the essence of sin to place them in opposition and thus to distort the design dominant in creation. And it is, we believe, the duty of thought to re-establish the unity endangered by human freedom in whatever way it can. If the work of the poet consists in hearkening to the murmurs of harmony through all the dissonances of being, that of the philosopher is to justify the finality which presides at the ordering of things as in the development of history and ordains that being, in spite of appearances, *is good*. Let us then finish this essay with some reflections upon the relation between profane and sacred love, still guided by the Sibylline saying: "There is but one love".

It is a law of this precarious world that the equilibrium of essences tends to collapse. Before wilful evil appeared, there was an imperfection of nature, a kind of degradation and, as it were, *entropy* of being, which has tended to become reversed or corrupted throughout its range. Now love can be considered as an essence with its own equilibrium: in that pattern of life the flesh should be at the service of the spirit, and that service is love itself. But this human love, too, does not possess its own order and end within itself: it also should be subordinate to a higher love which it symbolises and for which it prepares the way.

Such is the thesis which we have not ceased to maintain or at least to assume. Notice that this subordination is preservative; for the flesh is only truly flesh when it obeys the spirit; and human love is only true when it accepts its relationship to a more lofty and nameless love. Sacrifice, essential at each of these

stages, does not harm; it saves.   Thus, in love, the admirable
law that what is lost is found, that self-oblation and possession
are one and the same, is realised.   And it is not incorrect to
say that love can be conceived in three senses, according to
whether it applies to the flesh, to spirits or to God, that King of
spirits and Lord of all flesh.   But it is more true to say that there
is but one eternal love which is what God *is*, provided that He
is not represented as absorbing in Himself and annihilating the
other loves but rather as saving, purifying and, in truth, preserving them in the pristine purity of their being.   Like all
essences incarnate in time, love must be *recovered* and recon-
quered.   Its structure is mobile, fluid and subject to influences
which change it and secret motives which threaten to corrupt it.
No other function of human nature has more need of vigilance,
not to subdue or dominate it, but to keep it in conformity with
its pattern.

That is why love fares ill without a preservative, purifying and
nourishing atmosphere in which it can breathe; and such an
atmosphere cannot be very different from that which twenty
centuries of Christianity have afforded.   Supposing, therefore,
that Christianity did not exist and true love had none the less
developed upon earth, that love would certainly have created
the most favourable conditions for the spread of the Christian
religion.   But, in reality and in the order of history, although
the seeds and the scent of it have always existed in the world
(though only in a nostalgic form), it is Christianity which preceded love; Christianity made its way into the Graeco-Roman
world before love was known there; it made straight the paths
and developed the most propitious circumstances for love; in
every epoch, and in very different forms, it has restored the
conditions favourable for its expansion.   There is a secret
relation between this religion and the development of human
love; it is not that human love did not exist before its advent,
nor that the faith was necessary for the awakening of a sentiment
so much at one with nature, but because in fact it is under the

Christian influence that these pre-existing elements were planted and cultivated so as to produce the so-tender and so-precarious flower of Western love.

It is certainly the case that Christianity, like Judaism, has not been the religion of *Eros*; it had been taught from the first that sin was allied to the abuse of sex. Sexuality, with its delusive allurements, has seemed to Judaeo-Christians typical of the testing imposed upon men, and the most deceptive of illusions, since its semblance is so powerful that it paralyses the intellect before seducing the will.

But it must not be forgotten that the tender offshoot of Israel developed in violent and voluptuous civilisations in which sexuality was worshipped in a scarcely veiled symbolism and promoted to divine rank. In order that the religion of a jealous God might be instituted among these cults it was imperative that it should protest against them with an implacable vigour: for the hierodules had so often sullied the high places, sometimes even the holy place of the Temple! In practice, in order that Agape could appear, it was imperative that Eros should first be abolished and uprooted. Then only could it be reintroduced. It is this police-work which is necessarily the most obvious and consequently the most historic, in the ordinary sense of that equivocal term 'history'.

But under cover of this work another is increasingly to be found as a constant element in the Judaeo-Christian stream; it is that of arousing and re-arousing the sense of love, transfusing into Agape the fire and zeal proper to Eros. This was the meaning of the Christian mysticism which the *Song* heralded and which bore its first fruits with Paul, with Augustine and Bernard before its full fruition with the Spaniards in the sixteenth century.

But may it not be that the hour has come for Christianity to experience a new development and to manifest outwardly that which has not ceased to exist inwardly, behind the carapace of defences and prohibitions? Merejkovsky, that strange prophet of orthodoxy, says somewhere that paganism did not understand sex and that Christianity understood it no better. In this latter fact he sees the cause of the constant oscillation of culture between an excessive atomism of the individual and a monstrous collectivism. It remains, he says, at last to understand the value of conjugal society and to restore the mystery of marriage, in which the Russian mystique discerns a first sign of the spiritualisation and resurrection of the body. In its primary and literal sense marriage would thus be a sacrament of terrestrial generation in preparation for the eternal birth of beings devoted to death. In the secondary and spiritual sense, it would be a mystery of spiritual regeneration in preparation for the eternal and glorious life of bodies finally permeated with Spirit.

A type of Gnostic thought is recognisable there to which Russian orthodoxy is often addicted and which Western Christianity, in spite of Irenaeus and Origen, has neglected, no doubt with good reason. But Gnostic language may conceal a measure of truth. It is possible that the sacral mystery of love has not yet been brought to full consciousness nor accepted with full freedom. It may be that former civilisations, over-absorbed in the task of perpetuation of the species and social organisation, have not yet had the leisure to live out the mystery peculiar to love, nor to educate youth with a view to that mystery. It may even be that the religious life, displaying the characteristic signs of segregation, has prevented the mystics from understanding the resources for the religious life latent in human love. It may be, too, that the misogyny of the ancient sages of Israel colours our thought. It may be that the conditions proper for the independence of woman have not yet been realised; that virginity alone has been honoured and exalted and not yet maternity and the conjugal state. It may be then that lovely and mellow developments of the thought and feeling of Christian peoples will yet take place, shedding no new light but adding light to light.

That does not infer a third age in which the spirit would at last be manifest but rather a more profound understanding of ancient treasures still insufficiently explored. It would, however, justify apparently daring realisations which would afterwards be deemed to conform to the pristine type and perhaps to be even more like the customs of primitive Christianity than any other. Thus the old religion would be renewed by return to its sources. It is permissible to suppose that a simplification and greater inwardness in Christianity might lead it back to less rigid forms. They are those which humanity needs in the present phase of its history, in which it is not so much a question of repression or conservation as of establishment. A world in gestation and seeking its new equilibrium demands incentives, examples and ferments much more than regulations. For example, one may catch a glimpse of the rôle which might be played in the towns and countryside by households and families animated by a spirit of frankness and love and renouncing their self-centredness in order to give themselves circumspectly to the great common tasks. They would thus, in a new way, totally different in appearance but identical in inspiration, take up again the work of the monks in the West when they created the monasteries.

The cure for civilisation should have some resemblance to that claimed by barbarism! But it should also show some element of novelty. It may be that the reunion of the sexes in families of a new type might also recover, though without superseding, something of the excellence which the total segregation of the sexes according to monastic requirements produced.

The problem of our time is rather that of uniting than of disuniting essences. It is the property of religion, as it is the spirit of philosophy, to cause the same sap to circulate through contrary states so that the opposites, instead of excluding, assist and sustain each other. It is characteristic of Christianity that it has exalted the family founded upon love and has known how to develop an undefiled love beyond the bounds of sex and family. In short, it has never accepted the principle that either generative love or virginal love is sufficient; it has reconciled these two loves by affinities so profound that, as we have said, virginity needs the family and the family needs a parthenosphere.

We have said that the family institution could gain in richness by throwing itself open to the community with a love more fully conceived. For every deepening of inwardness must enlarge generosity, just as all isolation and all silence should render us more attentive to others and to the universe. At the same time it is to be hoped that, in a more adult humanity, virginity will be better understood by those who are strangers to it. For it will then appear, not as a mere morose isolation, but as a secret integration with communities more vast and more spiritual than the family. Communism is not mistaken when it reminds us that the energy immanent in love should be put to the service of the human community.

There are many signs leading us to believe that we are about to leave an era of enclosed and separate societies in order to penetrate into an era of communities in which individuals will be more fully integrated, and in which we shall recover, in a new and congenial form, that condition of coinherence of consciousness characteristic of primitive ages. In this sense, the world of to-morrow will be favourable for an extension of love. A partial explanation, perhaps, of the crisis of the Churches and the growth of an 'atheist Communism' among the nations, is the fact that religious society has long remained fettered by the ancient forms in which it is incarnated, whereas a political and social movement has no traditions to maintain. Now it is a tradition with Christians to separate the world of the soul into two hemispheres, that of the perfected who, on the mystical level, live the life of communion fully, and that of mediocre and ordinary folk called to occupy themselves with their affairs and to maintain the state of the world. The strength of Communist propaganda is that it denies this tacit partition and offers the bread of exaltation to the humblest. For it permits them to participate in the tragedy of toil and at the birth of a new world as the Church formerly succeeded in doing when Christianity could be absorbed in great communal tasks such as those of the Crusades or the cathedrals.

The difficulty consists in this, that the Christian ideal, no longer incarnate in institutions or social movements, is not sufficiently compact or concrete to attract or hold the worker of the world. From this point of view also, it seems that barriers between *states* of life and *classes* of society should be abolished and that, in conformity with the very law of love, all forms of love should intermingle. In a world which, as in the times of St. Francis of Assisi, has begun to grow cold, *frigescens mundus*, where ordinary folk are lifted to a latent heroism by rigour of circumstance and the loss of former securities, it is more than ever necessary that the elect should mingle with the masses. The characteristic of the age to come, and that in which it seems eschatalogical, is the necessity for choice between the two extremes, with no tenable middle course—either to grow great or to disappear. And this too will compel love to rise to the occasion.

We do not know in what kind of world we shall live. And we are equally ignorant whether the phase of mutation preparing a kind of third age in the history of the world will last for several decades or for several centuries. For the period of time necessary for the fulfilment of that future eludes the prophets of our day as, of old, it eluded the prophets of Israel with their constant announcement of the coming of the Kingdom on the morrow. But if it is certain that one day it will come, it is of little moment, save for that infirmity, our impatience, to know when an event will come to pass. What we do know is that human love has not completed its career. By its very nature it renews itself, meeting unknown problems with ever-new responses, never believing in cessation or catastrophe. Thus, in each world crisis, it assumes the grace of dawn and of a new venture upon the way of peace and promise. The further humanity fares, the more wide is the way; the more therefore is its cause for hope. And love and hope are akin.

Index

INDEX

ABÉLARD, 49–50, 112
Abnormal, the, 6, 17, 51, 56, 58, 128
Abuse, two kinds of, 136–7
Acarie, Madame, 142–3
Adam and Eve, 30, 135, 168–9, 189, 204, 230
Adolescence, 60–1, 66, 94, 102, 177
    prolongation of, 111
Adultery, 4, 14, 43, 108, 122
After-death state, 117–8, 178, 195
Agape, 25, 28, 44, 192–6, 233
Allendy, Dr., 7, 16, 41, 69, 107, 127
Amorism, 36
Aristotle, 28, 181
Attraction and allurement, 57

BEAUTY, 57, 107, 110
Being, nature of, 8–9, 57, 82, 167, 188, 231; reason of, 19, 154; sense of, 210–11 ; third dimension of, 216
Berdiaeff, Nicolas, 230–1
Bergson, 131, 146, 172, 182, 229
Biosphere, 156, 159, 163
Birth control, see Control of life
Body and soul, see Flesh and spirit

CAUSE AND EFFECT, 181–2
Celibacy, see Continence, and Virginity
Chance, 154, 183
Character, see Destiny and character
Charity, 43–4, 142, 194, 196–7
Chastity, see Continence, and Virginity
Child, advent of, 83, 99, 104; influence of, on love, 83–4, 90, 104–7; only, 83, 106
Christianity, and conflict of flesh and spirit, 5, 11, 41, 45–9, 51; and freedom, 204–5; and hypocrisy, 202 ; and love, 4–6, 9–10, 27–31, 65, 187, 197–8, 200–3, 232–3, 235; and nature, 172, 177, 206; and the infinite, 201; difficulties of, to-day, 9, 46–7, 237; future of, 200–1, 204, 233

Church, Catholic, and marriage, 119; and mysticism, 144, 202 ; teaching of, 118, 172, 187, 203, 236–7
Claudel, 7 (note), 30, 76, 123
Communism, 139, 164, 172, 214–6, 236
Comradeship, 63, 110–1, 115, 120, 139, 216
Comte, Auguste, 16, 141, 172, 229
Conception, mechanism of, 156, 187. See also Reproduction
Conscience, 5, 42, 103, 203
Contemplation, state of, 147–8
Continence, 127–34, 165, 171; concept of, 140 ; difference of, in man and woman, 127, 139–40; objections to, see Virginity
Control of life, 5–6, 106, 132, 187, 205–6, 213
Convention, definition of, 217
Coquetry, 74, 77
Culture, survival of, 220

DANTE, 30, 33, 118
Death, and love, 56, 90, 116–7, 219; mass sacrifice of, 178 ; preparation for, 149
De Chantal, Jeanne, 142
Descartes, 138
Destiny and character, 69–70, 78
De Vaux, Clotilde, 229
Development of love, 19, 88–125, 153, 199; 1st phase, 88–107; 2nd phase, 107–113; 3rd phase, 113–119 ; design of, 113
Divorce, 84, 115, 122–3
Dominique, 29, 31, 33
Dominium, 166
Don Juan, 32–3
Dostoievski, 181
Dreams, 68–9
Duality, in man, 40, 46, 51, 169, 188; of love, 57, 190–2, 203
Du Bos, Charles, 181
Duns Scotus, 3
Duty, 28, 120–1, 136, 173–4
Dyad, human, 124, 168 ; of love, 219

241